9/2006

UNDER CONSTRUCTION

UNDER CONSTRUCTION

How I've Gained and Lost Millions of Dollars and Hundreds of Pounds

NEW AMERICAN LIBRARY

NEW AMERICAN LIBRARY
Published by New American Library, a division of
Penguin Group (USA) Inc., 375 Hudson Street,
New York, New York 10014, USA
Penguin Group (Canada), 90 Eglinton Avenue East, Suite 700, Toronto,
Ontario M4P 2Y3, Canada (a division of Pearson Penguin Canada Inc.)
Penguin Books Ltd., 80 Strand, London WC2R 0RL, England
Penguin Ireland, 25 St. Stephen's Green, Dublin 2,
Ireland (a division of Penguin Books Ltd.)
Penguin Group (Australia), 250 Camberwell Road, Camberwell, Victoria 3124,
Australia (a division of Pearson Australia Group Pty. Ltd.)
Penguin Books India Pvt. Ltd., 11 Community Centre, Panchsheel Park,
New Delhi - 110 017, India
Penguin Group (NZ), cnr Airborne and Rosedale Roads, Albany,
Auckland 1310, New Zealand (a division of Pearson New Zealand Ltd.)
Penguin Books (South Africa) (Pty.) Ltd., 24 Sturdee Avenue,
Rosebank, Johannesburg 2196, South Africa

Penguin Books Ltd., Registered Offices:
80 Strand, London WC2R 0RL, England

First published by New American Library,
a division of Penguin Group (USA) Inc.

First Printing, January 2006
10 9 8 7 6 5 4 3 2 1

Grateful acknowledgment is made for use of the following: "Ain't No Stoppin' Us Now." Words and Music by Gene
McFadden, John Whitehead, and Jerry Cohen. © 1979 Warner-Tamerlane Publishing Corp. and Mijac Music.
All Rights Administered by Warner-Tamerlane Publishing Corp. All Rights Reserved.

Photo credits can be found on page 261.

 REGISTERED TRADEMARK—MARCA REGISTRADA

LIBRARY OF CONGRESS CATALOGING-IN-PUBLICATION DATA

Guerra, Jackie.
    Under construction: how I've gained and lost millions of dollars and hundreds of pounds/by Jackie Guerra.
    p.   cm.
    ISBN 0-451-21723-3
    1. Guerra, Jackie.   2. Entertainers—United States—Biography.   I. Title.
PN2287.G745A3   2005
791'.092—dc22   2005013937

Set in Filosofia, Gigi, and Helvetica Neue
Designed by BTDNYC

Printed in the United States of America

PUBLISHER'S NOTE
While the author has made every effort to provide accurate telephone numbers and Internet addresses at the time of
publication, neither the publisher nor the author assumes any responsibility for errors, or for changes that occur
after publication. Further, publisher does not have any control over and does not assume any responsibility for
author or third-party Web sites or their content.

To anyone who has ever wondered if they could . . .

Yes, you can!

¡Sí, se puede!

Have fun, laugh a lot, and be great!

IN LOVING AND GRATEFUL MEMORY OF
JOYCE GUERRA

There've been so many things that have held us down
But now it looks like things are finally comin' around
I know we've got a long, long way to go
And where we'll end up
I don't know

But we won't let nothing hold us back
We gonna get ourselves together
We gonna polish up our act
And if you've ever been held down before
I know you refuse to be held down anymore!

I know you know someone who's got a negative vibe (Euhh)
And if you let them
They'll only push you aside
They really don't have nowhere to go
Ask 'em where they're going
They don't know

Don't you let nothing
Nothing stand in your way!
I want you to listen
Listen to every word I say
Every word I say!

Ain't no stoppin' us now
We're on the move!
Ain't no stoppin' us now
We've got the groove!

Groove it!

—McFadden and Whitehead, "Ain't No Stoppin' Us Now"

Contents

Introduction

IT WAS A PERFECT DAY IN THE SAN FERNANDO VALLEY. Sixty-five degrees and zero humidity. I leaped into my car and was cranking my Beyoncé CD when I spotted my neighbor wrestling his leaky refrigerator into a moving van. Moments later I learned his beautiful home was being demolished and replaced by a huge stucco box with twenty apartments. Oh my God! Oh my God! I felt like I'd been sucker punched when I realized that for the next year I would be living next to hell. Better known as . . . a construction site.

I bolted back into my house and frantically called my city councilwoman's office. "They are building a monstrosity inches from my window. What can I do?"

She quickly replied, "You can go to a permit hearing."

I cleared my throat. "What exactly will I do at a permit hearing?"

She cleared her throat. "Argue for your 'quality of life.'"

"My 'quality of life'? Does anyone ever win with that argument?" I asked.

"Well, that's your best shot. Good luck."

"Thanks." Before I was even able to finish the one-syllable word she hung up. I was determined to show up at that permit hearing to argue for my "quality of life."

On my way to the hearing I called my cousin Jodi, who owns her own concrete-pumping business in San Diego. I was sure she would be able to give me some helpful tips or inside info about the rules that a construction crew has to follow in a residential neighborhood. She explained the schedule to me. "Anything else you recommend?" I asked.

"Yeah. Try not to be home too much during the next year. Other than that, close your windows and turn your music on loud."

"That's it?" I demanded. I knew that Jodi must have more advice for me.

"Just don't be one of those losers who show up at the permit hearings arguing for 'quality of life.' "

The hearing was held in a small hotel deep in the San Fernando Valley on a day when the temperature had plummeted from a recent high of 117 degrees to a breezy 103 degrees with about 300 percent humidity. The room was small and sandwiched between a *quinceañera* party (a Mexican "Sweet 15") on one side and a conference on California bankruptcy law on the other. Shocking how your past always finds you!

I walked into the stale room with no air-conditioning and realized that I was, to quote my cousin, one of three losers there to argue for "quality of life." I could see the deck was not stacked in my favor as I sized up the competition, which consisted of four lawyers to represent the developer, two mouthpieces, and an assistant, whose combined clothing allowance rivaled the GNP of a small country. Aside from me, my team consisted of a woman who apparently had no idea that it was brutally hot outside, nor that it was the year 2004. She wore a red velvet gown and a rain slicker. Her hair was piled high on the top of her head with about seventeen butterfly pins and barrettes scattered throughout. "Butterfly" carried three canvas tote bags spilling over with papers, file folders, and newspaper clippings. The other person on "Team Quality of Life" was a man who, through his hair and wardrobe, was apparently reliving his glory days during the disco era. "Disco Inferno" sported a fake-'n'-bake tan. You know, the kind of tan that can only be acquired by wearing out a punch card at the mini-mall tanning salon. His white tank top allowed just enough of his silver chest hair to pop over the top, to give his three pounds of gold chains somewhere comfortable to rest.

As the meeting began, Butterfly unleashed a high-pitched squeal, complete with an unmistakable Brooklyn accent. "Is this going to be made part of the public record or will it be buried like the Warren Commission hearings?" One down and two to go. Without skipping a beat, Disco Inferno hopped out of his seat and asked, "Will there be accessible Porta Pottis on the site?" It wasn't looking good for my team. I realized it was up to me to give us our comeback when I glanced at the sign-in sheet, only to see that Disco Inferno/Mr. Porta Potti didn't even live in my neighborhood. Apparently Disco Potti derives comfort from knowing the exact locations of public toilets. It was my turn to speak.

I felt like Julia Roberts in the movie *Erin Brockovich*. Remember that movie, where a regular citizen battles the big guys when she discovers a corporate cover-up? I was inspired. I announced in my best Erin Brockovich style, "I love my neighborhood and I specifically chose it because I work out of my home; I rehearse, I have meetings there, I design jewelry, and I am writing a book." No reaction from anyone. In my head I could hear the lonely sound of crickets. I continued, "I'm afraid that turning the house next door into a construction site for the next year is going to greatly affect my quality of life." Even Butterfly looked at me like *I* was nuts. Once again she blurted, "Is this going to be buried?" And then she looked at me and said, "Ya gotta talk their language, honey." And with that I knew there was only one thing left for me to do: go home, close my windows, and turn some music on loud. So much for my *Erin Brockovich* moment.

Six weeks after my disastrous appearance at the permit hearing, I woke up with the most annoying cold. I shuffled downstairs, still comfy-cozy in my favorite pajamas and slippers, to make myself a cup of tea. I put the mouth of the cup over my face to breathe in the steam from the hot water as I sat down in front of my computer and looked out my window. At exactly seven a.m., five men with sledgehammers and picks began tearing down the house next door. I watched them tear down in one day what had taken three families and four generations to build. That beautiful home held fifty years' worth of hopes, dreams, and memories. The giant tree in the front where kids had climbed was chopped down, chopped up, and hauled off in a Dumpster. Maybe it was the fact that I didn't feel well that made everything seem so much more dramatic, but it hurt me to witness what hours before had been a magnificent home become a pile of trash. And suddenly there was a big, empty, open, and vulnerable lot next door to me.

The first few days I watched as the squirrels that used to play in the trees just scampered around the empty lot in a crazy circle. The lot stayed empty for a few weeks. One morning while I was sitting at my computer and alternating between coughing and sneezing, I saw one of the squirrels standing in the lot that once held the trees where he used to play. He scurried toward me and perched himself on the fence that separated my house from the newly emptied lot and looked right in my window. The squirrel looked right at me, as if to say, "What happened? I feel so lost." I found myself talking to the squirrel. "I'm sorry, little squirrel, I guess your quality of life has been affected too." As I spoke to the squirrel I understood for the first time that I felt lost too. Also, I was on day nineteen of this twenty-four-hour bug.

I went to see my doctor, Dr. Sarang, that afternoon. While she examined me, I told her about my thwarted attempt to argue for my quality of life. As an added bonus to my visit, Dr. Sarang asked me to step onto my lifelong nemesis (music please: bahm . . . bahm . . . bahm) *the scale in the doctor's office*. My heart raced as I watched her slender hand slide the base number from 150 to 200 and then to 250. I stared at the prongs in their final resting place: 291. I could not believe it. There's no way. This is not possible. Aside from the last three weeks, I had been religiously following the Zone Diet for the last seven months. Seven months and $10,000 worth of prepackaged food later, I weighed more than I'd ever weighed in my entire life! Dr. Sarang put her arm around me and said, "Jackie, you are a confident, talented, and beautiful young woman. Aside from the fact that you've managed to turn a cold into bronchitis, you are in remarkably good health, but if you don't take off some of this weight, the pain in your knees is going to get worse and eventually you'll do permanent damage to your joints and possibly your heart. You're too young to have those types of problems, but you will. Don't you see what you're doing to your quality of life?"

Nobody had ever asked me that.

She gave me a stern lecture about my needing to rest, scribbled a couple of prescriptions down, and sent me home. I walked out of her office in a state of shock. Whether she knew it or not, Dr. Sarang's words sent me into a spiral of self-reflection.

I walked into my house with a bottle of antibiotics, an inhaler, and a new thermometer. I felt very scared and wanted some comfort, so I called my reassuring, deep-voiced dad in Mexico City to chat.

"Hi, Chimi." (I call my dad "Chimi," and he calls me "Mija" or "Chimi-Chimi.")

"Hi, Mija. How's my number-one daughter?" (I'm his only daughter.)

"I'm okay." I knew he wouldn't buy it.

"You don't sound too okay. Tell your dad what's the matter."

"I don't know. I guess I have a case of the blahs."

"That's not the Jackie I know. I didn't raise a 'blah' daughter. My Chimi-Chimi is a fighter who might get knocked down once in a while, but she comes back swingin'!" And then he asked, "What's the last thing that happened to you?"

"Nothing specific." And before I knew what hit me, I rattled off a whole laundry list of things that, until my dad asked, I hadn't even realized were upsetting me.

"My new Web site still isn't finished, and the guy I've already paid and is supposed to be building it isn't returning my calls. I just found out yesterday that my deal for a new show at CBS is over—they didn't pick up the script to shoot a pilot. I've had this stupid cold for three weeks, so I went to see my doctor today. Turns out I don't have a cold. I have bronchitis. Then I got weighed on the gross doctor scale. You know what, Chimi? After being on the Zone Diet for the last seven months, carrying my food around in little plastic containers in a big blue bag, seven months of parading around with the stupid 'bag of shame' and ten thousand dollars later, I weigh more today than I've ever weighed in my entire life!" I stopped to cough, and my dad stepped in.

"Well, Mija, sounds like you got a lot on your plate. You win some, you lose some, but you know what? You're in the game and that's what is most important. First you have to take care of your health. I don't like to hear you got so run-down you have bronchitis. What did the doctor tell you to do?"

"Rest, drink lots of fluids, take my antibiotics, and use an inhaler. And she told me that if I don't lose weight it's going to affect my quality of life." There was the long, uncomfortable but rather familiar pause as my father desperately flipped through the file cabinet in his brain trying to come up with something he could say to me that he hasn't said a hundred times before whenever the subject of my lifelong struggle with weight has reared its predictable and ugly head. I cut him off at the pass. "Don't worry about that." I immediately changed the subject, for which I'm sure he was relieved. "You know what also really sucks? Remember I told you that they tore the house down next door? Well, they've officially started construction on the gigantic twenty-unit apartment building fifteen inches from my dining room window. So for the next year my whole block will be under construction."

"But that's life, Mija. The building next door is under construction, you're under construction, your career and your Web site are under construction, the whole damned world is under construction. Don't overcomplicate things. Life is very simple; you're either laying a new foundation or you're building upon what you've got." Silence. I let the silence hang while I thought about how brilliant my dad was.

"Wow. If I let you talk long enough, every once in a while you come up with a gem," I said teasingly.

"Now get better."

"I promise I will."

I thought a lot about that conversation with my dad as the weeks and months passed, and I watched the construction crew next door show up every day and build upon what they'd done the day before.

As it turns out, we had record-breaking rainfall in Los Angeles that year, and the work that was being done by the construction crew kept getting interrupted by the rain. They'd work and work, and when it rained, they'd stop. But when the rain stopped, they'd come right back, clean up, and pick up where they left off. Watching this, I thought about how often we all get derailed when our plans get rained on. For example, since the day I stepped into show business, my goal has been to host my own talk show. I worked with a production company for a year. We planned and plotted and strategized. I attended a flurry of meetings on the West Coast and on the East Coast, participated in countless conference calls, appearances, and photo shoots. Everyone involved was excited, confident, and energized. The show was planned, the budget was approved, the staff was on board, and there were people scouting for apartments for me in New York because it was obvious this show was about to happen. And then the day before it all was about to be official, the rain came. The executive in charge of my deal was suddenly fired, and then another executive involved in the project was fired. Suddenly all the work and time and effort seemed wasted. But just like the construction crew after the rains, I had to get up, get right back to work, clean up the mess and keep building. Sometimes circumstances beyond our control thwart our plans, but if it's important enough, you keep building. Other times you need to take a moment to determine whether where you've been going is still where you want to go. Either way, when the rain stops, it's right back to work.

While I was forced to stay home and rest during my bout with bronchitis, I thought long and hard about my conversation with Dr. Sarang. I thought about all of the diets, the weight-loss programs, the shakes and the trainers and the nutritionists and the hypnotists and the fasts and the years I struggled with bulimia and diet pills and laxatives. I thought about all of my mother's pleas for me to lose weight, the bribes and the blackmail. It was a vicious dance that we had been doing since I was eight years old.

I began to cry as I thought about the construction workers with their hammers, axes, and picks tearing down the walls of that house, because I knew it was time for me too to tear down the walls I'd built up to protect myself from my own pain and possibly face an open, empty, and vulnerable lot in my own life. Was I finally ready to lay a new foundation and build my own dream house to live in?

As I watched the beautiful, cozy home with big, full trees and a large backyard being transformed into a gigantic building ready to give shelter to twenty new families with new hopes and dreams, I was acutely aware of my own transformation. In the beginning I was so pissed off about the construction next door. I thought that this noisy, filthy, intrusive construction site would rob me of my quality of life. But now I will be forever grateful to that construction crew that showed up day after day to tear down the old and rebuild the new. For it was while watching them that I remembered that life is a process of building and that I'm not finished—I'm *under construction.*

Today, one year later, I weigh 145 pounds. The guy I paid never finished my Web site, but I found someone else who did. I've turned my lifelong passion for jewelry making into a business, and I even host a TV show about it. I've worn stiletto heels for the first time, and I know that I'm smarter, healthier, and happier than I've ever been.

I'm not a licensed therapist. I am a Mexican-American Valley Girl who stumbled into show business. I've lost and gained the same hundred pounds four times in the last ten years. I've been a bulimic, a compulsive overeater, and a cellulite cream user. I have lived through family crises, including alcoholism, relatives going to prison, bankruptcy, being robbed, friendships ending, and dreams dashed. I've lived in my car. I held my own mother as she took her last breath on this earth. At times I haven't been sure if there was a reason to take another breath, or why I should even bother to get out of bed.

But I did.

Like everyone, I work every day to be a good person, fiancée, daughter, sister, aunt, friend, citizen. I try to be kind and focused, eat right, read the paper, wear sunscreen, pay my bills, be confident, follow my dreams, stand up straight, hold in my stomach, not to forget to say please and thank you—and have good eyebrows!

"Be confident!" "Love yourself!" "Believe in yourself!" Well, that's all great, but how do you do it? How do you really love yourself? How do you feel confident? How do you believe? How do you put your best foot forward—even when you need a pedicure?

I can tell you the answers aren't found in a store, the bank, or at an all-you-can-eat buffet. You can't buy confidence. The quality of your life is up to one person, you! So what's it gonna be? You want to waste your life trying to please others and be a watered-down version of someone else? You want to stand on the sidelines feeling bad while you watch others play? Then this book is not for you. But if you're ready to get into the game, be great and feel great, have the courage to be who you really are, clear the clutter in your life, get rid of old habits and old attitudes that no longer serve you, and to assume the role of superstar in the movie of your life, then *this book is definitely for you!*

Love where you live, but be open to a little home improvement. Let's make the world a better place one person at a time, starting with you. Life is a work in progress, and we're all *Under Construction*.

CHAPTER ONE

Camp Guerra

"Things do not happen. Things are made to happen."
—JOHN F. KENNEDY

I WAS ON THE PHONE WITH MY DAD THE OTHER DAY. For some reason we started talking about my brief career as a soccer player when I was a kid. We were laughing about what a terrible soccer player I was. "What was I thinking? I was terrible!" I said. "But you had fun and you gave it hell, Mija," he replied, laughing. For all of his wisdom, my father has always had a real knack for putting his own spin on commonly used phrases and expressions in English. For example, most people say, "What the hell?" My father says, "What the shit?" Most people say, "My contention is . . ." My father says, "My contingency is . . ." Truman said, "Give 'em hell." My father says, "Give it hell." He's an original!

We laughed and reminisced. "Remember the beautiful picture of you on that button that your mom and I used to wear?" he asked. Wow! I hadn't thought about that button in years. That button with a big ol' picture of me in my soccer uniform haunted me throughout my teenage years. My parents would pull it out and wear it in front of my friends to tease me. I was horrified. We laughed and cried and had a really nice talk, which ended with my dad's traditional phone closer, "Give it hell, Mija! I love you."

As soon as I hung up, I went to look for that button, and I found it. As I looked in the face of that chubby little girl in pigtails and braces staring back at me, I was struck by how happy and confident she was. There wasn't any apparent reason for that kind of confidence; my uniform was too small, my tummy was too chubby, my braces dominated my face, my pigtails were crooked, and my eyes were half closed because the photographer snapped the picture in the middle of my big laugh. I looked at the picture and realized I had had no idea I was a bad soccer player. I played because I loved it. It was fun, my dad was my coach, and it was pure joy!

I felt so proud every weekend when I'd put my uniform on and stride onto the field. And suddenly I was flooded with memories of my family going to practices, games, and award banquets. (The awards were mostly for my brother, John, who was and is a great soccer player.) My mom would cut oranges into quarters to take for us to eat during half-time, and bring a cooler of ice water and little tiny cups that she'd line up on the sideline so we could grab them and have a sip the second we came off the field. I could smell the smell of the grass. It was a glorious time in my life. As I continued my private little trip down memory lane, I kept obsessing about the fact that I had so much fun on that field and never even realized I wasn't any good at the game. And then the best memory of all came to me: I could see my mom's and dad's faces so clearly whenever I was on the soccer field and would glance at them on the sidelines. I could see them both with their big smiles drenched in sunlight, beaming at me and giving me the thumbs-up, and my mom shouting, "Go, Jacksie!" As I pictured them, I began to cry. I had a good, long solo "happy cry" that morning. And then it hit me: of course it didn't matter whether I scored a goal or blocked a goal; it didn't matter that I had braces and a chubby tummy. I was full of joy because I was on the field and I was *in the game*! My focus as a chubby ten-year-old on the soccer field was all about doing things I was excited about. I wasn't even aware of the resistance that exists in a world not necessarily made for chubby girls with braces who aren't good athletes but love to play soccer. My family loved me and they cheered me on!

Now I get it—even at ten years old, I was under construction. The same things that made me "successful" then are still what make me successful now:

You have to be "in the game" to win.

Don't wait to be perfect to get "in the game."

Win or lose, enjoy playing.

As a kid, I played hard and I played to win, but even when I didn't win, I still enjoyed the game. I didn't wait until I mastered the game, lost weight, got my braces off, and found a uniform that fit me perfectly to get out onto that field. I just did it. I understood then what I have to remind myself of now: in sports the only person that anyone is trying to stop is the one with the ball. I have to remind myself not to sweat it when I encounter pettiness, jealousy, negativity, or criticism, because chances are they're coming after me because I have the ball. Besides, when you're in the game there's always someone rooting for you. I always knew that even when I missed the ball or fell onto my rump, I could look over to the sideline and see the happy, loving, supportive faces of my personal cheering squad, my parents.

Both of my parents come from humble beginnings. My father is the middle child of seven from Durango, Mexico. When he was a young boy, his parents divorced. My grandmother and her seven children moved to Mexico City, where she could find work as a seamstress while raising her children as a single mother.

My mother is the oldest of six children from Inglewood, Colorado. My mother was never a child. Her parents divorced when she was eight years old and she went to work. She did odd jobs to help her mother financially with the burden of raising six kids on her own, and worked in the house to help raise her five brothers and sisters. My mother left home at a young age and went to Chicago, where she got herself a fake ID and went to work as a Playboy bunny at the famous Key Club. She didn't abandon her younger siblings when she escaped her childhood; she took her younger sister and brother with her. She used the one thing she had that people—men, in particular—seemed to admire: a hot body. She was a little girl living a big girl's life.

My father went to work to support his family when he was nine years old. Even at nine, he had an undeniable entrepreneurial spirit. He didn't like to work for anybody and wasn't waiting around for someone to give him a job. He made a job for himself by going to the *mercados* of Mexico City and unloading trucks for the local merchants for tips. At the age of nine he was hustling to help his family. At seventeen, he left his mother and brothers and sisters to come to the United States to build a life he had dreamed about back in his beloved Mexico.

H-O-T! ¡Caliente! *My mom posing for the camera.*
Being shy does not run in our family.

When I was seventeen, my world was consumed with my friends, school, what I would wear that day, and my many after-school (fun) activities. My mom at seventeen was in a new city working full-time and raising her younger sister and brother by herself. At seventeen my dad was alone in a new country learning a new language and working full-time to send money to his family in Mexico. Whenever I think of my parents as children working to help their single mothers survive, I am so proud to be their daughter.

In the mid-sixties my parents both ended up in San Diego, California. My mother worked as a cocktail waitress in a restaurant called Oscar's. My father was a dishwasher at that same restaurant. As the story goes, my mother (who was two years older than my father) thought he was "hot." My father, who spoke very little English and had only been in

My dad making his first holy communion and looking thrilled.
Hiding feelings does not run in our family.

the United States for a few months, thought my mother was *creida*.
That's Spanish for "full of herself." He thought she was a show-off. I
think they were immediately attracted to each other. My mother had a
convertible, which was a gift from an ex-boyfriend. One day when she

was not scheduled to work but he was, she drove her car to the restaurant with the top down, dressed in capri pants, a halter top, dark glasses, and red lipstick. She just knew she had it going on. My mother was there to sweep my father off his feet. . . .

She staked out the parking lot and waited for my dad's shift to end so she could make her move. As soon as he walked out of the restaurant, she did.

"Ramon! You want a ride home?"

"No, thanks. I like to walk." He began to walk toward the parking lot exit. No way was Joyce going to let her carefully laid plan end like this. She had put way too much time and effort into the planning, plotting, and scheming to get my dad to pay attention to her. And when my mom set her mind to something, it was on!

She let him walk a few blocks down the dirt road. Many times throughout my life I heard my mom tell this story. "He sure looked good from behind. His shoulders were broad and his butt was soooo cute and his hair was so thick and black and shiny. The sun was setting as I watched him, and I thought, 'He is so good-looking, no way is he getting away.' I pulled out all the stops!" (Hearing this story when I was a kid prompted a lot of eye rolling and shouts of "Gross, Mom" from my brother and me.) She let him walk a few hundred yards, and then pulled her car up next to him and popped open the console that divided the two front seats to reveal two crystal glasses and a bottle of wine.

"Thirsty?" she taunted. My dad has admitted he was flattered by her advances, but more than anything else he was curious about this cocktail waitress dressed up in her convertible with a bottle of wine and real glasses. He smiled, got in, and the cocktail waitress and the dishwasher drove down that windy, dusty road along the San Diego coastline and into their life together.

Though it was controversial at the time, they moved in together and were married two years later. My parents really loved each other and, much to my brother's and my dismay, had no problem with public displays of affection. As a kid I was disgusted with their constant dancing and kissing; now I am so grateful to have been witness to true love. They had pet names for each other. My dad called my mom "Chaparra" (shorty) and "Esquincla" (little brat), and my mom always called my dad "mi vida" (my life). Cute, right? Not when I was ten!

Neither one of my parents was ever handed anything. Both of them came from extreme poverty, broken homes, and pressures at a very young age to provide for their families. When they met each other, they fell deeply and passionately in love and determined to build a life that, as my dad says, "represents the American dream. That you can come to this country with nothing but dreams, ambitions, and the willingness to work hard, and within one generation achieve success." Both of my parents were willing to work hard and make whatever sacrifices they needed to in order to move ahead and build the life they dreamed about. I think that in each other they found an understanding of who they were and where they'd been that nobody else could relate to. My parents loved each other madly and were always affectionate with each other and with my brother and me.

My mother was obsessed with the Kennedys. To her, the Kennedys represented everything good and classy and everything possible about being an American. My mother dressed like Jackie Kennedy and took John Kennedy's call to action very seriously. She always handwrote thank-you notes because she read somewhere that Jackie did that. She volunteered to help anyone and everyone who needed her. My mother was the kind of woman who always spoke her mind and took great offense when she felt someone was being treated badly or unjustly. My father was impressed with the winning attitude and loyalty displayed by the Kennedys. He thought Joseph Kennedy Sr. was a genius for creating the opportunities to define his family the way he dreamed of them. They paid homage to the Kennedys by naming us Jackie and John.

My parents made each other better. My dad went back to school and got his high school diploma, and then attended college while working full-time. My mother was an autodidact. She read everything she could get her hands on. She read about foreign cultures and successful people and elegance and even the occasional trash novel. She loved to read because reading gave her a peek into the windows of homes she'd never been in. After my brother began kindergarten she went to school to get her real estate license and began to sell real estate. And sell she did.

We moved around a lot when I was a kid. By the time I was in sixth grade, we'd lived in San Diego, San Jose, Granada Hills, São Paulo, Brazil, Saugus, and Mexico City, and finally moved to Valencia, California. I loved moving. I loved the adventure. My brother hated it. We both learned to adapt to new environments and to make friends quickly because we had to. My brother always hated to leave his school, his sports, and his friends. I missed my friends too, but loved making new ones. My father was a young rising star in the Jack in the Box corporation in the late seventies, when they decided to open Jack in the Box in Brazil. So when I was eight years old, we packed up and moved to São Paulo. It was a magical time for my family. We lived in a beautiful house, traveled all around the country, and my mom and I became obsessed with jewelry making. After two years we came back to the United States, but continued to travel. My parents really wanted my brother and me to see as much of the world as possible. They took us to Colombia, Argentina, and Panama. We also traveled around the United States and got to see many of the great states of our country.

When I was growing up, our house was always full. My parents had a lot of friends, but we also have a lot of relatives. My parents always took in the stray relative: if someone came from Mexico, they stayed at our house; if someone fought with their parents, they stayed at our house; if someone was going through a divorce, they stayed at our house; if someone fell on hard times, they stayed at our house; if someone wanted to move to California, they stayed at our house. My parents felt that if they had something, they had something that could be shared. This was a big thing in our house. My parents also partied hard. There was always music and people and dancing and barbecuing going on. Pool parties were a way of life in my family. My parents loved to have people over. Sometimes our home seemed more like a frat house. My dad and his brothers would go out with my uncle Taylor and his brothers from Arkansas. My uncle Taylor had married my mom's sister, Judie. The combination of Mexicans and Arkansans was a lot of fun. They'd go out and have fun, but sometimes they'd come home a little bruised and with tales of some "ass whoopin'," as my uncle Taylor would put it. My mom, my aunt Judie, my cousin Jodi, my brother, and I would hang out together and sing and dance and play cards, go to movies, bake and laugh while the men acted like boys. . . .

One night we were at my aunt Judie's house while the Brewer boys and the Guerra boys went out. We were jolted out of our sleep by gunfire! There were some guys shooting guns at the front of the house! Apparently, my dad, Uncle Taylor, and their brothers were at a bar and some guy made a comment about there being "too many Mexicans" in the bar. Uncle Taylor and one of his brothers got up and told the guy to leave because there were "too many assholes" in the bar. And they were off! The fists started flying, and I guess the guy who made the racist comment got beat up pretty badly. He and his friends got mad and got into their cars and followed my dad and Uncle Taylor and the others home. My dad and his group started driving to Uncle Taylor's house. When they pulled into the driveway, they realized they were being followed, so they drove away. But the guys saw the house and came back before my dad and Uncle Taylor got home. They literally pulled out guns and started shooting up the front of the house while we slept. They shot up the roof, Aunt Judie's car, and the mailbox! Aunt Judie, who is all of four feet ten, grabbed a huge hunting rifle and lay on her stomach in front of the picture window that took up the entire front side of her house, with the rifle perched on the windowsill. We were all terrified. My mom put my brother in the dryer and tried to stuff me into the washing machine! I didn't fit, so she opened up a sofa couch and stuffed me inside of it. My cousin Jodi was shoved into the kitchen in between the refrigerator and the oven. Someone walked up to the front of the house. My aunt Judie yelled, "Who's there?" And a man's voice said, "Wyatt Earp." Aunt Judie said, "Wyatt Earp, my ass!" And she shot the gun. The entire picture window was blown out. The man went running down the front path, jumped into a VW Bug, and was so scared he couldn't even start the car. He was literally pedaling with one foot like Fred Flintstone to get away from my aunt Judie and her rifle. It was scary, but in the end, a great and funny story. And that was pretty much how my entire childhood was: exciting, funny, bizarre, scary, and different from everyone else's, full of surprises, activities, people and culture clash.

My father is an avid baseball fan. When he was a kid in Mexico, he was recruited to play on a minor league team, but never had the chance to fulfill his boyhood fantasy of becoming a professional baseball player because he had to work to provide for his mom and his younger brother and sisters. One of the things I admire most about my dad is that he has never shown any bitterness about it. He just always loved the game. As soon as he could afford it, we had season tickets at Dodger Stadium. Or as my dad calls them, "the Doe-yers." (I don't know what to tell you. He can say "Jackie," but he just can't quite make the same sound for the "Dodgers." To him they are, and always will be, his beloved "Doe-yers.")

During baseball season, we'd all pile into the car and make the "drive on the five" (Interstate 5), listening to the voice of the Dodgers, Vin Scully, on AM radio. On the way home, if the Dodgers won, we'd listen to more Dodger radio; if they lost, we drove home in silence—if we were lucky. When the game was close or my dad felt "the Doe-yers were robbed," he'd force us to listen to Chuck Mangione—no offense to Chuck, but not too many preteens and teenagers are lookin' to rock out to a trumpet. Now that I'm an adult and live and drive in Los Angeles, I am in awe of my parents' ability to organize two kids, two careers, and beat L.A. traffic to get us to every single game without a hitch. We rarely missed batting practice, let alone the start of the first inning. We went to the regular season games, the practice games, the All Star games, playoffs and World Series games, bat day, pennant day, hat day, and my favorite, old-timers' day. Our home looked like a Dodger apparel and memorabilia storage area. The Guerra family was a member of "the Big Blue Wrecking Crew!" Our seats were on the field level, near the Dodger dugout in between third base and left field. My brother and I were on a first-name basis with some of the team: Dusty Baker (left field), Ron Cey (third base), Bill Russell (shortstop). When we went to Dodger Stadium we'd each wear something in support of the Los Angeles Dodgers. And it was not optional!

During the early eighties, when the Dodger-Yankee rivalry was in full effect and Fernando Valenzuela was the star of Major League Baseball, my dad was in heaven. "Fernando-mania" swept all of Los Angeles, but in my house you would have thought he was a member of our family. "Fernando this" and "Fernando that"—it was an exciting time. During Fernando-mania we didn't go to Dodger Stadium; according to my dad we went to "Fernando's house." At every single game my dad would stand up and belt out the national anthem—albeit off-key, with a loud and proud Mexican accent. My brother and I would stand up and stare into left field at Dusty Baker while we worked to stifle our laughter. At the end of the song, at every single game, my dad clapped his hands together and shouted, "Play ball!" My mother always loved to sing "Take Me Out to the Ball Game" during the seventh-inning stretch. She'd jump up out of her chair and sing with the lack of self-consciousness usually reserved for kids completely unburdened by a need to match tone, key, or pacing; she did it for the fun of it. My dad and my brother talked stats and tried to catch fly balls; I was the family scorekeeper, and my mother provided a steady supply of peanuts, Dodger dogs, frozen malts, soda, and beer (for them). I looked at the game not so much as nine innings but as nine snacks. We had a lot of fun at those games, even if it was sometimes really embarrassing!

My mother loooved Elvis Presley! She grew up at a time when Elvis exploded onto the national stage, and she thought he was the most electric, exciting, talented, and sexy human being she'd ever seen. She believed the world lit up when Elvis showed up! To her, Elvis was the personification of passion and success. As a kid, whenever I'd be nervous or need a big dose of confidence, my mother would tell me, "Imagine you're Elvis Presley, the biggest star the world has ever known. People stand in the rain and snow and wind to wait to buy tickets just to be in the same building as you, to see you and hear you! People will trample over each other to get near you. Walk into a room like you're *Elvis Presley*!" When Elvis walked onto a stage, everyone was energized and excited. So she believed that if I imagined I was Elvis, I'd walk into a room with that same energy and excitement! This taught me many things: it taught me the undeniable power of visualization; it taught me that how others perceive me depends largely on how I perceive myself. If you *act* like you're Elvis when you walk into a room, the other people in that room are lucky because they get to be there to experience it. To build upon my mother's lesson, *people only know about you what you tell them*, so tell them you are fabulous! You tell people who you are by the way you treat yourself, your posture, your expression, the way you present yourself, your tone of voice; all of these things add up to say to the world either you believe you matter or you don't. I know you *do*! So walk into the room like you're Elvis Presley!

My parents firmly believed in "the Great Society." They believed in the American potential for greatness. Vigorous action, service to your community, hard work, and hard fun were the mottoes. My family embodied these traits. They won big and lost big. The word "no" was not in my family's vocabulary. We lusted for greatness. We took big chances. We were sometimes greedy. We wanted to win at any cost. No one gave an ounce of thought to what could go wrong. No one worried about the future. They all believed that in the United States, anything was possible if you're willing to learn, work hard, and take a chance.

As a kid growing up in Southern California, I was blessed with beautiful weather year-round. As a family, we spent many Thanksgivings and Christmas Days swimming and hanging out by the pool. Because it was always so beautiful outside, my mother had very little patience for anyone sitting indoors in front of a television or talking on the phone. Whenever my brother or I would make an attempt at lounging around inside the house, my mom would demand, "For the love of God, will you please get out and *do something*!!!"

My mother would do anything to be in the sun. She grew up in Colorado and hated the cold and the snow. When my brother and I wanted to learn to ski, my dad took us to Mammoth and my mom stayed home. "No snow for me, thank you." She loved to be outside by the pool, though never to just lie around—"that's lazy." She would work in the garden, water the lawn, sweep the pool, barbecue, do paperwork outside, make phone calls, anything that kept her in the sun, where she could work on her tan. She loved to be tanned and she loved being in a bathing suit. Of course she did—she looked great!

I didn't share her zeal for sun worship. I liked group activities. I did share her and my dad's appetite to learn and for doing volunteer work. "Of those to whom much has been given, much is expected," they've said approximately one million times in my life. I volunteered at church, hospitals, senior citizen homes, and an orphanage. I participated in an adopt-a-grandparent program and taught women at the seniors' center to tap-dance. At least that's what they let me believe; truth is, they taught me! If someone needed to raise money, I was there ready to wash cars, babysit, or sell cookies. I was a Blue Bird, a Brownie, and a Girl Scout. I loved being a Girl Scout. I really took the oath and the Girl Scout law to heart. I had the opportunity to do things as a Girl Scout that I would have never experienced otherwise, and in the process I learned a lot about myself and discovered things that I enjoyed and that I was good at. Speaking of cookies, I found out that I am a natural at selling products I believe in, and believe me, I believe in Girl Scout cookies! My parents have always said I'm a natural-born salesperson because I'll talk to anybody about anything, and according to them I have the gift for gab. It's true, I was a chatty kid, and as a teenager I was practically glued to the phone. My mom used to say, "You know, Jacksie, if you can figure out a way to get paid for talking to strangers and friends, you'll be a very wealthy woman."

When I was a Brownie and then a Girl Scout, I was in heaven! It was everything I loved: meeting new people, learning, being of service, and a little bit of competition to spice things up. Every time I earned a new badge, I couldn't wait to add it to my sash. As the sash filled up and I had to begin adding the badges to the back, I was thrilled. My mom was my troop leader when I was a Brownie, and I was so proud. My mom was really smart and funny and supercrafty, and everyone loved her. "Your mom is so cool," the other girls would say to me. I loved it. The first time I got to sell cookies was a really happy time for me. On a Saturday morning I got up early to take a bath and put on the uniform I loved so much. I brushed my hair into two tight ponytails and added ribbons and barrettes to match my uniform (I've always overaccessorized). I grabbed my order form and made my way around the neighborhood to sell, sell, sell. I wanted to sell a lot, but I *really* wanted to sell the most.

I came home that day with almost one hundred orders, but I didn't stop there. I begged my dad to take me with him to work so I could hit up each of his colleagues. I convinced my mom to let me go to the open house of a home she was trying to sell so I could charm her clients and their neighbors into buying some cookies too. I called friends, family, and relatives and begged them to place orders. I went to my brother's soccer games and baseball games to sell the cookies there. At the end of the sales period I had successfully sold 142 boxes of cookies, more boxes than anyone else in my troop. I won! When the boxes arrived on a Tuesday night, my mom and I carefully organized them in the garage and wrote out tags with the names and addresses of the people to whom the cookies belonged. It was a big project. My brother helped too—in that annoying six-year-old little brother way, but for the record, he helped. As we finished taping the last card to the last box, my mom pointed her finger at me and said, "These belong to other people—do *not* eat any of these cookies." And then she turned to John and said, "And that goes for you too, John-John." "Can't we have any?" I pleaded. "No. You don't need to eat cookies." "Whatever that means," I thought. We went into the house and went to bed.

I lay in bed thinking about all those cookies just one flight of stairs and three doors away in our garage. My favorites were the Thin Mints and the Savannahs (peanut butter). Apparently they were most people's favorites, because that's what was mostly down there. My mouth started watering just thinking about them. Once I knew that my parents were asleep, I quietly snuck downstairs and made my way from the living room to the family room, through my dad's office, the laundry room, and into the garage, where I flicked on the light and looked at all those cookies. I thought, "If I just open one box, nobody will notice. I'll just open one and take some money out of my piggy bank to pay for it and it will be fine." And then I did it. I opened a box and ate one, then two, then three, then before I knew it, an entire row of cookies! I took the wrapping and the rest of the box back upstairs and put it under my bed to hide the evidence, and fell asleep. The next morning when I woke up, I took the box into the bathroom with me to finish the cookies off before anyone discovered them. I turned the water on in the shower and sat on the floor and ate the cookies. I went downstairs and announced that I didn't want any breakfast because my tummy hurt a little. My mom took my temperature and gave me a glass of water. "Sip this, Jacksie. Do you need to go see the doctor?"

"Nope. I'll be okay."

When I came home from school, I went straight to the garage and opened another box and added more money from my piggy bank to the cash stash. This time I took it upstairs to my room and lay on my bed to quietly and privately enjoy my secret snack. That night I changed my routine. I realized that at this rate I would run out of money by the next day, so instead of taking entire boxes I started opening multiple boxes and taking one or two cookies out of each box. "This way no one will notice," I thought. I was sure as only an eight-year-old can be that my plan was foolproof. I mean, who would *possibly* notice one or two cookies missing from their box? I did the same thing on Thursday and Friday. On Saturday morning, when it was time to deliver the boxes, my mom went to the garage to start loading the boxes into the trunk of her car.

"Jacquelyn Marie Guerra!"

I knew my secret snack stash had been discovered, because whenever my mom used my full name it meant trouble. I started down the stairs and heard my dad in the garage with my mom. "What happened?"

"Your daughter has been eating the cookies," she told him. Whenever my mom was upset with me she'd refer to me as "your daughter." Whenever my dad was upset with me, he'd do the same.

"It's not a big deal, Joyce. So she had a few cookies. She's a kid," he argued.

"Not a few cookies. There are three entire boxes missing, and twenty-three more that have been opened," she announced.

I stood in the doorway until my dad saw me. "What happened, Mija?" He looked so sad and disappointed.

"I don't know. I was hungry." I had to give it a shot.

"You were hungry? When did you have time to eat all of these cookies?" my mom demanded.

"I don't know."

"Well, I know one thing. You're going to personally apologize to every single person who trusted you to deliver their cookies, and you're going to figure out a way to pay for them. I suggest you ask your brother if you can do his chores to earn his allowance."

"It'll take me twenty years to make enough money!" I protested.

"We'll figure out a plan with you, Mija." My dad was trying to keep the peace.

"I'm sorry," I said pathetically. My mom looked at me with such disappointment. I hadn't seen that look thrown my way too many times in my eight-year-old life, but the few times I had felt like blows to my heart.

And so what should have been my victory lap around the neighborhood to deliver the cookies turned out to be one of the most humiliating days of my life. The good news is that everyone whose cookies I ate was really nice about it when I made my apologies. I got a lot of "That's okay, sweetie," and "Believe me, if all those cookies were in my house, I'd eat them too." The bad news is that I didn't learn a very necessary lesson on the importance of portion control or anything to help me develop a healthy relationship to food.

That evening I stayed in my room sitting quietly at my desk, just thinking while my mom made dinner. I knew she was still mad at me. I didn't dare do anything to draw attention to myself. I could smell the delicious smells of her homemade white rice and refried beans. I wasn't sure what else she was cooking, but whatever it was, it smelled delicious. That's one thing about my mom: she was an amazing cook and loved doing it. "Dinner's ready!" My dad poked his head into my room. "Come on, Mija, time to eat!" He put his arm around me and we walked downstairs together. The smell of my mom's delicious dinner made me happy, and I was convinced that once we all sat down together at the dinner table, everything would be back to normal. I rounded the corner into the kitchen and saw that my mom had made one of my favorite things, chicken tortilla casserole. Yummy! I sat down at the table with my brother and my dad. My mom put the steaming food onto plates and set them in front of us: first John, then my dad, and then a plate at her place. And then the ultimate punishment—she put a plate of sliced tomatoes and cottage cheese in front of me. My heart sank, but I did not dare say a word. When my mom wasn't looking, my dad put some casserole onto my plate, and I inhaled it before she could see. Preview of coming attractions!

That night, after helping my mom with the dishes in silence, I went to bed without cookies for the first night in almost a week. I lay in my bed trying to fall asleep, but I could hear my parents talking downstairs.

"Joyce, you can't starve her. She's a little girl."

"I know she's a little girl. This is the exact time that she should learn to eat right. Do you want her to grow up to be a fat girl?"

"Come on, Joyce. She feels bad about the whole thing."

"She's going to feel bad if she keeps gaining weight. She has to go on a diet."

"She doesn't need to go on a diet. She's growing. So she has a little baby fat. She's strong. She's big-boned," my dad insisted.

"When she's eating a box of cookies every day it's not baby fat. She's going on a diet."

"Just don't say she's fat," my dad insisted.

As I listened to their conversation I realized that my mom wasn't mad at me because they had to pay for the boxes of cookies I'd eaten. She was mad at me for eating. I put my pillow over my face and cried myself to sleep.

The next day I was put on the first of what would be many, many diets and had the first of many battles with my mother about my weight.

My mom made every attempt to turn daily chores and goals into a competition between my brother and me. She documented everything on her "chart of stars." My brother and I got stars for punctuality, tooth brushing, feeding the dog, sweeping the pool, and proper water conservation bathing. I often had a chance to dominate the chart of stars: if I stuck to my diet, a star; if I lost weight, another star; if I went swimming after dinner instead of having dessert, more stars! It didn't work. The chart would be up and then it would disappear for a while, but it made a comeback throughout my childhood. She tried.

Despite our diet tug-of-war, my mom and I were very close. We're both Leos, so we'd argue often but we loved always. One of the things we shared was a love of crafts, especially jewelry making. She was unfailingly enthusiastic about all the pottery and paint and other projects that we'd make for her and proudly displayed every single one, including a frame I once made out of bobby pins, and a pencil holder my brother made out of Popsicle sticks! My mom and I would sit for hours making things. We could turn virtually anything into a piece of jewelry. One summer we collected the tabs off aluminum soda cans and turned them into necklaces and cuffs. It may not sound glamorous, but we thought our designs were gorgeous. We taught ourselves to bead and wire wrap and knot pearls. We'd buy broken jewelry at swap meets and thrift stores and turn them into something amazing. I loved planning, designing, and creating with my mother. She was deeply artistic and had a real knack for being able to look at something and deconstruct it in order to reconstruct it in a different way. I inherited her passion for color and design, and my brother inherited her ability to construct. John is an electrical engineer with a real talent and patience for arts and crafts. He has passed on my mother's enthusiasm for crafts to the next generation. I've received many gifts from my nephew, Aryton, and my niece, Jessenya, that have Joyce Guerra's influence all over them.

My dad trained and guided my brother and me like we were heavyweight championship contenders. "It doesn't matter how many times you get hit—it's how you react that determines a winner." My dad is a competitor and approaches life to win. He loves horses and boxing and baseball. He is tough and doesn't shy away from confrontation or a challenge, and occasionally he says things that are very politically incorrect where men and women are concerned ("a woman should look like a lady"). More than once, as I tried to walk out the front door, I was stopped in my tracks by a comment like, "Aren't you going to fix your hair, Mija?" He likes women to be clean, polished, and pretty. But the truth is, in many ways, my dad was ahead of his time. He never expected anything different from me than he did from my brother, and he certainly wouldn't stand for anyone else doing it either. When John played sports, so did I. When John was given karate lessons, so was I. When John was taught how to clean, load, unload, and fire a gun, so was I.

In tenth grade I was given an assignment in my history class to write about "Great Americans." I was really excited because we had just learned about the Freedom Rides during the sixties, and I chose to write about the slain civil rights activists Cheney, Goodman, and Schwerner, who lost their lives while registering black voters in Mississippi. I was very passionate about my choice and excitedly shared it with my teacher. He told me that I should stick to what I know. "Why don't you choose a more feminine topic? Why don't you think about writing about the president's wife?"

"Why can't I write about Cheney, Goodman, and Schwerner?"

"You're a young woman—write about a woman."

I was so annoyed with my teacher. When I went home and told my dad about the conversation, I learned what a mistake it was for anyone to pull the gender card with me. The next day my dad was at my school bright and early to greet my teacher.

"Can I see the books you give to the girls in your class?" my dad demanded.

"I don't know what you mean, Mr. Guerra. The boys and the girls use the same textbook," my teacher replied nervously.

"That's what I thought. So why would you tell my daughter to choose what she studies based on being a girl?"

I have to admit I was proud that my dad stood up to him, but I also felt bad for my teacher, who looked so scared. Before he even had a chance to answer, my dad continued. "Did you tell the boys to choose male subjects to write about, or do you just like to single out the girls?"

"I'm sorry, Mr. Guerra. I think Jackie may have misunderstood what I meant."

"She didn't misunderstand anything. You're the one who is confused. Don't ever tell my daughter or any other girl that she should study anything different than the boys in your class."

And with that, he left. Not bad for a man often accused of being a macho Mexicano!

That night I got a lecture about how "that's the last time I'm going to make that argument for you. You better toughen up, Mija. People are going to try to tell you what you should do and know and where you should go and who you are throughout your life. You better know who you are and what you want and speak up. Next time *you* ask him to pull out the boy textbooks and the girl textbooks. Do you understand?" I did.

One of the things that my brother and I have laughed about over the years is that my parents used to have a wall plaque that hung in our house that read, "Children learn what they live, not what they're taught." My parents most certainly taught us to be polite. They showed us to stand up for ourselves. They taught us to obey and follow rules. They showed us to question things and speak our minds.

My parents were young adults during the sixties, when massive changes were happening all around them. Everything they'd been taught as kids was suddenly open for discussion. The civil rights movement, the women's movement, birth control, the Chicano movement, the first Catholic president of the United States, the rise of the UFW, all of it had a profound effect on them, and they passed it on to my brother and to me.

My parents believed that society's rules were optional, but their rules were gospel. They believed that the most important thing for us to do as we made our way through life was to learn as much as we could while we figured out who we were. We were taught by example not to fear challenge or failure, but to learn from them and to strive to be better and stronger; with every choice and decision, we're laying the foundation for the people that we're capable of being. We're *under construction.*

CHAPTER TWO

Senator Hollywood

"Without leaps of imagination, or dreaming, we lose the excitement of possibilities. Dreaming, after all, is a form of planning."
—GLORIA STEINEM

EVER SINCE I CAN REMEMBER, I WANTED TO BE OF SERVICE; I wanted to *get out and do something!* When I was in sixth grade, my teacher asked the class what we each wanted to be when we grew up. Immediately a row of small hands shot up.

"I want to be a dancer!"

"I want to be a wrestler!"

Then the teacher looked at me. "Jackie, what do you want to be?"

I answered, "I want to be the first Mexican-American female senator from the state of California."

My fascination with government and public service was probably, as they say, in my blood. I remember the day my father became a United States citizen. We all helped him study for the test; U.S. trivia became our dinnertime entertainment. When the day came, we all went to the Federal Building downtown in brand-new coordinating outfits and watched my dad stand up with hundreds of other immigrants and take the next step in the American dream by becoming naturalized citizens. I'll never forget when my dad finished: my mother walked over to him and gave him the most passionate kiss, and said, "Now you can vote, mi vida." I knew from the way she said it and the kiss she gave him that voting was a really big deal. My mom always told us, "Voting is the great equalizer; rich or poor, everyone's vote is counted the same. You have to participate in the system to be part of the system. Your vote is your way of adding to the rich fabric of our country. You have a responsibility to give your country as much as you get." For my eighteenth birthday my mom had a license plate frame made for my car that read, "Register & Vote: Su voto es su voz" (Your vote is your voice). She often talked about "giving a voice to the voiceless." I loved it and knew that in some way that's what I wanted to do.

My first "adult" job was as an organizer for the Hotel Employees and Restaurant Employees Union (HERE), Local 11. Growing up I'd read about the civil rights movement and the Freedom Rides, the women's movement, Cesar Chavez and the UFW and all of the organizers who made such a difference in the quality of life for all of us. I dreamed of being part of something that could have that kind of impact on people's lives, to empower them and make them stronger. When I had the opportunity to work at Local 11, I didn't hesitate.

The members of Local 11 work in some of the greatest hotels and restaurants in the world, in Los Angeles, California. I was assigned to the contract negotiations for our members who worked at the Hyatt Hotels. Aside from organizing our membership, each of us on the Hyatt team was also responsible for making sure that contracts were enforced and for organizing new members, and in anticipation of an attempt by the Hyatt corporation to try to convince their employees to get rid of their union, we also ran weekly picket lines; we worked to gain support for our members at the Hyatt Hotels and in the Los Angeles community for our boycott, organized rallies, solicited donations, kept morale up, attended negotiations, ran information meetings, and did lots of paperwork. The work was constant, intense, and rewarding, and the results were often immediate.

During negotiations I met a dishwasher in his early fifties, a man who had immigrated to the United States from his native El Salvador. He worked the graveyard shift for eleven years, and told me that he had never received any overtime pay. Luckily, he'd kept every single pay stub he'd received. We filed a claim for back wages, and in one lump sum he received all the overtime he'd earned during his eleven-year career. As a result, he was able to make a down payment on a house. Today that man and his wife live in a home that they own, and their daughter is in college. By creating an environment where people are informed and able to speak up and stand up for themselves, the union provided a way for this man to completely change the course of his family's life. It was exciting and it felt really good to be of service and make a difference every day in the lives of our members. When people unite, they are never voiceless. It was exciting, all-consuming, and exhausting.

One night I came home after a very long and brutally hot California day. We had had an all-day picket line, followed by a four-hour staff strategy meeting. It was ten thirty p.m. and I was wiped out. I walked into my empty apartment, and my insane neighbor, Bobby the drag queen, was waiting to tell me a story about how our other neighbor, the drug dealer, had beaten up his boyfriend . . . what a day! When Bobby left, I went into autopilot, as I had done virtually every night since being assigned to the Hyatt campaign. I made an entire box of macaroni and cheese, grabbed my two-liter bottle of Diet Coke (what's the point? you ask. I don't know—it just made sense at the time!), a bag of tortilla chips, and plopped onto my couch. I turned on the television just in time to catch the eleven o'clock news. As I shoveled gigantic spoonful after gigantic spoonful of mac 'n' cheese into my mouth and washed it down with Diet Coke, the sportscaster was talking about an NFL linebacker who was apparently the "biggest" draft pick of the year. He weighed 260 pounds. The anchorman chuckled as the sports guy threw it back to him and said, "Wow, that's a big guy." And at that moment, sitting alone in my dark, depressing, and lonely apartment, listening to the sounds of Bobby the drag queen rehearsing his version of "Dreamgirls" and anesthetizing myself with chips, macaroni and cheese, and Diet Coke, I realized that *I* was an NFL linebacker—without the athletic prowess or the multimillion-dollar payday. I weighed as much as the NFL draft pick who was the topic of the news banter!

I felt like I had been slapped. I snapped out of my self-induced carb coma and looked around my apartment. I realized for the first time that I was dressed from head to toe in black. My couch was black, the table was black, my lamp was black, my dishes were black, and the handles of my silverware were black. Suddenly I thought, "Everything around me is black—*what am I in mourning for?*" Sadly, I realized I was in mourning for my life. I didn't have one. I had gained a hundred pounds, I lived alone, I hadn't seen my friends in so long I wasn't even sure I still had any, my parents and my brother had moved to San Luis Obispo, California, where my brother would attend college, I missed my family, and I was surrounded by everything black. I had to make a change.

A few days after I discovered that, apparently, I was in mourning, some friends of mine invited me to meet them for happy hour at a club in West Hollywood called Rage. I made the usual excuses and explained to them that I couldn't just "take off." I knew they were upset with me, and I was too. Finally around nine at night I drove to the club. On the one hand, I was so proud of myself for taking some "me" time. On the other hand, I was racked with guilt because I still had so much work to do. I parked my dirty, filthy car filled with picket signs, fliers, and parking tickets and walked into the club. There was so much life and activity! People were talking and singing and dancing and seemed so happy. I saw my friends and joined them. While I was hanging out— what a unique concept!—I noticed there was a talent show at this club. I thought, "Hmmm, I wonder if I could sign up for the talent show and tell everyone about the boycott? Surely if they knew about the boycott, they'd support it!" I signed up. When I heard the host call my name, I went onstage and just talked about my tough day on the picket line, including the idiot who felt that it was his prerogative to spit on me. I wasn't nervous. Didn't have time. I was focused on getting support for the cause.

But the most life-altering and amazing thing happened. For the first time in my life, I understood the word "seduction." When I was on that stage and every single person in the club was waiting for my next word, it was seductive! It was better than any sex or drug that I had heard of. (Of course, my sex and drug experience at that time rivaled Mother Teresa's!) It was intoxicating: the laughter, the lights, the applause. I guess I stood out. Maybe the crowd liked my passion. Maybe it was a good day for chubby Mexicans. Or maybe I got on that stage the way my mother had taught me to do everything, like I was Elvis! I walked up there and looked at all those people and spoke to them like I had the most important thing to say ever and they were damned lucky to be there to hear it. Whatever it was, I won! I won the talent show. By following my instincts and not worrying about what someone might think or say or how I looked, I had hit upon something. But the most incredible part happened when I got offstage: I got more signatures on my boycott petition after ten minutes on a cabaret stage in a gay club than I had gotten in an entire month on a picket line! I had inspired a big, unsuspecting group to *get out and do something*. I felt alive, and I thought, "Okay, change of plans; *this* is how I'm going to make a difference."

While I drove home, I replayed the evening and all of the excitement in my mind a thousand times. I realized that while the activist side of me was in overdrive, the part of me that liked to have fun and entertain was being completely ignored. It seemed to me that the perfect marriage for both parts of me would thrive onstage. I knew how very powerful it was to stand on a stage with a microphone and how much you can accomplish when you're given that privilege. I started to think about how much I'd learned about myself and about the world from other people holding the microphone. My mind raced with images of Roseanne and Oprah. I knew how excited and inspired they made me feel, and how important their words were; what a difference they'd made in my life. By the time I got home to what previously felt like a dark, gloomy dungeon, I was filled with a purpose. I actually said out loud, "This is how I'm going to change the world: I'll do stand-up comedy, I'll work really hard to build an act, and then one day I'll host a talk show, where I can do for others what good television has done for me, and then I'll help millions of people!" It seemed like a good plan. I called my good friend and fellow union organizer Karine. In my excitement I didn't realize that it was two in the morning.

"Karine, I'm going to do stand-up comedy!"

"What time is it?" she mumbled.

"I don't know, but I know that one day when I'm famous you're going to remember that you were the first person I told that I was going to be a comic."

"Can we talk about this in the morning?"

"Okay, call me when you wake up!"

"You're crazy. Get some sleep."

Good luck. There was no way I was going to sleep. I had a new dream and couldn't wait to get busy living it!

The one thing that stood between my current life and my new life was my work at Local 11. We were in the middle of heated contract negotiations with the Hyatt Hotel chain. I cared deeply about the job, the members, and my coworkers, and especially for my boss, the president of HERE Local 11, Maria Elena Durazo, who I called MED. I was sure that when I told her about my plan she would try to talk me into staying, or worse yet that she'd be disappointed in me. Both options made me nervous. Maria Elena is not just the president of Local 11—she is a member and she lives what she says. She is the daughter of migrant farmworkers and worked her way through college and law school, and chose to dedicate her life to improving the quality of life for working women and men in Los Angeles. To her it's not a job; it's a cause.

On my way to meet her, I must have downed about four cups of coffee. By the time I walked into her office, I wasn't just excited to tell her about my plan and nervous to see her reaction. I was completely wired from caffeine.

"MED, the most amazing thing happened to me the other night!"

"You met someone?" she asked. MED is a hopeless romantic. She's married to her best friend, Miguel Contreras, and wants everyone to be as in love as she is.

"No. I mean, not really. Well . . . kind of. I guess you could say that I met the real me!"

"What happened?"

I excitedly recounted my "moment in the spotlight" at Rage. As I got deeper into the story, she shifted in her chair and moved farther and farther toward the edge of her seat.

"You didn't!" She laughed. "You have some pair of *cojones* getting up in front of a bunch of people ready to party to talk about the boycott. Damn, you're good!"

"I want to be a stand-up comic." As soon as the words came out of my mouth, it was as if I could hear the sound of tires screeching. Her face, which had been smiling and laughing, was suddenly expressionless, and she sat back in her chair with such speed it was as if someone had pushed her. Finally, after what seemed like an hour but I'm sure was more like a minute, she said, "You what?"

"Just listen to me. I'm starving. Okay, clearly I'm not starving, but I need to do something where I'm contributing but also doing something that's good for me. When I was on that stage, I felt more energized, more inspired, and more alive than I ever have. I didn't even know I could feel that way." I could see by the way she looked at me that she was trying to figure out if I had truly found my calling in life or just needed some long-overdue time off to rest.

"Do you want to take some vacation time?" she asked, sounding concerned.

"No. I want to go and do this."

MED is a very passionate, thoughtful, and deliberate woman. She looked at me and said, "Jackie, you have a great future here. I know that you have planned for some time to run for office. The work that you've done and are doing is preparing you for that, and now you want to completely change your course to become a stand-up comic? I just want you to be sure that you've completely thought this through. I want you to be sure that if you leave, you're leaving because you are moving *toward* something and not because you're *running away* from something."

We sat and talked for a long time. I reminded her that I got more signatures on my boycott petition after ten minutes onstage than I'd gotten the entire month on the picket line. Imagine if I were on TV every day, I told her.

"You know, if you can do this, you really will make a difference." It was music to my ears!

"So you understand?" I asked anxiously.

"I understand that you have to do what's right for you. That's what we tell our members every day and it goes for you too: 'the better off you are, the better off we all are.'" And then she taught me a lesson I'll never forget. "You need to make a plan to leave. You have to tie up loose ends and explain to everyone why you're leaving so that they'll feel good about this decision. If affects them too. Remember this: *the way you walk out of one door determines how you enter the next door.*" As she spoke, I thought about how many times my mom had told me to "walk into a room like you're Elvis!" And now another woman I trusted and loved was teaching me to leave a room better than the way I walked in. I've had some good teachers!

It took me six months to "tie up loose ends" and leave my career as an organizer at Local 11 to take the next step in continuing to build my life. The people I worked with who had been my extended family for over two years were almost unanimously supportive. Even the ones who didn't necessarily understand what I was doing understood that it was the right decision for me. We won the Hyatt campaign, and today the workers at those hotels enjoy one of the best union contracts in the country . . . until the next negotiations! And so in the spring of 1993, I began my life as a full-time comic performing at every open mike, hotel lounge, bar, coffeehouse, and club that would let me. Elvis has left the building!

Most comics have war stories about their early days and all of the humiliation they had to endure to get ten minutes onstage. I can't compete with any of them. My early days of comedy were action-packed and a lot of fun. I started doing open mikes in Los Angeles. My comedy buddies and I tried to do at least two or three sets at different places. I made a lot of comedy buddies quickly because I had a car. (Believe it or not, there are people in Los Angeles who function without a car; they're called comics.) I spent my days writing material and hanging out with my new friends and my nights in search of stage time. Most of my comedy buddies were guys: Rich, Allen, Freddy, Peter, Bean, and Bill. I was pretty shocked at how segregated the world of stand-up comedy is; most clubs have a "Girls Night," a "Latino Night," a "Gay Night" and of course an "Urban Night." I don't know how it happened that in the art form made popular by Lenny Bruce, George Carlin, Richard Pryor, and Roseanne there is so much segregation. I was shocked at how few women were working in comedy, let alone Latinas. All those lectures that my dad had given me about being "as tough as the next guy" were really helpful, because comedy is still a boys' game and you have to be tough to survive. The world of stand-up can be pretty brutal, but when it's good, it's nirvana. Good stage time is like a drug. You feel high while you're on the stage, and then you spend the rest of your life trying to get more stage time to get that high again. It's really addictive.

Within five months of my doing stand-up for the first time, a very smart and aggressive agent approached me. She helped me put together an act and began booking me in colleges and universities around the country. I hit the road with my act, a tape recorder, a notebook, a camera, and a whole lot of enthusiasm. I was so happy to be performing and traveling around this beautiful country of ours. I was even happier to be reminded that there are places outside of Los Angeles where there is conversation beyond the latest diet, gym, colonic, workout craze, and so on. Places where people actually read books and the newspaper to know what's going on in the world and not just *Variety*, *The Hollywood Reporter*, and *Vogue* to know whose ass to kiss and which purse to carry. I was shocked that in many of the towns I visited there were people who had never met a Mexican. And forget about being able to pronounce my last name! But I was thrilled to go to cities like San Antonio, Texas, where the editor of the newspaper is a Mexican American, and Kansas City, Missouri, where there is a huge Mexican-American middle class, and Chicago, Illinois, where a Mexican American sits on the school board. It was an exciting time for me, and I was working on my act while meeting people all over the country, and despite the fact that life on the road can sometimes be a little lonely, I had fun.

About one year after I began to do stand-up full-time, I was offered, and accepted, a development deal by Columbia TriStar Television and the WB Network to star in my own sitcom. I was so happy and excited. I felt like I had hit the lottery, because I was going to be playing myself on television in a show that was based on my life. I thought I was the luckiest person in the entire world! Little did I know I was in for one of the most eye-opening experiences of my life.

A lot of miracles have to occur between signing a development deal and actually getting a show onto network television: find a writer for a pilot, get network approval of the script, cast the show, shoot the pilot, then hope the network decides it likes it and has room for the show on their schedule. Everything went smoothly getting the pilot written and approved. Then we began the casting process, and I realized I wasn't just starring in a network sitcom; I had to educate a lot of people about who I was and who Latinos are. One afternoon I sat in a room full of network and studio executives for a casting session for the actor that would play my best friend. The role was written for a funny Latina. A black Nuyorican (a Puerto Rican from New York) actress named Tracy Vilar came in to audition for the role and knocked it out of the ballpark. It was obvious the role was hers. But then someone in the room said, "But she isn't Latina."

I said, "Yes, she is. She's Puerto Rican."

Dead silence, followed by, "But she's black."

For the next twenty minutes I did my best impression of Mr. Mercado, my seventh-grade social studies teacher, to explain the ethnic and racial migration of Puerto Ricans. I drew charts and graphs and pictures, which I used to explain that in Puerto Rico the indigenous people are Indians, that the colonizers were Spaniards who were Caucasian, and the slaves they brought were Africans, so Puerto Ricans can be any combination of Indian, Spanish Caucasian, and black—or all of the above.

"But aren't all Latinas from Mexico?"

Out came my charts and graphs again! This was a roomful of successful, educated adults who wield a lot of power in the entertainment industry, and therefore shape the way we see ourselves on television. And all this happened in Los Angeles, which used to be part of Mexico! I honestly believe that they went through all of their years in school without ever learning this piece of American history. Their choices about who can and will play roles on television shows help shape how we see ourselves and each other! I got in my car to drive home and had to pull over twice to vomit.

Tracy got the role, and so this very talented and beautiful black Puerto Rican actor played the role of my best friend. The day that we taped the pilot was one of the most magical and thrilling days of my life.

Everyone I loved was there: my parents, my brother, Maria Elena Durazo, my friends. The network hired a family friend to cater the evening, and it was beautiful. I wish for everyone I know at least one night that is as perfect as that one was for me! A few weeks later I got a call from the president of the WB Network to tell me that our pilot was being picked up for a series. I was picked up in front of my apartment building by a stretch limousine and flown—first class—to New York (first time in first class). I arrived at my hotel room, which was bigger than my entire apartment, to find it filled with flowers from the network, the studio, my agent's husband, my business manager, my attorney, and my boyfriend. I felt very lucky and very special, and it was thrilling! Every time I picked up the phone to call the front desk, the person on the other end answered, "How can I help you, Miss Guerra?" I had arrived! I felt like royalty. I was living my dream!

First Time Out ran on the WB Network during the 1995/1996 television season. We were the number-two show . . . if you looked at the Nielson ratings backward. It wasn't a blockbuster, but it was an incredible experience. I got paid to learn about television production: writing, casting, budgets, network politics, studio politics, the meaning of syndication. (Ask any sitcom actor—syndication means "set for life.") I met some incredible people during *First Time Out* who became lifelong friends, and got to work with my childhood crush, Scott Baio, and my childhood idol, Rita Moreno. As a kid I must have seen *West Side Story* a thousand times. I know every song, most of the dialogue, and every dance routine in that movie. You can imagine my glee when I was told that Rita Moreno—the only Latina in the world to have an Oscar, a Grammy, a Tony, and an Emmy (actually two)—had agreed to play my grandmother on *First Time Out*! I was thrilled, excited, and very honored. I couldn't believe it! "Anita" from *West Side Story*, the legendary Rita Moreno, was going to play my grandmother, and I was going to share the stage with one of the women I admired most. This was better than a Lancôme gift with purchase!

The first day Rita was scheduled to work, there was no entourage, no fanfare, and no "rules" about not making eye contact or referring to her only as "Ms. Moreno." She walked right up to the woman who was in charge of the food on the set and introduced herself. "Hello. My name is Rita. Could you tell me where I can get a cup of tea?" I watched her make her way around the table of writers, producers, and network and studio executives. She spoke to everyone from the production assistant to the president of the network in the same casual manner and treated everyone with equal importance. I was so happy and relieved to know that the woman I admired is down to earth and truly someone worthy of being admired. What a class act.

When I finally introduced myself to her, she said, "Congratulations on your success, Hija. I hope you're enjoying it." Wow! Rita Moreno congratulating me? On my success? I think I said something really brilliant like, "Thank you. I am." Not my best one-liner, but it was sincere and I was in awe. We all sat down at the table to read the week's episode, and I could barely believe that this was my life. I was sitting and acting with Rita Moreno. Check that one off the "things to do before I die" list: act with Rita Moreno; check!

As the first Latina to star in a network sitcom, I became an unwitting role model for my community. I was an actress, activist, organizer—and scared. I found myself constantly putting out fires, doing press to promote the show (which I loved), working with the cast to make sure they were heard, trying to work with writers, take care of my family—all this and to star in a network sitcom—it was a lot! My brother was getting married, my mother was sick, and to top it off, I had a stalker, and the WB Network assigned a twenty-four-hour bodyguard to me. I got my first cold sore the day before a kissing scene with the brilliant actor David Ybarra, the executive producer that I loved had to go back to another show because of a contractual obligation, the new executive producer called me a fat f——ing c——t, and I was falling madly in love with one of the writers. In addition I had to maintain my schedule of comedy shows at colleges across the country, making personal appearances at every parade, festival, fair, or gathering anywhere in the United States to promote the show, doing a television show, taping promos, press interviews, media events, learning at the speed of light, and trying to eat, sleep, and brush my teeth! I was really busy.

People say that politics is dirty, but, believe me, it's nothing compared to the politics of show business. A Hispanic media watchdog group picketed *First Time Out* on tape night because, according to them, we didn't have enough Latinos working on the show. This was the ultimate irony since I had been turned into a full-time advocate and Hollywood activist for my community. I lobbied hard to encourage the network to hire as many women and Latinos at every level on our show as possible. As it turned out, we had more Latinos on our staff than any other show at that time. But for this particular group, it wasn't enough. The irony of someone picketing my show was not lost on me, but in this case the tactic was destructive.

First Time Out was the only show with two Latina leads—neither of whom was playing a maid, hooker, drug addict, or gangbanger. We had more Latino writers on staff than any other show, three of whom, as a result of their tenure on our show, became members of the Writers Guild of America and have gone on to successful writing/producing careers on other shows. Every week we cast brilliant Latino actors as guest stars. And we had Latinos on our production staff. It wasn't perfect, but it was a lot more than had been done in a long time on prime time. I was devastated that a group that claimed to be a civil rights group turned their organizing efforts on our show. I was reminded of a story that Cesar Chavez told a young organizers' training session that I attended in

Delano, California. *"La gente luchando para salir de sus condiciónes somos como el cangrejo. Cuando se pesca el cangrejo, se los meten en una cubeta. Todos los cangrejo se quieren salir y al momento que uno se sube, todos los demás lo arrancan para abajo. Deberiamos ser major que el cangrejo."* Here's the English translation: "Sometimes when a group is working to better their conditions, they act like crabs. Have you ever fished for crab? When you catch a crab you put it into a bucket. All of them will try to escape to get free. The minute one of the crabs climbs up the side of the bucket and is about to reach the top, the other crabs still at the bottom will pull him down. We should be better than crabs." No kidding!

Despite all of the drama and the trauma of *First Time Out*, I managed to fall deeply and madly in love with one of the writers on the show, Bill Torres. We started out as friends and grew into best friends. Several years later, he proposed that we spend the rest of our lives together in the most beautiful and romantic way, and then we celebrated at a wonderful party with our family and friends. Bill is my best friend and one of the greatest people on the face of the earth, my love and my rock. Who needs a sitcom when you've got a brilliant, kind, generous, foxy Puerto Rican hunk who makes you laugh and learn every single day? I'm in love—even though he can't dance!

I knew the end was near one Tuesday night when I read the week's script and discovered that my character would be going to Tijuana to have a tooth pulled cheaply by a stereotypical Mexican dentist. I called the network executive in charge of my show to express my concerns. Through tears of frustration, I begged her to step in. All she said to me was, "Jackie, you're a first-time sitcom gal. Go with the program. Keep your mouth shut and cash your check and buy yourself a present. One day all of this will be a page in your book." So, one night in December of 1995, I found myself on a soundstage in Culver City, California, sandwiched between *The Nanny* and *Mad About You*, in front of about 175 studio audience members, sitting in a dentist chair when the dentist walks in wearing a Charro sombrero and a serape. It was one of the most obnoxious and degrading moments of my life. My heart dropped into my stomach. I prayed for an earthquake to make it stop. I had no idea how I'd gotten to this place. But that not-so-helpful network executive was right: it is a page in my book!

Shortly after we taped that episode I was invited to dinner with one of the top executives of the WB. We went to a casual restaurant and had

I think you have a future in film.

a chance to get to know each other. Toward the end of the evening, I realized that we hadn't really discussed the future of the show, but I figured it was a good sign that she'd invited me to dinner, especially since we were waiting for the network to decide whether they were going to pick us up to do more episodes. Out of nowhere she said, "You have a classic face. Like a movie star from the fifties." Chills ran down my spine because I've heard only too many times, "You have such a pretty face." Translation: You should lose weight. So when I heard her words, I thought it was fancy network speak for "You should lose weight." But she surprised me again by saying, "I think you have a future in film. You have a film actress kind of presence." I thought this was an odd thing for her to say to me since I was the lead of a television sitcom on her network, but I was grateful and flattered by her compliment.

First Time Out debuted the same year as *The Wayans Bros*. That Christmas the WB Network sent out holiday cards and gifts to the stars of their shows. I figured out what the future held for our show when Shawn and Marlon Wayans received matching Range Rovers . . . and I got a card. As I looked at that card, I could hear that network executive's prophetic words: "I think you have a future in film." I was so busy being paranoid that she was telling me to lose weight that I completely missed the real message, which was that I didn't have a future on *First Time Out*! It wasn't so much a compliment as it was a hint. I guess we hear what we want to hear.

First Time Out was canceled three weeks later.

CHAPTER THREE

After the First Time Out

"The world is round and the place which may seem like the end may also be the beginning."
—IVY BAKER PRIEST

SHORTLY AFTER *FIRST TIME OUT* WAS CANCELED, I read a script for a movie called *Eat Your Heart Out.* I called my agent and told her that I really liked the script. She told me that the writer-director of the film was a wonderful director from . . . "Hmm, I think he's from Mexico. Yeah, he's a rich guy from Mexico and his father is funding the movie." Interesting! She called and got me an appointment to read for the role of "Julie."

The day of the audition was one of those perfect days in Los Angeles, the reason that so many people from all over the world move here. The weather was perfect and bright and crisp and everyone seemed to be in a good mood. I loved the script, I loved "Julie," and I loved my outfit. I drove from Studio City to Santa Monica with coffee in hand and the Los Angeles skyline in front of me. I sang along with Mary J. Blige, Lauryn Hill, and Marc Anthony at the top of my lungs, a fantastic car concert! When I arrived at the audition, I walked into a waiting room full of very recognizable faces, all there to audition for the same role. As I looked around the room I realized two things about my "competition": one, I outweighed everyone in that room by about fifty pounds; and two, I was the least famous person there. The odds didn't look good.

When my name was called, I went in to meet the Mexican director, Felix Adlon. I asked him why he called me in to read for the role of "Julie" since, based on the other women who were there to audition, he obviously had a different vision in mind. And by vision, I meant skinny! He explained to me that what he was looking for in "Julie" was an essence, and that the actress who had been cast as the lead in the movie, Pamela Segall, had suggested that he meet me. I didn't know

Pamela but I already liked her! During my audition both the director and the casting director laughed a lot and I had a great time.

I got the part and I was thrilled. I called my parents to tell them that I was going to be in a fantastic movie produced and directed by Mexicans! I was going to play "Julie, a gregarious, outspoken, opinionated makeup artist who does not fear a little cleavage." Big stretch! *Eat Your Heart Out* is the first film I was ever cast in. As it turned out, it was one of the best experiences of my life, too.

The first clue that it would be a wonderful experience came when I got a call from the costume designer. After the perfunctory chitchat about sizes, she informed me that the director and the producers wanted my character to look beautiful and sexy. Whaaaat? I was in absolute and total shock! This after my experience on *First Time Out*, where my wardrobe fluctuated between overgrown, chubby third-grader and gigantic, flowing, sparkly, "mother-of-the-bride" wear! And way too frequent comments, like "You'd have more options if you dropped some weight. There isn't much to choose from in your size." It was a new day in this actress's life.

My first day on the set happened to be the first day of filming for the entire cast and crew. We were shooting on the UCLA campus. I got to the set early and saw my trailer (with my name on the door—it was superexciting), and then went to the producer's trailer, and, in my best Spanish, introduced myself to Felix's father, Percy. He didn't say much, but seemed to be amused by my enthusiasm, and gave me a very warm "welcome" hug. Hmmm, Percy is a very unusual name for a Mexican. He spoke to me in English, with a very thick accent. I immediately called Bill to tell him that I was on the set and just met the wealthy Mexican producer named Percy. Bill replied, "Percy Adlon?"

Jackie: *"Yes!"*

Bill: "Percy Adlon, the award-winning German director of *Bagdad Café*?"

Jackie: "What? I thought he was Mexican."

Bill: "No. He's German and he's a genius."

Jackie: "Oh, that explains the weird look on his face when I spoke to him in Spanish."

So as it turns out, Percy is not a wealthy Mexican who decided to bankroll his son's vanity project. He is an accomplished director and producer serving as the executive producer of *Eat Your Heart Out*, the funding for which came from traditional investors, and Felix is an accomplished writer who was set to make his directorial debut. No free rides here. Boy, was I wrong about who these people were!

The first scene to be shot was my audition scene. I knew every beat of that scene. During the audition, I got laughs exactly where I expected them, and since then I'd rehearsed the scene over and over with Bill and found it even more funny! All of my experience was in stand-up comedy and on a sitcom with a live studio audience. I knew how to get laughs and I was there to deliver "the funny." I got dressed, went through hair and makeup, and walked onto that huge soundstage at UCLA confident and ready for "the funny"! I was bursting at the seams to hit it out of the park. I just knew that the lighting guys, the grips, the sound guys, everyone on the crew was going to crack up when we did the scene.

I heard Felix yell, *"Action!"* And I flew into action. I hit the first beat in the scene where there is a funny moment and . . . nothing! Suddenly, the cameras are rolling, the lights are beating down on me, I'm dripping in flop-sweat, and totally aware of my surroundings, and therefore not present in the scene. We finished the scene, and I didn't get even one little chuckle. You know the nightmare of showing up at school naked and being in the quad with everyone in the entire school staring at you, pointing and laughing? That's *exactly* the way I felt! Everything that eight minutes earlier had seemed exciting and magical was now horrible. Luckily, there was a sound issue and Felix asked us to do the scene again. To my horror, he said to do it *exactly* the same way. What? Didn't he understand that it totally sucked and *nobody* laughed? Well, he's the director. I got myself together the best I could and did the scene all over again, hoping for the best and . . . nothing! Again, not even a sympathy giggle. When Felix yelled, "*Cut*," I seriously thought I was going to be sick. The crew needed to work on something, so we took a ten-minute break. I ran out of that soundstage so fast. I turned a corner and saw a pay phone. I called my agent, sobbing, and told her that the filming was going terribly and I was sure I was going to be fired. I asked her not to fight it because I just couldn't be funny and I didn't know why. I begged her to just let them fire me, thank them for the opportunity, and let's move on. She asked me what happened and I told her: I did my scene twice and both times I hit every comedic beat that I'd rehearsed, and both times the scene was met with deafening silence! She took a breath and said, "Jackie, this is not a comedy club or a sitcom in front of a live studio audience. This is film and the people on the set have to be silent! They can't make noise and laugh and cheer— it's a movie, not Comedy Central!" That was twice in one day that I managed to be the ultimate show-business schmuck! Let's review: not a spoiled Mexican guy directing a movie bankrolled by his daddy, and no laughing on a film set. Okay, I was ready for my close-up!

As I made my way back to the soundstage, I finally met Pamela Segall. Aside from the fact that I knew the only reason I had my first role in a film was because of her, I immediately fell in love. Pam is about five feet tall and weighs about ninety pounds, most of which is hair and attitude. She has a deep, raspy voice and the most insane sense of humor. The day I met her she was wearing six-inch platform boots, a T-shirt with the name of some obscure band, thrashed jeans, had a cigarette dangling from her lips, and leather cuffs climbing her forearms. Pam immediately made me feel comfortable and completely at home. I walked onto that set a new person—Elvis was back!

I now understood that on a film set, the only reaction that is necessary is the reaction that you solicit from your fellow actors in a scene. It's about shutting out all the noise and everything else around you and just focusing completely on listening and communicating with the person in front of you. Just paying attention to your own emotions and allowing yourself to feel what is real—not what you imagine, not what has happened before in similar situations, not what you think is going to happen, not what you've been told may happen, but being totally and completely present and allowing what is supposed to happen, happen. That is paramount for an actor and very useful in life. Be present and listen. React to what is and not what "should" be. No expectations!

It reminds me of when my dance teacher would say surrender to the music. Feel the music. Think less and feel more. It's like when you really look at a painting and you just sink into it. Just be in the moment. Give in to the moment. Give in to the good part of the moment. Not the smelly part of the moment. For example, let's say you wake up, your body's stiff, you have a billion things to do, it's a million degrees outside, and it's rush, rush, rush, and no fun is in sight. Slow the game down a bit. Grab your coffee. Feel the warm cup. Bring it up to your nose. Close your eyes. Smell the aroma. Sip it. Enjoy the fact that your nose is in the cup. Feel the heat. Feel the wet brew touch your lips and your tongue. Listen to the sound of the sip and feel and hear it going down your throat. *Enjoy* that moment, dammit. It's calming and soothing. Get in touch with your senses. This will help. And don't forget to stretch, breathe, and relax.

It is said that elite athletes in crunch time see the game in *slow motion*. That is why they are elite. The athletes they defeat in crunch time *rush and panic*. The more urgent the situation, the more you need meditation. Be the calm in the middle of the storm.

At the end of that first day I went home to Bill and recounted my day. He was amused and supportive. He had gone to the video store and rented *Bagdad Café* for me to watch. We watched it together and I understood why I had been feeling so fabulous on the set. It was simple: Felix and Percy have an appreciation for women in all forms. The star of *Bagdad Café* is a delightfully Rubenesque woman with an appetite for life. That is the essence they were looking for and the reason they kept treating me like I was some kind of goddess! On *First Time Out*, I was reminded of how fat I was every single day by anyone who felt like commenting on it or doing really passive-aggressive things, like putting a treadmill in my dressing room (subtle) or writing scenes where my thin roommates were in miniskirts and belly shirts while I was covered in layers of clothing and a coat for no apparent reason. On *Eat Your Heart Out* my wardrobe was tight, bright, and bold. I wore plunging necklines in fuchsia, orange, yellow, and electric blue. No smocks, no layers, and no tricky placement behind furniture to hide my hips. I was treated for the first time in my professional life like a beautiful woman. Further proof that beauty is in the eye of the beholder. Felix and Percy are European and not tainted by the narrow American ideal of who is beautiful. I love them for that and for allowing me to feel beautiful. It was fun!

The days that followed on the set of *Eat Your Heart Out* were filled with great times. I spent a lot of time with Pam and really got to know her. I felt so happy to have a new friend. One afternoon while we were filming at an ultracool loft in Venice Beach, my parents came to visit me on the set. Pam took them all around and introduced them to everyone. My dad made a point of telling everyone who would listen that I thought Felix and Percy were Mexican and joked about how well they spoke German—for Mexicans! Even though I was an adult, costarring in a feature film, on the set where I work, my dad has the uncanny ability to make me feel twelve! Thanks, Dad!

During the filming I heard from a friend of mine that Gregory Nava was going to make a movie about the life of Selena Quintanilla Perez, the brilliant Tejano singer whose career was cut tragically short when the president of her fan club murdered her. I had seen Selena and her band in concert and it was an amazing show. When I heard about the movie, I called my agent and said, "I have to be in this movie. I'll sweep floors, I'll work as a production assistant, but I have to be involved in this film." I felt an intense connection to this project. My agent tried, but the director wasn't interested in seeing me because my background was in comedy and *Selena* was to be a drama. He also mentioned that Selena and her family had very indigenous features and were very dark-skinned, and he felt that I wasn't physically right for the part of

Selena's sister, Suzette. This ticked me off because I saw Suzette at the concert and was shocked at how much we looked alike. We were just about the same height, same weight, same body shape, and we definitely had a similar vibe. We even had on the same earrings, the same shoes, and the exact same shade of lipstick. I called my agent back and said that all I wanted was an opportunity to read. She said, "The door is closed."

But two months later, I got a call from my agent saying that they would see me. I showed up on the lot in full stage makeup and a long-sleeve black T-shirt with a crisp white shirt tied at the waist (very Suzette) and black pants; it was about 105 degrees.

I walked in knowing that this was my part to lose, and I gave the best audition of my life. I walked out, got in my car, called my agent, and said, "I nailed it. Let me know what my call time is." I went back to work on *Eat Your Heart Out* and told everyone that I got the part. The next day I learned that another actress was hired to play the role of Suzette. I was disappointed, but somehow I knew I was going to play that role. Even after the entire cast was in Texas rehearsing, I kept telling people I was going to be in the movie. I was obsessed. About five weeks later on a Sunday afternoon, I came home from brunch with my parents and found seventeen messages on my voice mail and nine faxes in my machine. My agent, my lawyer, and the casting director from *Selena* were trying to reach me. My agent told me that I needed to be on a plane in two hours to read for the part. Bill drove me to the airport, I said good-bye, and I was off on a very excellent adventure.

When I arrived in San Antonio, I was taken from the airport to the hotel and told to go to my room and wait for a call from someone in production. I was not to leave my room, not to go to any restaurants, not to go to the gym, not to walk around, and not to speak to *anybody* because they didn't want anyone to know I was there. I was in an actor's version of the witness protection program. Unfortunately the actress cast as Suzette was still in San Antonio and didn't know she was being replaced yet. All night I sat in my room, read and reread the script, and pretended not to notice that I was so nervous that I couldn't sleep.

The next day, I sat in a huge soundstage by myself, waiting for my audition with Jennifer Lopez. It was freezing and I was nervous. Just twenty-four hours earlier I had been sitting in a restaurant with Bill and my parents in Studio City, California, trying to decide what to order and making plans for the week, and now here I was in Texas, waiting for Jennifer Lopez, Gregory Nava, and the family of one of my musical favorites, Selena. And despite my nerves, I thought about how much I love the miracle of life; each day when you wake up you never know what miracle may occur or who may enter your life. It's so exciting!

I also thought a lot about Selena. I knew that she had been in this same soundstage many times with her brother, AB; her sister, Suzette; and the rest of the band. I could picture them there, full of hopes and dreams, joking around, rehearsing, planning their week too. I thought about how precious life is, and how the last time Selena drove to this soundstage, she had no idea that it would be the last time.

Just then Jennifer walked in with her best friend, Arlene Rodriguez. Arlene is a funny, mouthy, no-nonsense, streetwise, loving person with a bullshit detector that's always on "high alert." She is Jennifer's lifelong best friend from the Bronx, and, at that point, Jen's assistant too. It was really comforting to see them, because until then I had been completely alone since arriving in San Antonio. I was dying to talk to someone and Jennifer and Arlene were it! I had met Jennifer a few times at auditions and parties in Los Angeles. I knew her to be really focused, a hard worker, and a really nice person. Now I was blown away by how much she looked like Selena. Her hair was dyed jet-black and pulled into a tight ponytail. She was wearing large silver jewelry on her fingers and neck, and had on huge hoop earrings and bright red lipstick. This was not the Jenny from the block in Los Angeles that I knew—this was Jennifer bringing Selena to life. Amazing!

We talked about how rehearsals had been going and she filled me in on her crazy schedule—dance rehearsal, band rehearsal, scene rehearsal, workouts, hair and makeup tests, fittings, tanning, meetings with the Quintanilla family, reviewing videotapes of Selena performing as well as family videos, press interviews, all in the heat and humidity of summertime in San Antonio. And then she said the most generous thing that an actor can say to another actor before an audition. She told me, "Do whatever comes naturally to you during the scene. If you want to touch me, punch me, hug me, whatever, if it makes the scene better, do it!" I was genuinely touched and grateful. It's kind of an unspoken rule in acting that you don't touch the person you're reading with. She gave me the freedom to just "be" in the scene and not worry about rules. Then she grabbed my hand and told me to have fun and that she "had my back." I knew that two other actresses had read with Jen that day and that I was the last one of the day. Before I could gather my thoughts, Gregory Nava, the writer-director of the film, the same one who refused to see me a few months earlier, swooped into the room and told me to "come with him." I followed Gregory into a room where Jennifer and Arlene were, along with a camera operator and a producer. Gregory asked me if I had any questions; I didn't. I mean, I did, but I couldn't remember them. He told me that the scene he wanted us to do was a scene that defined the relationship between the two sisters. And the next thing I knew, I heard "Action," and Jen and I were in the middle of an argument that takes place on Selena's tour bus. I grabbed Jennifer and threw her on a couch in the room, pounced on top of her, and began to whine, "Selena, you ate my chips. Those were my chips. Selena!" When we finished the scene, Jennifer hugged me tightly and mouthed the words, "You got it." I will always be grateful to Jennifer for what she did for me during that audition. It was a scene all about "chemistry," and she controlled 50 percent of it.

Greg thanked me and said, "Good job." Then he asked me the same question that the casting director and my agent had: "You can play the drums, right?"

"Doesn't everybody?" I replied.

Then he told me to go back to the hotel and not speak to anyone and wait for the Quintanilla family to come meet with me. Selena's family had cast approval. "They *have* to like you," he said as I walked toward the door.

I went back to the isolation of my room and the "actor's protection program" to wait. I could barely breathe. I sat on my bed and didn't move for about four hours: no music, no television, no nap, no phone. I ordered room service, and just sat there and stared at my food. I couldn't eat—that is rare! Off the top of my head I cannot recall another single time in my life when I was so nervous that I couldn't eat. Usually when I'm nervous, I can't stop eating. This was different; I was nervous and I wanted it so badly. I just played and replayed the audition in my head and couldn't figure out anything I would have done differently. There was nothing I could do but wait, and wait I did. Finally, at about six fifteen p.m., my phone rang. It was my agent calling to tell me that assuming the Quintanillas liked me (no pressure), I had the part—oh, and I'd need to begin work immediately, so I would not be able to go home to get clothes or anything else a person might need when she leaves her home for four months. But I didn't care! I was in the movie I'd dreamed about! The Quintanillas *had* to like me!

At nine thirty, Selena's parents, Suzette, and her husband, Billy, called me from the lobby of my hotel—*showtime!* I brushed my teeth, put on some lipstick, fluffed my hair (that's the beauty of naturally crazy, curly hair; just fluff and go), grabbed my purse, took a deep breath, and got into the elevator. The ride down to the lobby seemed to take an eternity! As the doors opened, I immediately spotted Suzette. Just like when I saw her at the concert, we were wearing the exact same brand and shade of lipstick (MAC Russian Red), we had on the exact same earrings, and our shoes were almost identical. Her husband's name is Bill, and my Bill was waiting for me in Los Angeles! All of them, Abraham, Marcella, Suzy, and Billy, gave me warm, gigantic, Tex-Mex-style hugs. We sat down and started talking and laughing as if we'd known each other all our lives. We were having such a wonderful time getting to know each other that I didn't realize that almost three hours had gone by. Abraham looked at his watch and called it a night. It took us another forty-five minutes to say good-bye. As they walked me to the elevator, Abraham gave me a big ol' hug and said, "Welcome to the family, Mija." Marcella kissed me, and Suzy said, "You better get your butt to the tanning salon 'cause you're pale, girl!" After four hours (and many, many shots of tequila), they liked me and I loved them! I got into the elevator knowing that my life was about to really change.

It was almost one a.m. but I couldn't sleep. I don't know if it was because I was hungry, excited, or a combination of both. I just know that my mind was racing. I called Bill to tell him all about my meeting. He was so proud of me. I missed him already. I lay in bed and thought about everything that had happened in the previous thirty-six hours; it was incredible. Every dumb cliché that you hear but don't really pay attention to came flooding into my mind—a closed door leads to an open door, an ending is just another beginning, things like that. When *First Time Out* was canceled I felt devastated and hurt and angry and scared; now I knew that if it hadn't been canceled, I would not have been available to do *Eat Your Heart Out*, and I wouldn't have been available to fly to Texas at a moment's notice to audition for Gregory, meet the Quintanillas, and get the role of "Suzette." And that is both the miracle of life and the reason that clichés exist, because just as one of my S-heroes, Scarlett O'Hara, says in *Gone With the Wind*, "Tomorrow is another day," and we never know what gifts the Universe has in store for us.

I finally drifted off to sleep sometime around three or four a.m. The phone began to ring at eight a.m.—six a.m. for me because I was still on California time—and I woke up to my agent telling me that the deal was done and I had to be ready to be picked up in thirty minutes to go meet with the costume designer, hairstylist, and makeup artist, and then go to band rehearsal. Band rehearsal. Oh shit! I had to learn to play the drums fast. I had no idea how to play drums. Before *Selena* the only drumstick I'd ever picked up was on Thanksgiving! I hung up and immediately called Suzette and woke her up. "I'm so sorry to call so early, but I forgot one thing. I don't know how to play the drums!" After she stopped laughing she told me not to worry; she'd call her old drum teacher and work something out with him. That's Suzette, always calm, cool, and confident. (I'm proud to say that if you need someone to play "Funky Town" or "Bidi Bidi Bom Bom" today, I'm your girl.)

The weeks and months that followed were a whirlwind of activity and excitement. The time we spent making the movie is very special to me and filled with many wonderful memories. I made a lot of new friends and fell in love with Texas—big hair, big food, and big livin'—my kind of place. I am so proud to have been part of a film that I love so much.

The spring of 1997 was a magical time for me. I was madly in love, *Selena* was in the theaters, my parents seemed to be doing well, my weight

(Left to right) Jacob Vargas, Abraham Quintanilla, Jennifer Lopez and me at a photo shoot during the making of the movie Selena. *Is it me or do I look like the Mexican Patsy Cline? It's the hair.*

was down, and the offers were pouring in for all of us involved in the movie. I was being offered movie roles, personal appearances, television appearances, premieres, parties, and big events. It was all very exciting, and just the beginning of really incredible things to come. One afternoon I got a call from Dick Clark, the music and show-business legend.

Dick is famous for his New Year's Eve show, for *American Bandstand*, and for being a major power broker in the music and television business for over fifty years. I walked into his office and into the living history of American pop culture. As Dick has often been quoted as saying, "Music is the soundtrack to our lives," and his office is the physical manifestation of that quote. There were the lightbulbs that had dominated the *Sonny & Cher* set, Elvis's cape, gold records, platinum records, Beatles memorabilia, and pictures of Dick with every conceivable musical legend of the last fifty years. Although I probably should have been intimidated, the place seemed somehow "homey." Maybe it's because Dick's wife, Kari, a beautiful woman with perfectly coiffed blond hair, sparkling blue eyes, and a sweet smile, is the office manager and has a remarkable way of putting you instantly at ease. There is a fireplace in the office, and their dogs roam freely and absolutely rule that kingdom. The office had the buzz of a place where many people are doing things they're excited about. Dick has an amazing staff, and has surrounded himself for years with people who share his passion for music and entertainment. He's very smart about how he assesses people; he trusts his instincts. As soon as Dick makes an assessment about a person, he moves quickly and swiftly and doesn't waste time second-guessing himself. I noticed this immediately about him, but had no idea how directly his loyalty to his own instinct would affect my life. After about a five-minute wait and a lovely conversation with Kari, the legend himself walked into the room. Now I know that everyone says Dick is ageless, and it's not like I don't know what he looks like—I mean, the man has been on television regularly since it was invented—but still I was surprised at how young and fit he looked and how energetic he was. He asked me what I wanted to do—more films? I told him I did, because I'd had such a wonderful experience making *Selena*, but I really wanted to do a daytime talk show. We talked about the many people who had come and gone as daytime talk show hosts, and he said that the reason some shows work and that others don't is because "regardless of the studio, the bells and whistles, the producing, in the end the most important thing that a daytime talk show needs is a host who has 'it.' " Then Dick Clark told me that he thought I had "it." I don't care who you are, when someone with as much experience in television tells you that you have "it," it's a good day. And then he told me something that I'm sure he meant as a compliment but seemed very strange at the time. He said, "I've only known two other people who were meant to visit people in their living rooms through TV: Ed McMahon and Al Roker."

What? Did he just compare me to Ed McMahon and Al Roker? I mean, obviously they're both talented and hugely successful but . . . Ed McMahon and Al Roker? Of all the thousands and thousands of great stars that Dick has met and known over the years, I most reminded him of Ed McMahon and Al Roker? I decided to just focus on the fact that the man who first put Madonna, Sonny & Cher, and Little Richard on television thought I had "it." We talked for almost two hours, and by the time it was over, we'd agreed to start developing a daytime talk show for me.

Dick and I and our respective teams got busy in the next few weeks and months working on developing a talk show. We hired a staff, came up with a concept, and started meeting with the studios to pitch our idea. We sold our concept to Buena Vista Domestic Television. The work was exciting, but watching and learning from Dick was fascinating. It was very apparent to me early on why Dick has survived at the top for so long in a business that eats people up and spits them out the second they get crow's-feet. Dick is a consummate businessman who doesn't take anything for granted. He is the least wasteful person I've ever met; he doesn't waste his time or his money. I learned a long time ago, while working as a union organizer, that you can tell what is important to a person by what he spends his time and his money on. It's a simple truth. So when Dick was willing to spend his time and money on me, I knew that our project was as important to him as it was to me. Dick has enjoyed success at a very high level for over fifty years and made millions in a cutthroat and competitive business, but still keeps an eye on the small details of his empire. I once watched him gather a stack of reusable plastic champagne glasses after a mini-celebration when we signed our deal, walk them into the kitchen in his production offices, and hand wash them for use another time. Some would call that cheap, but I see it as his overall vision. He sees everything and wastes nothing. You can't argue with his success.

The weeks and months flew by as we prepared to tape our pilot episode. I was both elated and frustrated, because although I really had a shot at what I'd wanted for so long, things around me were beginning to crumble. My agent and Dick were constantly fighting and could barely be in the same room together. Both of them have extremely strong personalities, and both of them have great vision, and both of them were fighting for what they truly believed to be the best conditions for a successful show. The show we were trying to get on the air was a talk show that no one could agree on. I take full responsibility. Part of my team wanted it to be serious; they felt I should be interviewing antiestablishment revolutionaries at a bare table, in the dark. Part of my team wanted me to sing show tunes and do splits. Since I was the team cocaptain with Dick and was unwilling (at the time) to choose one side over the other, both suffered. Needless to say, that show never made it; back to the drawing board!

It was extremely stressful for me because I loved my agent, who had been so instrumental in the development of my career and had come to be a friend as well. Meanwhile, Dick had a lifetime of success under his belt, and I had tremendous respect for him and great reverence for his opinions. I found myself in a place that I cannot stand to be in, the middle.

Whenever I hear people say that they're "in the middle" or I find myself thinking that way, it really bothers me because being in the middle is just a safe way of saying, "I'm not taking a position." I know it's very difficult to tell people they're wrong. One of the most challenging things in life is to accept the consequences of your choices. I think that's why so often people feel stuck in the middle. It's a lot easier than choosing a side and facing the consequences of that decision. It's also very difficult to be true to yourself, especially when you're caught between two strong personalities to whom you have an allegiance. I felt extreme loyalty to my agent, who had believed in me for so long and sacrificed so much to get me every opportunity to work and thrive in my chosen industry. And I felt a deep loyalty to Dick because he had given me the opportunity of a lifetime. I spent hours and hours every single day listening to each of them separately and trying to make each of them see the other's point of view. But I never felt great about my attempt to "keep the peace." I didn't feel that I was honest. I allowed things to be said and decisions to be made on my behalf that I knew didn't serve me. I kept my mouth shut for too long because I wanted it so bad. "Never sell your soul to get something you want because you just might need it one day," my aunt Judie had told me once; I should have listened.

I knew I had real problems when Dick asked me one afternoon to meet him for coffee—alone. When I told my agent, she flew into a rage and told me that he was going to try to convince me to fire her. I met Dick at a coffeehouse, and I played with my spoon as he told me that he wanted me to see him as "the old guy who had made it to the top of the mountain and had some wisdom to share." Then, just as my agent had predicted, he went on to tell me that she was hurting me and my career more than she was helping. I felt sick. Mostly I felt sad because I couldn't argue with anything he said; all of it was true, but it was an unbalanced snapshot of the passionate woman I knew. I desperately tried to get him to see her through my eyes. After letting me ramble on about all of her good qualities for about fifteen minutes, Dick put his hand on mine and said, "Kiddo, loyalty is sometimes overrated when it's practiced as a principle and not because it's earned." I tried again to explain to him that I wasn't being blindly loyal for the sake of loyalty. I cared deeply about her and believed in her. I felt that her good qualities far outweighed what Dick referred to as her "aggressive nature." I even played the "woman in Hollywood" card. "Quite frankly," I said, "if she were a man we would not be having this conversation, because she would be seen as tough and powerful, not aggressive and abrasive."

"When you have to explain the behavior of people who work for you, you have a problem," he responded.

I thought I had a great solution: "I will make sure you aren't in the same meetings. From now on I'll deliver any information from her to you and from you to her." I didn't take a position and stand up for what I believed in. I thought that by playing the middle I'd be safe. I learned that playing the middle meant I could never be safe. I lost out on a huge opportunity because I was afraid to live by the consequences of my choice. Dumb, dumb, dumb!

I didn't understand the magnitude of what Dick had been trying to tell me. In my mind the answer was clear: we're a new "blended family" and we need to find a way to get along. Dick doesn't have time for games or elaborate plans to "get by." Dick is a businessman and a visionary with a lot of heart. He believes that it is a waste of time to try to "fix" people. He has a model for success that works, and he doesn't waste time questioning it. Even though he is not a young man, the fire burns inside him like a teenager on the brink of building a life because he is fueled by his passion. He's excited to wake up every day.

One of the most interesting personal philosophies Dick ever revealed to me is his yearly New Year's Day ritual with his wife, Kari. Every New Year's Day he wakes up after ringing in the New Year for the entire country on television and he and Kari clean out their closets. They prepare things they don't need or haven't used to give to charity. This alone is a great act of kindness and charity, but Dick has a philosophy and a very personal reason for doing it. "Every year on New Year's Day, Kari and I clean out our closets and get rid of the old stuff and the things that we don't use to make room for the new. If your closet is stuffed with useless things there is no room for new and useful things to come into your life." I love that! When he first said it to me, I thought about this and how true it is across the board in life. If you're lugging around things, beliefs, people, and attitudes that no longer serve you, you don't have any "space" for the things, beliefs, people, and attitudes you need. The clutter can be superdamaging. When you lose a loved one, or an opportunity, you may have a hard time figuring out what happened because you can't see through the clutter. Unfortunately, at this time in my life there was too much going on, and another opportunity was going away and I could do little to stop it. All of this came during a family crisis, and I was incapable of losing another person. I knew what Dick wanted me to do, but I just couldn't give up my friendship with my agent—I needed her too much emotionally. Dick told me he understood, and he pulled the plug on the show.

Essentially I chose my agent over Dick Clark. I chose loyalty, my personal needs and a friendship over starring in my own daytime talk show. In a "feel good" movie with a tidy happy ending, I would go on with my agent, win an Emmy, and have a star on the Walk of Fame. However, this did not happen. As it turned out, my agent and I parted ways a few months later. Permanently. In effect two windows of opportunities had been closed. I had to do some serious career and life rebuilding.

So my life as an actor is not so different than my life as an activist. Every day I pick up the pieces. I add a little more to the framework of my house. I put in another door and a few more windows, and I make sure I like the way they open. I keep my eyes open and I keep on building. That's my job. Movin' on.

CHAPTER FOUR

Baby, You're a Star!

*"Cherish forever what makes you unique,
'cuz you're really a yawn if it goes."*
—BETTE MIDLER

MY PARENTS HAVE ALWAYS BEEN MY BIGGEST CHEERLEADERS. My mother was my rock. She had the uncanny ability to believe and keep going in spite of anything. Both of them believed in me so fully and consistently that it rarely occurred to me that I couldn't do whatever I set out to do.

While I was preparing for my pilot with Dick Clark, my good friend Beth was preparing to give birth to her first child. She was my first friend to have a baby, and the experience was wild. Beth is one of the most loving and generous people I've ever known, and I adore her. I was working fifteen to eighteen hours a day, but my mom and I planned to spend the weekend before Beth was due cooking food to stock her freezer and refrigerator so that when she, her husband, Ronnie, and their new baby came home there'd be plenty to eat and they wouldn't have to worry about grocery shopping or cooking. My mom and I discussed and planned the menu a hundred times. My mom was totally into it; she loved to do things like this.

I got a call on July 3 that Beth had gone into labor and was headed to the hospital. I called my mom to tell her we had to get to work because the baby was coming! The next day, Beth and Ronnie welcomed their first child, Julian, into the world. Bill and I went to the hospital to meet Julian. It was really beautiful; Ronnie had his boom box in the room playing Earth, Wind & Fire's "Hearts Afire." Beth looked beautiful, Ronnie was beaming, the song was perfect, and Julian was healthy and gorgeous. It was such a perfect moment in time. As we left the hospital I called my mom and made plans to pick her up early in the morning to go to the grocery store to prepare for our cooking extravaganza! The next morning I woke up full of love and hope and the optimism that usually comes with the birth of a new life full of promise.

Mom got into the car and I knew immediately that something was wrong. My mother was a chatterbox. I used to call her "Chatty Cathy" because usually the second she'd get into my car it was nonstop talking. "Did you see Oprah?" "What do you think about this outfit?" "Did you do something to your hair?" "Your father . . ." Nonstop! But this morning, she was a little quiet. When I asked her what was wrong, she just said, "I'm just a little tired, Mija. Pay attention to the road." We went to the store and bought enough food to feed the entire floor of new moms at Beth's hospital. But that was the way my mom did it: completely plus 10 percent! We got to my house to begin the cooking extravaganza. As soon as we walked through the door I began to put the groceries away. After about fifteen minutes, I walked into my living room and saw my mother lying on my couch. My mom was usually a firecracker, the kind of woman for whom multitasking was a way of life. She took care of everyone, always had twenty things going on at once, seventy-five dreams and ideas and plans, and was always figuring out a way to do more and better, always! She was rarely sick, and even when she did get the occasional cold she *never* took a day off or lay down in the middle of the day. "I'll rest when I'm dead" was her motto. Now it was eleven a.m. on a beautiful July day and she was lying down. Something was very wrong.

"Mija, I think there's something wrong with me. I'm just so tired."

"Don't worry, Mommy. I'll get started and you rest." I went into the kitchen and started washing, chopping, and organizing the food.

About an hour later I checked on my mom, and she was sound asleep. This was really odd. I called my dad and told him that she was sleeping and said she didn't feel well. My dad said to let her sleep. "She'll be fine," he said. "She's just tired. You know your mother. She overdoes everything." It made sense. But a few hours later, my over-achieving, never-complaining mother asked me to take her to the emergency room because "something is really wrong." I was terrified.

We drove to the emergency room and waited, and waited. After an hour and a half, a doctor saw my mom, and immediately checked her into the hospital for tests and observation, which is code for *something's wrong but we don't know what.* There weren't any beds immediately available, so we had to wait. My mother looked so small and scared lying on the emergency room gurney. The nurse wheeled her into a corner in the hallway, between the room where the sick and devastated were being treated and the admissions area. It was three p.m. and my mom was being admitted into the hospital, and nobody could tell me why. I called my dad, and he said he'd get there as fast as he could. My mom was desperately trying to be brave, but the fear was in her eyes. I kept trying to talk about silly things to keep her mind off of the depressing and terrifying events that surrounded us.

When my dad and my uncle Pepe showed up after work, we were still in the hallway. At midnight, we were still in the hallway. We'd been there for ten hours before they finally had a room for her. As soon as she got settled, she started coughing up blood. It was the most terrifying thing I'd ever seen. My mom, who was so strong and full of life, lying in her hospital bed, looking so tiny, coughing up blood; it was more than I could handle. I burst into tears as the doctors came running into her room.

My dad, my uncle, and I were asked to leave and stood in the hallway in silence. I am not a doctor, but I'd seen enough movies and television shows to know that coughing up blood is not a good sign. Finally the doctor came out and told us that she needed to rest, and there wasn't anything they could do for her but help her to rest comfortably. I didn't want to leave, but my dad convinced me that I needed to go home and rest and get a few things for my mother, so at about two thirty a.m., I made the long drive home. I was scared, but I just knew my mother would pull through. I went home to the comfort of Bill and told him everything that had happened. I didn't even realize I was sobbing. Bill just held me and said, "Your mother is very strong, baby. She is going to be okay, but you have to get some rest." I looked at the kitchen full of uncooked food and burst into tears all over again. How did this happen? I had woken up that morning with plans to spend the day with my mommy doing what she loved to do, and eighteen hours later my entire world was turned upside down. I went into the bathroom to wash my face and just cried and cried.

I watched the clock all night long and called the hospital every hour to check on my mom. Each time I called the attending nurse said the same thing, "No change, she's resting." Somehow, it didn't make me feel better. Finally the clock read 7:00. I got up, got dressed, and headed to my parents' house to get some of my mom's personal items. I had a cup of coffee with my dad, who also seemed so scared and pale. I got to the hospital around eight thirty and went right up to my mom's room, where she was sleeping. I lay down in the bed next to her and held her, as she'd held me so many times. It was the first time in almost twenty-four hours that I felt a little better.

When the doctor came in to check on her he asked me to go outside with him. Then he asked me the question I had feared: "How much does your mother drink?" There it was: the one topic that was seldom, if ever, discussed openly in our house. My mother was a wonderful and loving woman who had spent her entire life trying to obliterate the pain of her childhood in a bottle of wine or vodka. I knew she had a problem; my dad knew it, and so did my brother. We each tried at different times, sometimes alone and sometimes together, to get my mom to stop drinking. We'd been to therapists, group meetings, rehabs; you name it, we had tried it. But in the end, it was my mother's only way of coping with the pain she had never completely dealt with, and, like everything else in life, the only one who can ever change anyone's condition is the person herself, and my mother was not ready or not able to feel what she felt and face her pain without the aid of alcohol. *I* know there were other options for her, but this is the choice she made, and she couldn't see any other way. After a few awkward moments, I said, "She drinks every day." The doctor explained to me that her liver was very weak and there was nothing medically that they could do. He suggested that I take her home, make her comfortable, and make sure she didn't drink any alcohol. I agreed. I would have agreed to anything to make my mother feel better.

I went into my mommy's room and told her that I was going to take her home. She was so happy and, as usual, concerned about me. She asked me why I wasn't at work. Work? How could I possibly work when she was alone in a hospital? "Let's go home, Mommy. Everything will be fine. Stop worrying about me. You have to get better." I dressed her, gathered her things, and drove her home.

Once I got my mom home and into bed, I faced the reality of what I had ignored for the last forty-eight hours. I was taping a television pilot in less than three weeks, and there was a whole staff of hardworking people waiting for me who depended on me. In the other room was my mother, who needed me. My father had just started working at a new job and couldn't take off. It was up to me. I called my agent and explained to her that for the next few days I needed to be with my mom from six in the morning until my dad came home at three thirty. So I could only be available to work in the late afternoon and early evening. Everyone was very supportive and rearranged rehearsals and meetings to those times so that I could be there. As soon as I hung up the phone I went through every cupboard in the house and emptied countless bottles of vodka, wine, scotch, tequila, and whiskey. And then I went through the closets and looked inside my mother's purses and threw away all the tiny bottles of vodka I found. I loved my mother deeply and just wanted her to be better. I would rather her be mad for a few days than ever see her in a hospital bed coughing up blood again.

For the next week I had my routine of taking care of my mom and then going to work. It was really difficult to be the scared daughter of a very sick mother from six to three and then the peppy talk show host from four to ten. But if it helped my mom get better, who was I to complain? The morning of July 16, I arrived just as my dad was leaving. I kissed him good-bye and went into the house and started loading dishes into the dishwasher. I heard a really loud thump in the bedroom and ran in to find my mother sprawled out on the floor semiconscious. Although my mom was only five feet tall and weighed about 105 pounds, I couldn't lift her and she couldn't lift herself; she was weak and incoherent. I immediately called the hospital, and the doctor told me that she was probably detoxing, and to put her in the bathtub and let her body temperature cool down, and then she would wake up naturally. I couldn't lift her, so I put a sheet on the floor, rolled her onto it, and dragged her to the bathroom. I was crying, she was crying, and I was terrified. Through some miracle, I was able to get her into the bathtub, and just rubbed her back and talked to her. She tried to answer me but her speech was slurred, and she wasn't entirely able to focus. I called the hospital again, and again the doctor told me that this is normal when someone stops drinking cold turkey. I loved my mother deeply, and at that moment, I was mad at everyone who ever hurt her, I was mad at all of the adults who should have loved her and protected her, and I was *really* mad at her for drinking all those years. I wanted my mom back and didn't know what to do with this weak, incoherent person who couldn't lift herself. I was so scared. Suddenly my mom looked at me and said, "You know, I'm really ready to stop drinking. I'm going to take care of myself." I had waited my entire life to hear her say those words.

Bill came over as he had every afternoon to spend time with my mom and me. He sat down next to her on the couch and rubbed her head and held her hand. She looked at him and said, "I sure do love you, Bill." I thought my heart would burst. I was so grateful: for my wonderful mother, for an amazing guy like Bill, and that they loved each other. That moment was truly a gift from God. When it was time for me to leave, I went to kiss her good-bye and she grabbed my hand. "I love you, Jacksie," she said.

"I love you too, Mommy."

The next morning my phone rang at five ten; it was my dad. "Mija, the paramedics are here. Your mother stopped breathing, so I called 911. They're working on her now."

"We'll be right there."

My mom and Bill during a very happy time.
My heart is full whenever I look at this picture.

Bill and I flew out the door and got to their house just as the ambulance was leaving. There were a few paramedics still packing up, and they told us to go to Saint Joseph's emergency room. I have no idea how fast I drove, but I know that we got there in less than five minutes. Finally the doctor came out and told us that my mother was in a coma, and they were putting her into the intensive care unit.

"What does that mean?" I kept asking every doctor and every nurse. "What does that mean?" Of course, what I meant was "How long will she be in a coma?" "How can we get her out?" "What are you going to do?" I kept asking the same thing and getting the same answers and understanding nothing. I felt numb and scared, and I went into total protection mode. I wanted her to have pictures of the people she loved in her room, I wanted her to have her nails done and her feet warm, I wanted music she loved playing, smells she enjoyed—anything to jump-start one or all of her senses. I sat by her bed and stroked her hair and talked to her nonstop. I became the Chatty Cathy she'd always been.

Friends and relatives came to see her and show their love and support. When my uncle Taylor arrived I prayed that my mom knew he was there. My mother loved him very much. They had grown up together and shared a lifetime of memories. Uncle Taylor was trying to be calm and strong but he was devastated. He is a man of few words, but he looked at me and said, "That's a good woman right there." He was right; she was exceptional.

I appreciated all of them and it gave me great comfort to see friendly and familiar faces among the sea of doctors and nurses, but I just wanted to be with my mom. I needed to stay with her just in case she woke up. I wanted to be there just in case she could hear me or feel me or smell me. I didn't want her to be scared or alone. I only left from midnight to six a.m. because the doctors insisted that I go home to sleep, and even then I set my alarm so that I'd wake up to call the hospital to check on her every hour. No change. On the third day my mom caught a fever and they had to pack her in ice. My mother *hated* to be cold, and it tore my heart out to see her covered in ice. I know that if she was aware, she was pissed!

When I arrived at the hospital on the morning of July 21, 1997, the doctor told me that I needed to gather my family because he needed to speak with us at ten o'clock. At ten, Bill, my dad, my brother, his wife, and I met with my mom's doctors, a priest, a social worker, and a hospital administrator, who informed us that my mother was not breathing on her own and it was only the machines that were keeping her alive. He told us, "There is nothing else that we can do for her medically," and that according to my mother's living will we needed to make arrangements to remove the life-support machines. I cannot possibly describe what I felt in that moment. I kept saying to no one in particular, "How is this possible? She was supposed to be getting better! Why is this happening? It's not possible that there is nothing else that can be done." I felt heavy and cold. I couldn't move. I couldn't process what they were saying.

Dad said, "Your mother has always said that she didn't want to be kept alive by machines." I knew this was true. I'd heard her say it many times—every time we'd hear about some poor soul lying in a hospital bed being kept alive by machines. I could hear her voice: "I never want to be kept alive by machines. When it's my time, let me go. Don't keep me alive by machines and make everyone who loves me suffer." I knew that her wishes were most important, but I couldn't breathe! I kept thinking about the things my mom wanted to do that she would never have the chance to do. She'll never go to Ireland, she'll never see me get married, she won't know my children, she'll never see Barbra Streisand perform, she won't ever again lie on the beach, she won't grow old with my dad. I thought about my nephew, Aryton, my parents' first grandchild. How happy he made her and how much he loved her and how she loved him madly. I pictured their faces pressed together laughing and being silly, riding on trains, playing guitar, playing restaurant, reading and kissing and hugging. For some reason my mind raced with images of my brother and me as kids, and I thought about how my mom would not be here to guide and love Aryton and his new baby sister, Jessenya, the way she had John and me. And then I thought about Bill and me and our wedding and having kids, and that my mommy would not be there. And I thought about how much I needed her. I thought about all of the plans we'd made and the things we'd dreamed about. I felt frozen.

Somehow I made it out of that dreadful little room and found myself calling my mom's loved ones to tell them the doctor said we had to disconnect the machines. I was on autopilot as I relayed the details to my aunts, uncles, grandmother, cousins, and friends. I don't know what I said, but I know that people came from all over the country to say goodbye. I still didn't believe it was really good-bye. I kept praying for a miracle. I went into my mom's room, took off my shoes, and got into bed with my mom and cuddled with her like I used to whenever I needed an extra dose of her love and comfort. I couldn't stand the thought that she didn't know we were there. I needed to believe that she knew we did everything possible to help her. My biggest fear was that somehow in the darkness of her coma she understood what was going on and couldn't tell us. I was so afraid she was in there trying to say, "Help me! Don't give up on me! Please, forget about my living will. Help me!" I prayed and cried and held her. I fell asleep lying next to my beloved mother. It was delicious, familiar, and surreal. When I woke up about forty-five minutes later, Bill told me that the doctors were going to start her on morphine, so that when the machines were disconnected she wouldn't be in pain. As he was telling me the "plan," the nurse came into her room and started her morphine drip. It was the single most chilling moment of my life.

My father, my brother, my sister-in-law, Leticia, Bill, and I gathered around my mom's bed and talked to her while the morphine dripped and the machines were disconnected. The priest came in and gave my mother her last rites. My mother looked beautiful, so peaceful and small and sweet. We each took turns telling her stories, talking about the things and people she loved and the funny and wonderful things she'd done and all of her remarkable accomplishments. Through our tears and our fears we even managed to laugh as we talked to her about how many ways she'd touched each of us. We laughed because my mother was genuinely funny and so many of the stories were funny.

I looked at my dad, who has always seemed so big and strong to me; in that moment, when he was standing next to his best friend, his partner, his lover, the mother of his children, holding her hand and recounting "how far they'd come, Esquincla," I saw someone so vulnerable and so scared. I knew that my mom would have wanted a moment alone with him, so we all left for a minute so he could say good-bye to the woman with whom he'd shared his life for thirty-five years. When we came back, I stroked·her hair and whispered in her ear that I loved her, and I thanked her for being a great mom, my rock, and the best cheerleader anyone could ever imagine. I told her that I knew I am the person I am because of the life she gave me. And at three o'clock on July 21, 1997, my mother took her last long gasp of air and died as I held her head. I knew that nobody would ever call me "Jacksie" again and that a piece of me was gone forever.

And then, for the first time in my life, my knees buckled and I collapsed onto the floor and sobbed. I just sat there as the nurses and doctors came in to do what they have to do when someone passes away. We asked them to let her stay in her room until my aunt Judie could get there. Aunt Judie lives in Las Vegas and was on her way, desperately trying to get there in time to say good-bye to her sister and buddy. Finally, at about eight o'clock, Aunt Judie arrived, and the nurse took her in to say good-bye. When she finished, I went back into my mom's room and saw her lifeless body lying on top of what looked like a black garment bag. That was the last time I ever saw my mother.

What followed was a dizzying flurry of creepy activity. I couldn't get over the fact that my mother had done so much in her short years, affected so many, loved, raised two kids, traveled the world, won, lost, dreamed and lived, and then they just put her in a black bag, zipped it up, and put her into a drawer in the hospital basement. I was furious: That is my mother! That is the woman whose love and life defined me, and now she's in a drawer? I couldn't deal with it.

And I didn't.

For a long time I was crippled with grief and anger and a sorrow so deep I felt like I was constantly cold and couldn't get warm. I completely lost myself. I lost sight of who I was and where I was going. I didn't feel that I mattered. I lost my focus and my drive and stopped dreaming and believing—big mistake!

In my grief, I lost sight of the things that really mattered, and I fluctuated between long periods of time lying on my couch watching television in silence and eating everything in sight. I went from my recent low weight of 185 pounds to a new high of 260 pounds in what seemed to be five minutes! Before my mother died, I hadn't had red meat for about ten years. The day after she died, I went through the Jack in the Box drive-thru and ate two Jumbo Jacks with cheese before I made it home. I went right back to what I call "memory food." I ate everything I could that reminded me of my mom. I knew what I was doing. Once again I was soothing myself with food.

And then I hid from my life. My brother and father were desperately trying to pick up the pieces of their own lives. The Dick Clark deal was officially over. I essentially quit show business. I stopped living. I just barely existed. I filled my time with things and people where I could just fade into the background, because on some level I was punishing myself. I got involved in friendships and relationships that made me feel lost and unimportant. I became a background player. I was an extra in the movie of my own life.

Bill was worried about me, my dad was worried about me, I was worried about me! My dad and Bill decided that I needed to "get out and do something!" They went and bought me a bunch of beads and crystals and encouraged me to do something I'd always loved to do, make jewelry. I began to make beautiful pieces. Each bead and each crystal was a moment shared with my mother. Each time I completed a new piece of jewelry or a barrette, I could hear her voice cheering me on: "Oooooh, that's beautiful, Jacksie!" It made me happy for a moment and gave me a reason to get up in the morning; it gave me a purpose and a focus. Beading and making jewelry had always been very therapeutic for me. It's a way to be creative and, believe it or not, a great way to meditate and reflect. It's just me and my beads and my imagination and my thoughts. Even when I'm feeling yucky and maybe a little ugly, I'm reminded that there is tremendous beauty inside of me just waiting for a chance to get out when I finish a beautiful piece of jewelry. Instant gratification: I love it!

While working on my jewelry I thought a lot about all of the fun I'd had doing stand-up comedy, television, and movies; the people I'd met, the places I'd been, the dreams and the goals I hadn't yet met. Gradually I realized I'd essentially stopped dreaming and stopped pursuing my passion, and that I still had a lot to do. I began to see my life as a movie and wondered what my character should do now. How did I want *my movie* to end? I felt like a loser and I was acting like a loser—what a waste and what an enormous insult to my mother's memory. That was not the daughter my mother raised. I could hear her saying, *"Baby, you're a star!"* I realized that if she was right, I better start acting like it. If my life is a movie and I'm the *star* of *my movie*, I better make sure that the script is good, because I want *my movie* and *my life* to be great! In my fog of sadness and despair, I decided to put my mother's words and encouragement into some life strategies I could use immediately. I decided to use my mother's life as the fuel to help me get out and do something. I decided to put one foot in front of the other and try to make the movie of my life a blockbuster. I decided that all of us have a duty to live life and go for the gusto. So I put together some ideas on how we can all be *stars*.

Your life is a movie and you are the writer, producer, director, lighting technician, costume designer, casting director, and star! Sometimes you have to pull cable and sweep the floors, but never forget, *baby, you're a star!*

To begin, you have to get into the habit of *playing the part* as you imagine it and with confidence. You have to project confidence. As the *star* of your movie you have to *act* confident. Remember the old commercial that said, "Never let them see you sweat"? That's key! Confidence isn't something someone can give you, you catch, you're born with, or you can buy. Confidence is something you have to work to have every single day—but it's no harder than brushing your teeth, and you do that every day. (At least I hope you do!) If you *act* confident then you'll eventually *be* confident. Though it is difficult, you have to persevere and "fake it till you make it!" There isn't a damned thing worth doing that isn't, on some level, hard.

I was asked to speak at a very exclusive all-girls school in Beverly Hills. The girls were around seventeen or eighteen years old. I was having fun, telling stories, and the room was jumping. I told the story of how in high school I was so catatonic about getting the perfect prom dress that I threw up all over my lab partners and myself during third-period chemistry. The teacher made some weird joke about "chemical reactions." Whatever, it was traumatic. I also told how in eighth grade my mother refused to allow me to shave my legs. All the other girls were shaving, but I couldn't. So I refused to leave the house for a week in protest. Now of course I wish I didn't have to shave. The point of those stories was that no one remembers about the puke or the dress or the hairy legs of an eighth-grader. Not once since high school has anyone ever asked me, "What did your prom dress look like?" I promise that at no point has any prospective employer, new friend, or potential date ever asked, "How much did you weigh in high school?" When I've filled out credit applications, I've never seen the question, "How was your tan during high school?" All that matters to anyone as you make your journey through life is, "Who are you? What do you want? And what can you do for me?"

Then one of the brilliant young women asked me, "What do you know now that you didn't know the day you graduated from high school but wish you did?" I was suddenly stopped in my tracks. I scanned the room. I had the attention of four hundred impressionable young women who were about to enter the demanding and frequently brutal world of adulthood. I gathered my thoughts, considering what I would have liked to have heard when I was the semi-innocent, seventeen-year-old Jackie, on her graduation day.

"Aside from the fact that I should never rim the inside of my eyelids with eyeliner?" The girls laughed. "What I really know now is: Life is wonderful. Every single day is miraculous and filled with infinite possibilities. It is also really, really, incredibly difficult! There are heartaches and disappointments and loss and tragedy and pain that I could never have imagined as a high school senior, but, despite all that, it's amazing."

Yes, life is difficult. Holidays are difficult. Four-inch heels are difficult. Standing in lines is difficult. Raising kids is difficult. Carrying groceries in the rain is difficult. Being consistent and honest with yourself is difficult. Writing this book is difficult! But I persevere because this is the script I've written, and in my movie, my character is a bestselling author.

SHOWCASE AND PROMOTE YOURSELF

You are a star! So get into the habit of doing everything you do with total *star power*! All great stars play a variety of roles—just like we do in our everyday lives. Sometimes you are the protagonist, sometimes you play a supporting role, and that's fine. Regardless of the role, do it like a star! Personally, I really enjoy being of service. It genuinely makes me feel good to help people and to give a little of myself. But if I don't watch myself, I have a real tendency to put others before myself, and before I know it, I'm an extra in someone else's damned movie. I think that being kind is important, and I love to be helpful, but in the past I have definitely suffered from what I call "chub gen." Chub gen is short for chubby generosity, a term I use for doing something no one would ask of anyone except the chubby girl, the nerdy guy, their single friend, the out-of-work relative, and so on. The chubby is especially taken for granted: "Hey, can you watch my purse while I dance?" I suppose on some level I have put up with more than my fair share of obnoxious requests, because as a member of the chub gen club I felt I had to. "Can you go to my house and check on my new dog while I'm at the Grammys?" "Since you don't have to worry about buying a gift on Mother's Day, can you wrap the gifts I got for my mom?" "I need you to pick me up at the airport at five p.m. on Friday, and, oh yeah, did I mention it's the day after Thanksgiving?" I did all of these things because I'm essentially a good person who likes to help, regardless of the tolls and soaring gasoline prices. No more! Users and abusers will always take advantage of generosity. Being dependable doesn't mean being a doormat. It's noble and generous and a testament to your ability to be a friend, but there's a gigantic difference between being taken advantage of and being a friend. The question you should always ask yourself is, "Would my friends do the same for me? And have they?" Remember, someone else's bad planning is not your problem. You should only do for others what they inspire you to do. Do nothing that offends your soul because *baby, you're a star!*

Doing things like a star doesn't mean that it's always all about you and therefore you should behave like some jerk celebrity you read about in the tabloids. I think that many people confuse being a star with acting like a petulant child. A very-well-known actress once told me, "Act like a bitch and they'll treat you like a star." I know that there are many people who subscribe to that kind of thinking, but I don't. To me, being a star is about dreaming big, committing to the work, and giving an all-out performance whether it's in front of millions or an audience of one. Being a star means being on top of your game.

DEFINING YOUR CHARACTER

You don't have to be in show business to be a star! Your life is your own personal movie and *you* are the star of your movie! In life, just like in movies, success is determined by character. So before you do anything else, you have to define your character. Who are you? What do you want? What do you value? Who do you love? What are your dreams? How far are you willing to go? What in your life is negotiable and non-negotiable? What are your fears? What do you love to do? What scares you? What thrills you? These are all questions that define who we are and what our characters are. In order to answer these questions effectively, we have to be able to visualize our success and work backward to meet ourselves where we are today. It doesn't matter where you start as long as in your mind's eye you can fully picture your character's success. No one is going to hand you a part in anything. To succeed in a project you have to use your brains and your heart. You have to create, visualize, and write a plan. In movies it's called a screenplay. Now, I don't mean *you* have to sit down and write a screenplay. But it helps to see your plans on paper. A plan reinforces your goals. It's easier to re-member. It also makes you disciplined. For me, to sit down to write and create every day takes extraordinary discipline. I do the comedy and the jewelry and the performing, but sitting for hours at a time and staring at a white screen with a blinking cursor line is *sick*. I practice writing. I only write for five minutes. Then I allow one minute of dis-traction. Then I write for six minutes with a two-minute break. Then I write for seven minutes with a three-minute break. Can you follow this complex pattern? I'll stop while you catch up. I will now sing . . . "Stop, in the Name of Love"!

Okay . . . we're back.

The plan you're going to create takes just that kind of focus and dis-cipline. You can do it.

Many of us have a little critic in our head that is very judgmental and nasty and bitchy. He could very well mock the plans you are trying to make. Give the little critic a name, let's say Alfonso. When Alfonso starts criticizing you, kick Alfonzo in the *cojones* and order a latte.

Don't get scared by the amount of work it may take to get from here to there; it's your movie and your character is going to enjoy the jour-ney. Here's one thing I know for sure: time doesn't stop. You can worry about how long something is going to take and how much work you have to do and get nothing done, or you can fill your time with the things and the people that move you closer to your goals—your choice. Time will go on either way, so make the most of it and have a good time and learn a lot along the way! You're going to get older even if you simply lie around on your couch and watch television. The question is, *Are you willing to get wiser as time goes on?*

YOU ARE THE ONLY *YOU* THE WORLD WILL EVER KNOW, SO DON'T CHEAT US OUT OF THE GREAT *YOU*!

I have been thinking about my character. People always say, "Just be yourself." That *drives me crazy*! We are all many different things to different people. Like a diamond, each of us has many different facets. The more facets a diamond has, the higher its value. So don't get frustrated by the different roles you play in your life! It's up to you to decide who you are at this moment on this day. You can *never* depend on anyone else, no matter how much they may love you or how much you respect them. There's a showbiz cliché, "You're not as great as your best reviews and you're not as bad as your worst." This is *the* reason not to let anyone but *you* determine who you are and how you feel about yourself. We are all different people to the different people in our lives. We are children, parents, friends, partners, nieces, nephews, students, coworkers, employers, neighbors, and teachers. Consider this: My brother, John, is not just my brother; he is a son, a father, and a husband. He's also a soldier who served bravely and honorably in the Gulf War. To those of us who are privileged enough to live in the United States, he is a hero. To the people who met him in the foreign land where he was deployed, he may be a savior, an invader, an intruder, or even a murderer. So which is he? It depends who you ask. I went to a meeting the other day with a very powerful television executive. When I asked my agent, "What are they looking for?" she said, "Just be yourself." This made me think, Be myself? What does it mean to "be myself"? Yesterday I was doing a photo shoot. Last year I was 291 pounds and feasting on fries. Three years ago I was unemployed and penniless. This morning I'm happy. At any given moment of any given day, we are all different people. And that is my point. You can't *ask* anyone other than yourself to determine who you are. If you rely on anyone other than you to tell you who you are, you'll set yourself up for a never-ending ride on an emotional roller coaster. So get tough and get busy defining *your character*!

What defines a character in a film is not what he does and with whom he does it, but rather why he does what he does. Haven't you heard the joke about the bad waitress? There was a really bad waitress, and whenever the customers would complain, she'd say, "Oh, I'm sorry. I'm not really a waitress. I'm an actress." So finally her boss said, "Then *act* like a waitress!" She asked, "But what's my motivation?" And that's the question you have to answer for your character. What is your motivation? Who you are and what you want changes all the time. Who am I today? Am I same the person I was one hundred pounds ago? I used to be on a dance team with big hair, but does that mean that's who I'll always be? Am I being honest about what I want and what I value? Figuring out your motivation is about listening to yourself. We usually can find our truth when we strip away the lies.

In studying characters that have stood the test of time, I find myself drawn to Joseph Campbell's work on mythology. I am attracted to his writing based on my own belief that since the beginning of time people have had the same dreams and longings. People have always wanted meaning in their lives, the ability to pursue their dreams—and an occasional dessert! Specifically, we need heroes and legends. Every generation has its heroes. Every movie has its hero, and *you* are *the hero* in *your movie!*

THE TRUTH SHALL SET YOU FREE

In *The Power of Myth*, Joseph Campbell writes, "The writer must be true to truth. The only way you can describe a human being truly is by describing her imperfections. The perfect human being is *uninteresting*. . . . It is the imperfections of life that are lovable. Perfection is a bore; it's unhuman. The imperfection, striving, living . . . that's what's lovable." This philosophy is *perfect* for me because I am sooooooo *not perfect*! Not perfect? That's just another word for lovable, according to Mr. Campbell. Where has this guy been all my life? He knows that we are all under construction.

WHAT A CHARACTER!

Have you ever noticed that people always say that someone is a "character" when that person is interesting or particularly noticeable? Hmmm . . . interesting! An interesting character is one whose writer (also you) is honest about the character's flaws and imperfections. So as the writer and star of my movie, I have to be honest about my flaws.

What? What flaws? This self-improvement stuff is tough work! Now I have to come up with a flaw just to be interesting. Hmmm, let me see what I can do about that!

Here's some hard-core honesty about my character's flaws and imperfections: I'm always late, I'm frequently distracted, and I get my heart broken easily. I throw pity parties and I don't like the word "no." I hate budgets. I can't stand limits. I really don't like to rush and I can't stand sweating for no reason. I don't like to answer the phone. I watch way too much twenty-four-hour news and Court TV. My house is often a mess with all of my jewelry-making and crafting projects. My clothes can usually be found all over the floor. I lose my keys a lot. I panic when I can't contact certain people immediately. I love to cook but hate to clean. I do too many things on too big a scale. I order too much food in a restaurant. I overextend myself and overschedule myself constantly. I spend way too much money on candles, shoes, purses, and lattes. Bill says I'm demanding and bossy and never admit to being wrong (though I don't ever recall being wrong). Wait, I love Bill, but in my movie I get to define myself. I'm a woman, I'm Mexican-American, I have big dreams, a big mouth, and a big ass, and I expect greatness from myself and for myself. I have a lot to do in my life and I refuse to keep quiet about it. I love my life and I love my fiancé, Bill. And I'm as excited as I am afraid about tomorrow.

I'm far from perfect. Isn't it better to know that you're not perfect and stop pretending that that is the goal than to be a bundle of stress and nerves and beat yourself up constantly because you can't get it "right"? When you define yourself and your life with courage and character, you'll fall in love with yourself and others will soon follow. Get it done, don't get it right. Perfection and imperfection are who we are. Saints and sinners are both fascinating.

What a character!

EVERY *GREAT* CHARACTER IS A LITTLE MESSED UP!

Think about the people you most admire. I'll bet there are parts of them that are great and there are things that make them highly flawed—it's called being human! Think about the characters in your favorite movies; I'll bet they are highly flawed people, but that's what makes them, a-hem, "unique!" All interesting characters are complex and not perfect.

Some of my favorite movie characters are highly flawed women who are called to action by a burning desire or an unfulfilled dream, just like you and I are. They find themselves in the adventure. Their character is defined by their challenges—this is always the case! I adore characters who, despite their circumstances, have a burning desire to be more: Scarlett O'Hara in *Gone With the Wind*, Vivian Ward in *Pretty Woman*, Tess McGill in *Working Girl*. All three of these women believed there was a whole big world out there waiting for them to do something big in! And each of them was highly flawed, or, as I like to say, "unique." But they focused on being the star of their own lives and not on what they weren't or what they didn't have. When you focus on the "nots" and the "don'ts" in your life, then that's what you have: nothin'! When you focus on the possibilities, the dream, the plans and the goal, then that's what your life becomes. Beginning with yourself, treat everyone as the person they are capable of being.

Let me take a moment to be very clear about something: being honest and acknowledging your flaws to yourself is not the same as telegraphing them all over the place! People only know what you tell them, so if you spend your time telling people everything about yourself that you'd like to change, fix, forget, or deny . . . who the hell will want to pay to see you star in a movie? Don't do it! It will *always* come back to haunt you. Your personal to-do list is for your eyes only!

Show business can eat you alive, which is ironic, because in showbiz if you eat too much you could lose a job! Honestly, it never occurred to me that I wouldn't be successful as a performer because of my weight. I have been overweight virtually my entire life. I guess you could say I was "born to be wide!" I come from a long line of big-boned people, but I've never allowed my weight to stop me from pursuing my dreams. I got into this business because I had something to *say*, not because I thought I was so beautiful that people should pay money to see my face on a big movie screen. What does the way I look have to do with being funny or interesting or being a good actor? I'm always being asked, "How does _____ affect you professionally?," whether it's about weight or ethnicity or being a woman in Hollywood. I don't know, because I've never been anything other than a chubby Mexican-American woman. I don't know how my life would be different if I were someone else. I'm not stupid; I mean, I notice things like there aren't too many people who look like me winning Oscars and/or making the "50 Most Beautiful People" list, but that doesn't matter because in my movie, my character chooses to see opportunities, not obstacles. I have other things to do. In Hollywood, the land of the skinny and the beautiful, even the smartest and the most talented can end up on the *Whatever Happened to Them?* show. Hollywood is a tough town—for everyone! Believe me, it's not easy for the thin and the beautiful either. There are thousands of them showing up every day. My appearance is one of the things that in the land of the thin and beautiful makes me unique.

So I've decided that my character is a kind, loving, driven, wise, passionate, interested, inspired, fun-loving, confident, crafty, fashion-loving, activist, generous, creative, and proactive woman who chooses to see her "flaws" as something that makes her "unique." There are plenty of examples of how this works: Barbra Streisand has a "unique" nose, Jennifer Lopez has a "unique" booty! Can you imagine if Barbra Streisand had stayed home and brooded about the shape of her nose? All the joy and comfort that Barbra's talent has brought to so many over the years would be lost. And how selfish would that be? So don't be selfish! Share what makes you unique with the world because *baby, you're a star!*

IF YOU DEGRADE, YOU WILL FADE—
R.I.P. JOHNNIE COCHRAN

I try not to judge others or myself. It's important to practice this as best you can. When you judge others, you limit yourself. When you constantly criticize others—for example, for the way they dress—you put yourself on the block to be criticized, judged, or even ridiculed when you wear something new, different, or original. I used to work with an actress who is considered by many to be real and down to earth. I know from personal experience that those descriptions are pure image and have little to do with reality. Although she is attractive and successful, she spends her free time criticizing and judging others. It is exhausting. She criticizes people's weight, sexual orientation, religion, teeth, whatever occurs to her in the moment. She desperately wants to be considered strong, loyal, funny, beautiful, and real. But unfortunately she is crippled by her judgment of others. I'll give you an example: I know she has a strong desire to be perceived as a trendsetter, but she only wears what is featured in magazines or displayed on store mannequins. She is literally incapable of choosing her own clothes because she is so fearful of making a mistake. This is not perfectionism; it's a result of being so critical and judgmental. Because she criticizes so many so often, she is unable to express herself. She is paralyzed by what other people may think of her because she knows that she judges so harshly, and so she assumes that others do the same thing. It's a vicious, destructive, and sad cycle. It's a sad thing to see someone with so many gifts and blessings be reduced to living in a fearful prison of her own making. This is what criticizing and judging others for living their desired lives and starring in their own movie will do. Don't do it. Stop judging others, and soon you'll find that you stop judging and criticizing yourself. Imagine if you spent the time you spend thinking about and talking about other people working toward your own dreams and goals—how much more quickly could you cross the finish line? Give it a shot.

When I first started doing stand-up comedy, I was shocked at how many comics were divisive, and how comics who picked a group to humiliate seemed to be successful—at least in the short term. Hatred, jealousy, prejudice, and degrading groups of people will always be tactics used by some. The adrenaline it produces is seductive, but it's fool's gold! It seems we always need a group to blame our misery on. But how will that help us? I'm not going to pretend that there isn't an audience for meanness. There is always an audience that is so unhappy that they laugh as others suffer. But how will degrading someone else's movie improve your box office? Degrading is draining. And where is the profit in hate? Can you buy a new car with bitterness and hate? You are the star of your movie. You are the heroine. You are a leader and not a follower. Do the opposite of the miserable, the destructive, the numb, and the bullies. Drive on the "jerk-free" highway. After all, the jerks don't pay rent to live in your life, and they won't add to the value of your movie. You don't have time to suffer fools. You have a movie to star in!

YOU ONLY GET ONE CHANCE
TO MAKE A FIRST IMPRESSION

When you show people who you are, they'll believe you! You tell people who you are in many different ways. The way you look tells people a lot about you. You don't have to look like you're going to the prom or walking the red carpet every day, but, just like in a movie, your character is largely defined by the way you walk, talk, and dress. If you walk into a room like you're Elvis, then you are the biggest star. If you act like a loser and you don't matter, then you are and you don't. Your choice!

Do you look like the star of your movie? Being "camera ready" isn't about your hair and makeup. Being camera ready means being prepared whenever opportunity presents itself. You've heard the old saying, "Luck is when opportunity meets preparation"? Always be prepared for your close-up!

My mother always used to tell me, "Do your best at everything you do because you never know who is watching. No job, no chore, and no task is too small or beneath you; it's just an opportunity to be great." I think about this a lot.

MOVIES REQUIRE CONFLICT

Your dreams and your goals are just that—yours! Don't expect the rest of the world to make them happen for you or to be as enthusiastic about them as you are. But if you are surrounded by people who constantly tell you "you can't do that" or "that's stupid," you need to do some serious recasting of your costars. It's not easy, it's not comfortable, but it must be done so that your movie will be great.

My friend Sonia always says, "Remember the goal: maximize passion and minimize resistance." Mucho passion and minimal resistance? Good goal!

Whenever you make a change in your life, whether it's your attitude, your hairstyle, or your habits, you will be met with conflict or resistance. It's inevitable. Know that it is going to happen and prepare for it.

Conflict shows up in our lives in many different ways. It can be as seemingly innocent as a passing comment from a friend—from "Oh, you got a haircut" to "Who do you think you are, J-Lo?"—or something even more obvious, like "You're weird" or "You're a loser." It can also show up when you're trying to break old habits, especially when you're trying to change a social behavior like eating or drinking or smoking. I have a group of girlfriends I go out with a lot. Some of us drink wine, some smoke, but we all love to eat! Every single time one of us decides to stop drinking, stop smoking, or go on a diet, it's so predictable: the others feel personally insulted and make "friendly" comments about the inevitable failure of the effort. I've been at the mercy of the group many times during my professional dieting days. One of my "friends," who, by the way, is tall and thin, said, "Oh, I don't know if I can be friends with you if you're thin. It just won't be the same. Why are you doing this? You're fine the way you are. I never think of you as fat." Well, to quote Julia Roberts in *Pretty Woman*, "You just did." This is the conflict my character had to face in order to keep my movie going. But I've seen it happen over and over in all kinds of circumstances, and every time I think about the great scene in *The Godfather* when Michael Corleone is older and trying to enjoy a more quiet and simple life, and his family needs him to "take care of business." He looks at his sister and says, "Just when I thought I was out, they pull me back in." And that's the conflict and resistance that we can each expect when our character grows and evolves.

MOTION PICTURES HAVE TO HAVE MOTION

Movies have to move. Movies show characters dealing with challenges. Frequently a challenge leads to self-discovery. When you stop challenging yourself, you stop being who you are. When you are not being challenged you're being complacent. When you're complacent you are vulnerable to other people's agendas that may take you away from your own. Don't sell your soul for something you want, because you may just need it one day. Without a challenge you are just "hanging out." Then you'll find yourself in one of those "hanging out" slacker movies of the nineties. This is the new millennium. Move on.

Keep moving. Create action. The rolling stone gathers no moss. Objects in motion stay in motion. Too many naps will make you a sap. Be true to your school.

HOW DO YOU WANT YOUR MOVIE TO END?

Live your life so that people will say cool things at your funeral. Also, you want something cool on your tombstone. Something like "She was a *star!*" Either that, or "She was a great friend as long as you didn't ask her to pick you up from the airport during rush hour on the Friday after Thanksgiving!"

CHAPTER FIVE

Don't Weight to Live!

"How wonderful it is that nobody need wait a single moment before beginning to improve the world."

—ANNE FRANK

THE SUMMER BEFORE EIGHTH GRADE WAS MAGICAL. I spent the entire summer swimming, dancing, playing soccer, and going to Dodger games with my family. Many of my thirteen- and fourteen-year-old friends had already discovered boys and become "women." I hadn't, and still enjoyed the naïveté of childhood. I wasn't yet burdened by people's perceptions of who I was, or what I was or wasn't capable of. Everything seemed possible. I loved my life. I loved my family. I loved my dog and I loved the summertime. I had no idea the realization that I was fat—and, therefore, in some small minds, not expected to be active and happy—was right around the corner. I was busy playing soccer, swimming, and dancing. I didn't have time to feel self-conscious or the patience to wait to be skinny to get out and do something. I had a summer to fill!

I know that no matter how much you love yourself and envision your perfect life, we still live in an imperfect world that is obsessed with image, status, and success. But when you really break it down and think about it, the world is only a bunch of people—people just like you and me with dreams and ambitions and fears—so what is there to be afraid of? Your ability to live a great life is up to you—now! There is a great axiom that writers use in Hollywood, "Don't get it right; get it written." The idea that someone would wait for things to be perfect to live is abhorrent to me. I cannot stand to hear anyone (especially women) say things like "I'll do that when I lose weight," or "If I had a boyfriend, I'd do that," or "I'd be happy if I had money." What an insult to the people who would like to have one more day of life!

For me, the most consistent challenge I've faced all of my life has been my battle with my weight. But when I say, "Don't 'weight' to live,"

I am talking about all of the weight that we put on ourselves by creating these if-then situations: "Well, if I had a boyfriend . . ." "If I were a supervisor . . ." "When I graduate . . . !" "If I were rich . . ." "When my kids are older . . ." "I would, but . . ." The burden of expectation is what weighs us down and keeps us from soaring. It is the "wells," "buts" and "ifs" that make us think we should "weight" to live. *Don't do it!* This is it, your life, your movie. The audience is watching and rooting for you—give 'em a great show!

I've worked hard to live fabulously despite being severely overweight. But my weight is a very personal and difficult internal struggle. I'm not delusional. I know that what I look like is the first thing people see, but I also know that how I feel about the way I look has determined the way people react to me and treat me. As you know, regardless of what *they* think, I act like I'm Elvis! Why would I ever give someone a reason to say no to me by acting like my life should happen after I fulfill someone else's ideal of how I should look? That kind of boring, dated, and stale thinking drives me insane! It just doesn't make any sense to my character! Believe me, I understand it. I just don't agree with it.

There have been times in my life when I have been hurt or disappointed or believed that my life might be easier if I were thin. I mean, everywhere you turn it seems that the message is pretty loud and clear: skinny people are happier, better, more successful, and more loved. If you don't believe me, check out the commercials on television for antidepressants. Who do you see? Usually it's an overweight woman sitting alone or walking alone along the beach, looking really lonely and sad. Compare that to the commercials for things like birth control that are supposed to make you feel vibrant, alive, and sexy. Those commercials feature thin people surrounded by friends and fun, having a blast, dancing and succeeding.

Have you visited the plus-size department at your local department store lately? Let me tell you, the message is very clear. First of all, pack a snack—you'll need it because it's a long, long walk. The plus-size department is usually located at the farthest point from the main entrance of the store, either on the top floor, all the way in the back, or in the bowels of the store, all the way in the back. On your way to find the "women's sizes," you'll pass the juniors department with cool club lighting and music blaring through the speakers and well-dressed, happy-looking mannequins who seem as though they've stopped to pose while living it up on a dance floor. The mannequins are gathered in groups, as if to say, *When you look like this, you'll have lots and lots of friends!* Keep going, because you have a long walk ahead of you to find the plus-size department. You'll pass the perfume and cosmetics department with their pictures, products, and promise of a more beautiful you—if you look like the super-skinny, super-glamorous, super-happy models who are usually being admired or feted by handsome men or adoring children, whose images glare at you as you walk by, as if to say, *Use my products and you can be beautiful and gorgeous like me. Then people will admire you and shower you with love and presents!* You'll then have the joy of passing by the lingerie department, where the lighting is warm and the music is elegant and classical. The mannequins are poised and long and lean and sexy and feminine. Clad in bras and panties and peignoirs and stilettos, as if to say, *Wear this to smooth, lift, conceal or reveal. If you do, you'll be swept away to exotic and beautiful places. Your beauty will be timeless.* As you make your way past this department your head will swarm with the intoxicating smells of potpourri, which you must place in your lingerie drawer so that the pretty things you wear to feel pretty will smell pretty too!

But keep walking!

Past the gowns, past the designer wear, past the china, past the household appliances, the luggage, and the human resources department, all the way to the back. When you're close to the plus-size department, you'll notice that the music has stopped. It doesn't look like you're at a fun club with your friends. It doesn't feel like an exclusive yacht filled with classic elegance or the promise of sexy delights. You'll know you're there when you see short, stocky mannequins standing, arms to the side, totally inactive, alone and expressionless. They're not laughing and dancing, surrounded by their girls at a club. They're not posing and reveling in their own mystery clad in beautiful lingerie. They are bored, tired, uncomfortable, alone, and pissed off. The lighting is dim and you half expect to see tumbleweeds scurrying across the floor, because it looks like an unfinished construction site. The dressing rooms are poorly lit, and even the salespeople seem depressed at being assigned to Siberia. It's painful to think that the people who design department stores are more than willing to take our money, but seem to want us hidden from their other customers. It makes me feel like they're trying to shove us into a "fat closet." Maybe it's some conspiracy to make us walk farther to burn calories. Either way, the message is clear: small sizes are happy and plus-sizes are depressing.

But what does that mean? Does that mean only skinny people have the right to live? Only skinny people have the right to be successful? Only skinny people have the right to love? Only skinny people have the right to their dreams? Only skinny people have the right to happiness? Only skinny people have the right to be fulfilled? Only skinny people have the right to be celebrated? If that's the case, then why not take that premise a step further? How about only rich people, or white people, or left-handed people? Make no mistake about it: the assault on overweight people in the United States can be devastating. The challenges and discrimination I've faced as an overweight woman are not that dissimilar to those faced by people of color, immigrants, or gays and lesbians. I would be a total liar if I said my weight didn't affect me. Of course it does. Who we are is shaped by the sum total of our life's experience, by everything about us, including where we come from, what we've learned along the way, and what we look like. All of it affects the way we view, value, and judge others and ourselves. This in turn affects how we treat ourselves and how we allow others to treat us. There are times when I am overwhelmed by the aggressive messages that surround me about fat people. The difference between me and some people I know who struggle with weight is that I have refused to put my entire life on hold until I'm thin. I know that regardless of the size of my butt, I am bright, talented, and deserving, and that what I do and who I am is not based on the size of my jeans. I have a choice: I can wait for the world to change and tell me that I'm good enough to be happy and to achieve my goals, or I can be determined to be the best me possible right now regardless of current circumstances; I can write my script for my own happiness and success and be great during my own construction. For me the choice is clear. I'm not "weighting" for the world to change, I'm changing the world by living now. Even while I'm under construction, I have a responsibility to myself to do my best, be my best, and feel my best. I don't believe anyone should ever "weight" to live!

If I'd waited until I lost weight to start living I would never have played soccer. (Sure, I was the world's worst soccer player, but that never occurred to me because I was having fun.) I never would have been on a dance team, performed as a ballerina, taught tap, been in love, traveled around the world, started a jewelry business, succeeded in stand-up, starred in my own sitcom, acted in movies, modeled, written for magazines and books, worked as a union organizer, shared the stage with Cesar Chavez, Jesse Jackson, senators, presidents, and so on. . . . I live life now and I don't "weight" for anything.

When I say I don't "weight" to live, I mean it. Don't "weight" for the circumstances in your life to be perfect in order to fulfill your destiny. Don't be burdened by the weight of expectations: *If I were (fill in the blank), then I could do or be (fill in the blank).* Nobody is going to hand you your dream. Believe that! Aside from Ed McMahon coming to your house to give you a check because you've won the Publishers Clearing House sweepstakes, nobody is going to knock on your door and give you the confidence, love, stability, recognition, peace, wisdom, or self-esteem you crave and deserve. You have to work to build a life filled with those things yourself. You have to know who you are, know what you want, write that script, and take center stage!

One of the people in my life whom I respect the most is a dear friend in her early sixties who has raised two amazing children and enjoyed a

At a photo shoot for Torrid. . . .
Oh, yeah, I'm a model! Loooove Torrid!

loving marriage of thirty-six years. She is smart, loving, generous, kind, very organized (she's a Capricorn), and very honorable. She has a very full and impressive résumé of career experience, which ranges from grant writing to media buying to being a successful television producer. I admire her very much. One day she was at my house when I got some bad news about a project I'd been working on. I was really tired and overworked and felt sorry for myself—I had put so much into the project during the previous year, and with one phone call it ended abruptly. I said, "Sometimes I wonder how long I can keep believing that this is going to happen. I'm so tired of the risk and the uncertainty. I wish I had a little more stability in my career and in my life."

Without skipping a beat she told me one of the most wonderful things anyone has ever said to me and reinforced a strongly held belief of mine. She told me, "Welcome to show business. It's a hard life. The fact that you keep going and you're willing to take risks and stay committed to your passion and your dreams is what makes you really admirable. I've really enjoyed my life and I'm proud of what I've accomplished, but the one thing I regret as I look back is not taking more risks. I wish I'd taken more chances on myself." I thought it was so brave and beautifully honest of her to share that with me. I think about her words whenever I think I'd just like to stay home and take it easy. I think I better get out onto the field of life and risk missing the ball in order to score.

So what are you "weighting" for? Be honest. Do you secretly believe that if you just had something or could just do something, your life would be perfect? Are you "weighting" for something to happen or for the circumstances of your life to magically change in order to be the person you are capable of being? Most of us have these feelings, but the trick is to realize it and work to create the circumstances for your own success and happiness. Too much "weighting" and delaying can kill an opportunity and a dream. The only regrets you'll have are for the things you don't do. The saddest people I've ever known are those who wished they had done more, loved more, and lived more. The most fascinating people I've known are people who create their own breaks. Remember, in movies people move! There is a movie called *The Terminator*. There is not much of a demand for a movie called *The Procrastinator*. Procrastination comes from lack of belief. You have got to believe in yourself. If not you, who? What are you "weighting" for? What further proof do you need that you deserve all of the happiness you can imagine and are willing to work for? Remember, it's called a to-do list, not a " 'weight' until I have it all and then I'll do it" list!

My mother always told me, "You don't have to be book smart, but you do have to be smart about yourself." She wasn't formally educated, but she valued knowledge. To me the knowledge about who I am as defined by me is the most valuable lesson I can learn, teach, and remind myself of every single day. Happiness is directly connected to knowing who you are. When you're connected to the person you are, you are better able to make the choices and decisions in your life that you need to make in order to take yourself where you want to be. You don't waste time doing things or being with people who aren't in line with your goals and dreams. But if you're waiting for a moment in life for everything to be perfect, you lose, and you deprive the world of everything you have to offer right now at this moment. It's an excuse to not try. It's a shame and a waste. It's an excuse not to commit to your passion and to the person you are capable of being!

A few months ago I appeared on *Entertainment Tonight*. After my appearance, I received thousands of e-mails and letters from people all over the world. One letter in particular really struck me:

Dear Jackie,

I recently saw you on Entertainment Tonight *and really like your attitude. I especially like your "seize the moment" approach to life. I am a 53-year-old mother of 3 boys (31, 26, and 23). All my life I've wanted to write a screenplay. I've read about many screenwriters who took up to 3 years to write a screenplay. In 3 years I'll be 56. I don't know what I should do. Do you have any advice for me?*

A new fan,

Louise

Do I have any advice? ¡*Por favor!* Read on:

Dear Louise,

I'm thrilled to know that you enjoyed the piece on ET *and even more happy to know that aside from raising three wonderful young men (No small accomplishment. Those of us who share the world with them are very grateful to you* ☺), *you have a dream of your own. Do I have any advice? Hmmmm, let me think about this . . . YES, I DO!*

Louise, here's the deal: in three years you're going to be 56 whether you write your screenplay, and feed your soul, or not. You can spend the next year or three years or ten years writing your screenplay and fulfill your dream, or you can just get a year, three years or ten years older and not be closer to personal fulfillment. I am sure that you are too smart to let life pass you by. Don't "weight" one more second of your life to live it!

And by the way, I assume there will be a fabulous role for a fun-loving, chubby, Mexican-American woman in your screenplay! I'll expect your call!

Good luck, laugh a lot, and be great!

The difference between dreamers and doers is that doers don't see obstacles; they see opportunities, and they go for it. The best we can do for ourselves is strive to be both. Unfortunately, I think we're often stopped from *doing* because we get weighted down with negative thoughts. We start thinking that if we take a chance and do something, people might talk about us or judge us. We are burdened by the weight of self-consciousness, and we're burdened by the weight of fear, and we somehow lull ourselves into believing that *not doing* or *not trying* is more comfortable.

This kind of thinking is paralyzing and doesn't allow us to be the original piece of art that each one of us is. And since we are all originals, we all have a little bit of pioneering spirit that we need to tap into. If we are each unique, then it stands to reason that occasionally we'll find ourselves in unfamiliar or new territory. We may wait for someone else to show us the way to our dreams, and feel we need to do only what has been done before. What if all of the people who ever did anything for the first time felt this way? How would anything ever be invented, improved, or created for the first time? I am the first Latina to ever star in a network sitcom. On the one hand, I'm very proud of that, and on the other, I think it's a sad statistic that not until 1996 was there ever a

Latina who starred in a network sitcom. I'm often asked, "What made you think you could be the star of a sitcom when no other Latinas had done it before?" The answer is simple. I wanted to do it, I had the opportunity to do it, and I went for it. I didn't "weight" for someone else to be the first. I was the first.

Leopard print? Bring it! Cleavage? Oh, yeah! Why "weight"?!

As a former Girl Scout, I enjoy working with Girl Scouts. Recently I had the opportunity to speak at a recruiting conference in Boise, Idaho, where I also conducted jewelry-making workshops. There were over two hundred girls there, and I am very happy to share that although only a handful of them had ever made jewelry, they were very willing to learn and to *try* to make a necklace. As I walked around the room filled with Girl Scouts excitedly beading their necklaces, I came upon one of the girls sitting motionless in her chair.

"Why aren't you making your necklace?" I asked her.

"I don't know how to do it," she replied.

"Do you want me to walk you through the instructions again?"

"No," she said, "I know what I'm supposed to do. I just don't want my necklace to look stupid."

"What do you mean, 'stupid'?" I asked, a little shocked. I looked into her perfectly made-up face and thought about how when I was her age my mom wouldn't even let me shave my legs, let alone leave the house with a face full of makeup. I noticed that her clothes were perfectly coordinated to her accessories and nail polish, that she had perfectly manicured acrylic fingernails, and that her hair was perfectly arranged in a tight ponytail at the top of her head, with a fountain of cascading curls perfectly arranged at her crown. Obviously a girl who takes a lot of pride in her appearance. I realized this was a little girl who was so burdened by the weight of her own expectations to be perfect that she was unable to try anything new. She was petrified of being singled out as different or ridiculed for doing anything that hasn't been done before.

"Make something that you'd like to wear," I suggested. And then the floodgates opened up.

"I don't want to make something that people will think is stupid! Can't I just copy what you're wearing?"

I sat down next to her. "If you make it and you like it and you wear it, that's all that matters. There is no wrong way or right way to make a necklace—there's just your way."

"But I don't want people to talk about me," she pleaded.

"What do you care if people talk about you?" I asked. "If someone else's life is so empty and pathetic that the best they can do is try to knock you down by talking about you, you should feel sorry for them. If they're such losers that all they have to do is talk about you, then, good, you've given them a purpose." At this she started giggling. "Consider it a part of your public service project if they want to waste their time talking about you. The only reason you're even an issue to them is because you have the ball, so run with it!"

"Well, before I do it, I want to plan my design so that it won't look stupid when I put it together."

"I gotta tell you," I said, "I don't know what a stupid necklace looks like. I don't think I've ever seen a stupid necklace. Why don't you just make your necklace, and then if it's stupid, which I highly doubt, you will win the award for the first stupid necklace ever made in the history of jewelry making? If it isn't stupid, then you end up with a beautiful new piece of jewelry to wear. Either way you win, right?"

She laughed and got to work. By the end of the workshop she had a beautiful necklace. She walked up to me and said, *"I didn't even know that I could do this!"*

I was so happy for her, because I know the next time she is faced with a situation that is unfamiliar to her, she will remember the time she thought she was going to make a stupid necklace but chose to try rather than sit and stare at her beads. She proved to herself that she is capable of rising above the weight of what others might think, her own discomfort, and whatever feelings of vulnerability she may have had to create something really beautiful. Probably for the first time in her life, she did something for herself without "weighting" to be perfect, and in the process had a lot of fun and learned something about herself she didn't know at the beginning of the day. And so I'm happy to say that the award for "first stupid necklace in the history of jewelry making" is still up for grabs.

The pursuit of perfection is incredibly self-destructive and a recipe for disaster. The best we can do is face our fears and keep moving forward. All we can do is be and do our best and not "weight" to be perfect to live; remember, we're under construction.

"Weighting" also limits our ability to learn and grow and live and succeed when we "weight" for perfect circumstances in order to move forward with our goals. This is a lesson I learned in a highly unorthodox way while working as an organizer for the Hotel Employees and Restaurant Employees Union, Local 11.

I had a very tough but brilliant boss named Victor Griego, who is most definitely a dreamer *and* a doer. Some of the abilities I like most about myself are the result of my tough boss pushing me beyond my own perceived limits. One day while working on a national campaign, he asked me to pick up some very important fliers that were at the printer. We needed these fliers for a big event the next day with the Reverend Jesse Jackson, Martin Sheen, and many other dignitaries from all over the country. I had a million things to do that day—all very high priority—and needed about nine more hours in the day to complete half of them. But I agreed to swing by the printer's to pick up the materials. I called the printer to find out what time they closed. The owner told me they close at nine p.m., and that he was going to leave promptly because it was his anniversary and he and his wife had dinner reservations at nine thirty. I went about my day and knew that no matter what, I needed to be at the printer's before nine p.m.

At about eight forty I headed toward the printer's. On my way, I was pulled over by one of my friends in local law enforcement and reminded by way of a hefty moving violation that it is not legal in California to make a right turn on a green light when there are pedestrians in the crosswalk. I kept my mouth shut and tried to get the officer to hurry up and give me my ticket so I could be at the printer's by nine p.m. I was back on my way at eight fifty-seven. I arrived at the printer's at nine oh three—and guess what? The lights were out, the doors were locked, the place was closed, and the printer was gone! The event was scheduled to begin the next morning at seven a.m. and I didn't have the materials. I was in so much trouble! I panicked, I cried, I called one of my colleagues, and she suggested I call my tough boss and get it over with rather than show up the next day without the materials.

I called Victor and explained what had happened. I knew there was nothing I could do about it; I was just confessing my screwup.

He said, "If the store is closed you have two options. You can wait for it to open tomorrow and you'll be able to pick up the fliers after the event is over, or you can get the owner to open up for you so that you can get the fliers and fulfill your responsibilities."

"What a dick!" I thought. "What does he expect me to do?"

"Find out where the printer lives," he continued. "Go to his house and get him to open his shop for you. Do it now—you don't have the luxury to wait."

I immediately remembered that the printer was at a restaurant with his wife. I drove to the restaurant without knowing what this man looked like, horrified that I was about to interrupt his celebration. But I was even more horrified that I'd failed at such a simple task for such an important event, which so many people had worked so hard to make a success. I knew I needed to come through.

I marched into the restaurant and stopped a hostess. "I'm looking for someone I don't know. I don't know what he looks like and he's not expecting me, but I need to find him." This absurd moment was interrupted by fate, luck, or a miracle. A sweet-faced gentleman walked right up to me and said, "It sounds like you're looking for me." I explained who I was and that I'd missed him by three minutes. I apologized profusely for interrupting his anniversary dinner, and asked him if there was any way to get into his shop and get the materials before the morning. I fully expected him to tell me I was out of line and who the hell did I think I was disrupting his anniversary dinner with his wife. Instead, he chuckled. "I wish my employees had half the hustle you obviously have." He gave me his cell phone number and agreed to meet me at six thirty a.m. at his shop. I was there at six twenty a.m. waiting for him when he arrived. He gave me the materials *and* offered me a job. I thanked him, hugged him—I think I may have even kissed him! As I was leaving, he said, "I'm going to remember your name because I know I'm going to be hearing about you in the future. Anyone who is as determined to get things done as you obviously are will probably be president one day." Nice thought, but at that point I felt like a loser who *almost* blew a major event, got a ticket, and interrupted a total stranger's anniversary dinner. But for the first time in my life I consciously realized there is no reason to "weight" for things to happen. When you just ask, it's amazing how willing people are to help. Everyone wants to participate in success.

Even if you ask someone to do something that isn't the norm, if you have good reason, people will try to accommodate you. Why? Because people are essentially good and want to feel helpful! Remember this and use it responsibly.

Occasionally you will come across people who are completely unwilling to deviate from the norm. You know the expression, "Think outside the box"? This is what anyone who is successful does. Otherwise we're just sheep staying in line and never trying anything new or different. Tragic. The people who "weight" to live until someone gives them a title, a ring, a diploma, or whatever else they perceive they need in order to be whole are strictly "think-in-the-box" thinkers (TIBs)—and until they get out of their own way they'll *never* do anything of significance and will *never* feel truly fulfilled. I realize we all have to step around these human landmines, but that's okay. Soon enough they will be in your rearview as you blow by them on the highway of life. Their problems and limitations are theirs. You have your potential to unleash on the world because, don't you forget, *baby, you're a star!*

I may have cursed my boss many times under my breath. I may have lost sleep and had stomachaches over blunders—that was the old me. The "new Jackie" realizes that my boss wasn't unappreciative. He was making me see my goals as something I control. I am supergrateful to him for this lesson. Take control of your circumstances and take control of your life; don't "weight" for the store to open—get it opened! Don't be a TIB and don't let the TIBs get in your way.

DON'T "WEIGHT" TO BE
THE PERSON YOU WANT TO BE

Act like the person you want to be. Don't act like your worst nightmare. Act like that person who has had a brisk walk and a shower and is glowing. You have the glow. Just turn on the light. Just flick the switch.

I realize that even good situations are temporary and all of us get stressed. Every day we fight noise, pollution, stress, anxiety, being late for a deadline, and the dread of loneliness and despair. We fight the negativity that comes from being tired of having an unkempt home and an out-of-shape body. We can't control the world around us, but we sure can control the way we react to it. Sometimes you have to be the wise one and just step away from the stress. It's a great thing to remind ourselves. Personally, I've always loved the expression, "If you can't stand the heat, get out of the kitchen." (Although a toasty kitchen is usually a good-smelling kitchen, which generally means something yummy is being made. Nothing wrong with that!) Unfortunately, people often use this expression in a negative way—to emphasize where someone may fall short or be too stressed to perform. Personally, I think there is another way to look at it. Sometimes in the thick of things, or the *heat of the moment,* so to speak, we need to just step away from the "heat." Be a voice of reason for yourself. When you're stressed, don't do anything out of your normal routine: don't overeat, drink too much, or pollute good relationships with bad situations. Don't hurt your body or spirit because of the stress that surrounds you. Release it all by remaining focused on your goals and sticking to your script! Just step away from the car!

Don't "weight" to be great . . . it's never going to be easier than right now!

Don't "weight" for obstacles to disappear or for anyone to give you permission to grow and evolve. Whenever you decide to make a change and take control, there is a cause and effect. If you've spent every Sunday morning on the phone with your friend gossiping about everyone you know, and now you've decided that your character spends her Sunday mornings working out, your friend is going to feel the void. Even the people who love us will sometimes try to knock us off our "high horse," not because they don't love us, but because on some level we all understand that when someone close to us raises the level of their game, we have to work harder to keep up. It's very basic and consistently true. When you are striving to be better and feel that the people around you are attacking you, picking on you, criticizing, ignoring, or trying to knock you off your game, remember: In football, the *only* person everyone is trying to knock down is the guy with the ball. So when people are trying to knock you down, realize it just may very well be because *you* have the ball! Hang on to that ball, keep your focus on the end zone, and exude confidence. That makes you the star! Know that!

DON'T WAIT FOR A CAMERA TO BE CAMERA-READY

Don't you admire the person who comes into work every day and manages to be "camera-ready" every single day? She's current on the latest books and movies, remembers to send thank-you notes, and is seemingly always happy. The only difference between you and her is that she isn't "weighting" for anything to be the person she wants to be. It's not a matter of wearing the latest trend, or expensive clothes, or tons of makeup; it's a matter of treating yourself like the star you are, being your own best friend, and doing the things that make you more you, right now! If feeling good means wearing a nice pair of shoes—wear them. Don't "weight" for the prom to wear them. If spending an extra hour a day reading a great book makes you happy, read it! Without question what is most attractive is the confidence you feel when you're truly comfortable in your own skin. What are you "weighting" for?!

We come to love not by meeting a perfect person, but by seeing an imperfect person perfectly. And this means you. Don't "weight" to love. I am not saying to become some kind of weirdo who loves everyone and everything and walks around in a cultlike stupor. I'm saying that when you don't take the time to truly know and love yourself, I would bet just about anything that you're incapable of really loving anyone else. By seeing yourself as you are and loving yourself enough to nourish and protect yourself as you construct the person you intend to be, you allow yourself to see others as they are, to love them as they are, but to treat them as the people they are capable of being. This guarantees a lot of riches! By contrast, people who constantly hammer away at what bothers them about the people they claim to love are putting up barriers between them and their own personal fulfillment. They're "weighting" for the perfect people and perfect circumstances to be the best person they can be.

I have a friend I truly love. She is a wonderful person with a big heart. She wants what we all want: to be healthy, loved, successful, and acknowledged. The problem is, she cannot get out of her own way to save her life. She keeps "weighting" for things to happen. She comes from a good, loving, supportive, and successful family. Unfortunately she is "weighting" for a husband and for the acknowledgment of others to be happy. She is weighted down by short-term and unfulfilling relationships. She is weighted down by the fact that she is unfulfilled in her work, but won't leave because she has no idea who she would be or what she would do if she didn't have a fancy office in a fancy building with an embossed business card. She has the kind of family that most people dream about, but is always upset with them because "they don't know her." She is frustrated by the fact that she is not yet married, but she constantly says that she "doesn't have time to socialize or chitchat." She is very bright and always says the right thing, but rarely lives it. She has filled her life with so much activity but hasn't taken the time to really get to know herself, and that's why no person, no job, no gift, no friendship is ever good enough. Nothing makes her feel loved or cared for or fulfilled. She describes herself as nurturing, but is resentful of anyone who asks her to do anything, even when it's her job. She is constantly frustrated, hurt, disappointed, or feels that she is unappreciated. She is "weighting" for life to make her happy.

This is a recipe for disaster. Until she gets to know herself and is truly able to identify who she is now, she will never be able to build the life she desperately wants, with love and passion and intimacy and happiness. If she were an actor, the director would yell "Cut!" and she would be labeled a terrible actress, because in acting what you do is never as important as why you're doing it. In life, just as in acting, the character you play has to *be* in order to *do*. If what you're doing is what defines you instead of who you are, you're in trouble. My friend cannot sit still and just be, because she doesn't know how to make herself happy. When we "weight" for something outside of ourselves to make us happy, we are sure to be miserable, because until we know what we need and what we want, how will we ever know it when we see it? She needs to slow down, stop saying what she thinks people want to hear, stop filling her time with activities that don't nourish her soul, and start being. She is "weighting" for someone else to make her happy. But as my mother always said, she needs to "become Mrs. Right and Mr. Right will find her."

CREATE A "NO-WEIGHT" PLAN WITH BIG IDEAS

Let's discuss ideas. What is an idea? It could be a system or thought, scheme or method or plan to better the universe. Remember when you help one person you can motivate that person to help another, and before you know it many are affected by one act of selflessness. An idea can be a solution. It can be a proposal ignited by inspiration. An idea has energy. An idea can be motivation and inspiration that comes from a belief in something. But it is definite energy that when delivered thoughtfully and carefully and passionately will take on a life of its own and attract the people and the resources we need to give it life. What pushes you forward besides the stuff you have to do? If you're living and dreaming and creating your circumstances for success, then you're giving life to your ideas. For example, my jewelry making started as a passion, and turning it into a business began as an idea. . . .

THE JEWELRY BUSINESS

People told me to "weight" for the economy to improve before I started my business. They said I should "weight" to get a bigger space. But what is the right time? If I don't value my own passions enough to make them happen now, then when? How long should any of us "weight" to live? Life is right now, and I'm not "weighting" for the perfect time. I'm creating the circumstances for my own success as I define it, now!

It makes me happy to pursue my passion. I am thrilled when something I've created puts a smile on someone's face. This is my only life. I can't "weight" for a perfect home, a perfect economy, no cellulite, whatever; I can't "weight" to pursue my dream!

And now, I live in Cluttersville, U.S.A.!

December 2004. Our home is not really a home but a storage facility filled with tools, crystals, hardware, pearls, semiprecious stones, sketches, lists of ideas, boxes, and samples. When you walk around my home you have to take small steps. You don't want to step on a tool kit, or an outgoing order box, or the exercise bike, which is next to the dresser-chest, which is next to the ottoman, which is next to the couch and sofa and tons of gifts, books, magazines, lit candles (I am a scented candle fanatic ☺), a computer, blankets, throw pillows, press kits, videotapes, DVDs, CDs, and more stuff. There is an open box with piles of bead mats, tool rolls, and a huge bag of biodegradable packing peanuts. It's been sitting there for at least a month. It is the centerpiece of my kitchen–dining area. This open box is two feet wide and is the bridge between my stove and my dining room table. My guests enjoy fabulous fine dining next to hardware and jewelry-making materials. Instead of reading a menu they can read my personal and business mail, which is located on a filing cabinet behind my dining room table.

They can also read fascinating receipts from suppliers from all over the world, not to mention my eclectic assortment of store coupons, because I am obsessed with sales and discounts. Everything is conveniently located. Everything is close by. Everything you might need on earth can probably be found in a few seconds: food, phone, Internet, and tools are what I'm about. Nice and cozy. If you stretch you could get rice from the stovetop and not have to leave your seat at the dining room table. With my back to the wall I write this book. I write at my kitchen table. I am inches from the window, which is inches from the massive construction project next door, now in its seventh month. I look outside and see a man with a mustache a few inches from me. He smiles at me. I nod. He says Happy Holiday, and comments that I have gifts everywhere. He tells me I have no space. He also says I shouldn't go to sleep with the television on. Who is this? Note to self: Call local law enforcement.

As a result of my job as host of *Jewelry Making* on the DIY Network, where I showcase jewelry makers from all over the country, I have been getting orders for some of my jewelry and tool kits. At the beginning of most businesses there is little profit. We are no exception. It's a lot of investment, or, as they say in business school, "sweat equity," which is just a fancy term for "work for free." Bill must make boxes and help with the packaging and tape the boxes according to my exact specifications before taking them to the post office. He is losing his mind. He has threatened to end our engagement. But we both know he just wants to vent. I have maintained my cool (except when I am yelling). It's not easy. But at least I didn't "weight."

Fast forward to April 2005. I now have partners and a workspace, and although I am still investing "sweat equity," my commitment to my passion has attracted some incredible people who are going to help me make my dream come true: a jewelry line, do-it-yourself jewelry-making kits, and a book about jewelry making. Why? Is it because they're nice people who want to help me? Absolutely not! Yes, they're

nice people, but they realized that I am so passionate about these projects and didn't "weight" for the perfect time or the perfect circumstances to make it happen that they were ignited and fueled by the
passion. And that's what happens when we don't "weight."

As I conclude this chapter, I hope that you'll take the time to draw up
the plans for the house you're building—yourself. This is it. This is your
life. Do not regret yesterday and don't fear tomorrow. Keep growing
and keep building. And I hope you'll decorate your "house" with a piece
of my jewelry!

CHAPTER SIX

My Best Friend, Jackie!

> *"Have no friends not equal to yourself."*
> —CONFUCIUS

I HAVE A SECRET WEAPON THAT I PULL OUT WHENEVER I NEED HER; it's *my best friend, Jackie!* Now I know it may seem a little wacky, and at first it may feel uncomfortable, but let me explain. . . .

Every single day everywhere you look there is someone saying you're too thin, too fat, too ignorant, too this or not enough that. The truth is, we are each perfect just the way we are, this moment, this day, as is! But we have to know in our hearts that we are perfect, and tomorrow we can become even more perfect!

My best friend, Jackie, reminds me that a compliment is someone's gift to us. So just like with any gift, take it and give thanks. If you reject a compliment you are signaling to the world that you don't deserve praise or to be celebrated. Puh-lease!

And it's annoying. Have you ever complimented someone's hairstyle, only to hear, "Uh, ah, shucks, uh, ahh, it's nothing, really, are you sure? I'm so fat. My hair would look better if I had passed algebra." This is a colossal waste of time! Can you imagine if Gandhi was like that?

You: Gandhi, congratulations, you freed millions of people.

Gandhi: Yeah, that's great. But it doesn't change the size of my schnoz. My nose is ridiculous. What a honker. I am gross . . . and, while I'm thin, I have cellulite.

Absolutely absurd. And believe me, we're always teaching people how to treat us. If you tell people by your words and actions that you're unable or unwilling to accept their praise and compliments, they'll pay attention to you and eventually they'll stop. Nobody wants to fail; let them be successful! When someone gives you a compliment, practice saying a simple phrase: thank you!

If you tell yourself that you are fat, boring, and untalented, then that's it—you've sealed your fate because you are what you think you are. Remember: "Watch your thoughts as they become your words. Watch your words as they become your actions. Watch your actions as they become your character. Watch your character as it becomes your destiny" (Byrd Baggett). Besides, would you say such mean things to a friend? Then why are you saying them to yourself? So be nice to your friend (you) and tell yourself how amazing and unique you are. And don't forget to exfoliate!

My best friend, Jackie, consists of the best parts of me that sometimes I forget to share with myself. Whenever I have something to do and I put it off, my best friend, Jackie, reminds me to get it done. Whenever I get an idea and then think, "That's stupid," my best friend, Jackie, reminds me that my ideas are as valuable as anyone else's. Whenever I forget to do something and I start to beat myself up about it, my best friend, Jackie, reminds me that I can do something about it now. Whenever I am tired or scared and I start playing those ugly old tapes in my head, my best friend, Jackie, reminds me that I can choose whom I listen to and turns the tapes off.

The beauty of being your own best friend is that you're never alone and you're never limited to the negative thinking or fear of the moment. There are times when we are incredibly stressed out, and what happens when we're stressed out or scared? Human nature: we revert back to the most familiar and sometimes destructive behavior. Personally, I have a terrible habit of eating late at night. Whenever I am looking into the refrigerator for the seventeenth time at eleven forty p.m., my best friend, Jackie, pops up to remind me that I am capable of making better choices for myself and that maybe it's time to go to bed so that I don't make a mistake.

Sometimes we just need someone to listen or hold our hand through a task. Sometimes it's something very important, and sometimes it can be as simple as returning a pair of shoes we bought and never wore or didn't like or spent too much money on. Haven't you been in a situation and thought, "If only I had someone to go with me" or "I wish someone would do this for me." Done! You as your best friend can pick up the slack for the real you. Have you ever had to make a phone call you didn't want to make, go to an event that should have been fun but stressed you out, ask for a well-deserved raise or stand up to someone in your life who is sucking the life out of you? I know there have been many times when I was faced with doing something I knew would seem a lot easier and a lot less burdensome if I just had a friend to stand by my side or to hold my hand. That's when I called on my best friend, Jackie.

In the past I have not been my best friend, Jackie. I forgot that I have a responsibility to do my best and be my best and take care of my house. Once my house is in order I can help others with their construction.

Let me tell you how I learned this lesson the hard way:

In 1996 I found myself in the very fortunate position of making more money than anyone else in my family. I was working on a network sitcom, where I made more money per week than my parents made in a year. I felt very fortunate and wanted to share my fortune with everyone I loved and cared about. My father ran into some legal problems, and (fortunately) I was in the financial position to help him out. My mother needed a lot of medical care, and I was (fortunately) in the financial position to help. A friend of mine was going through a nasty divorce, and I was (fortunately) in the financial position to pay for his attorney. The father of another friend was dying across the country, and I was (fortunately) in the financial position to buy him numerous plane tickets, rental cars, and a cell phone so that he could be with his father during those last months. My brother got married, and I was (fortunately) in the financial position to help him out. A friend of mine got his truck repossessed, and I was (fortunately) in the financial position to help get it back. My neighbor needed to get out of a terribly disastrous relationship and felt that she couldn't leave because of finances, but I was (fortunately) in the financial position to give her the money to start her new life. I did all of this willingly and lovingly and am glad I was in the (fortunate) financial position to give them what I thought they wanted and needed, and honestly it made me feel good—at the moment.

I learned very quickly that it doesn't matter how much money you make—you take yourself and all of your problems everywhere you go. Read on. . . .

I had been broke for so many years that when I began to make money, I just spent it! Imagine you're starving for a long, long time. Then one day you wake up and you have a full-time chef who prepares five-star meals for you three times a day. And you gorge yourself! You don't just overeat: you stuff yourself until you cannot move, and you're so uncomfortable you can't believe what you've done. That's exactly what I did with money. Because like the person who was starving, I had dreamed about making money and being able to go to a mall and buy something just because I liked it and wanted it and not because it was on sale.

I spent the rest of my time and money worrying about everyone else and how I could help them. And again, I felt great about it in the moment, and I certainly reaped the benefits of making my loved ones' lives a little happier and bringing some instant relief to them. But I woke up one day and my show was canceled and I had no income, and I found myself in the (unfortunate) position of having made a lot of people I loved financially dependent on me, and I had no money.

When I realized I had spent all of my money and didn't have anything to show for it—I didn't own a home, I didn't even own a car, I didn't have any investments—I felt terrible. I was devastated and I was terrified. I had been so busy putting financial Band-Aids on everyone else's lives that I lost sight of my own needs. I had panic attacks for the first time in my life and would wake up in the middle of the night with night sweats. What had I done? I spent a fair amount of time feeling sorry for myself, and then I got mad. I was mad at all the people who had had their hands out while I was making money, and were suddenly all gone when the money was gone. I was mad because there was nobody for me to turn to for financial help. I was especially mad at myself. Why didn't I ensure my own financial stability before handing out money like it grew on trees? And where was the friend who could have reined me in and warned me to take better care of myself? I spent the next couple of years trying to play financial catch-up. I made enough money to live a nice life under normal circumstances, but once you're in debt it takes a lot to get out of that financial hole and be able to live comfortably.

Once I got over the initial "feel sorry for me fest," I decided to get out and do something! I needed to come up with a plan so that this would never happen to me or anyone I care for. Not if I could help it!

It took a while, but I realized that my mistake was *not* in doing and giving. My mistake was in not doing and giving to myself *first*! So when the party was over and I forgot to have a good time, I was really pissed about cleaning up. I was not a victim of anything. My circumstances, my decisions, and my choices are all 100 percent and completely in my control. Once I understood, accepted, and believed that, then the rest was easy.

And that's when I became my best friend, Jackie!

If we're smart and we choose our friends wisely, then we choose people who complement our best selves. A friend should be a person who makes you better. A friend is honest but kind. A best friend reminds you that you are better than your worst day and more than your latest mistake. A friend encourages you to be your best self. A friend is loyal. A friend is a good listener and a friend protects you.

Let's discuss the qualities of a best friend a little further. . . .

Your best friend should listen to you and truly *hear* you. Being heard is not the same as being right. If you ask me the most important gift someone can give to another, it is to say, "I value you and I hear what you're saying." The person who is speaking will think, "I am being heard, and so I don't have to keep saying the same thing over and over." This is truly valuable when you are faced with a decision or crisis. I know there have been times in my life when I have felt very scared and/or desperate about a situation and have confided in people who did not hear me.

Being my best friend, Jackie, helps me deal with relationships that are out of balance. Relationships that deplete rather than strengthen. Bad relationships usually involve bad communication. Someone usually is not being heard.

For example, I had a friend who seemed to be fearless. She didn't put up with much and was very comfortable calling people on their bad behavior. As we grew closer, I relied on her to resolve issues in my life that I didn't feel comfortable confronting. I had a weakness: I wasn't comfortable with confrontation. Our communication was pretty good. We were both being heard.

In the beginning we were very much equals, both working actresses. As time passed, her career took off and my life fell apart; my mother died, my father moved back to Mexico, I wasn't working, I had gained about seventy-five pounds, my home was burglarized, my car was broken into, my computer crashed, it was Mother's Day and I was completely broke and scared to death. We were on very different paths, and it was hard for us to *hear* each other. I needed my friend to hear me and understand what I was going through, and I didn't feel that she could. As a result, I found myself constantly trying to convince her of how difficult my life was. This is *always* a recipe for disaster on both sides. For her, how completely annoying must it have been to constantly hear the same "woe is me" song? For me, it was debilitating to constantly have to repeat and amplify my problems and fears in an effort to get her to acknowledge that she understood what I felt. It was a breakdown in communication that ultimately led to the end of our friendship. I had to find someone who could hear me. It wasn't easy but I listened, heard my inner voice, and moved on. I was taking care of myself in the long term.

This is just basic human nature. If you ask me, "How are you?," and I say, "I have a headache," and you say, "Hey, turn up the music. This is my favorite song!," clearly you haven't heard me. When we're not heard, we repeat our problem over and over and over to whoever will listen to us *until we're heard*! If you don't believe me, watch a kid. When a child needs something and is whiney or crying, and you say, "Don't cry, baby," he'll keep crying. But when you stop, look at him, give him your full attention, and say, "What's wrong?," when you hear him and repeat it back to him, acknowledging a problem even if you can't offer an immediate solution, he usually stops crying immediately. Why? Because he's been heard!

LOVE THE ONE YOU'RE WITH. THAT'S YOU!

My mom always said, *"Love yourself the way you want to be loved."* Treat yourself the way you want to be treated. The same is true for being my best friend, Jackie! Take care of yourself the way you would take care of your best friend. You wouldn't allow anyone to attack your friend or tell her that she is bad, stupid, ugly, and worthless. So why would you do that to yourself? Be your own best friend. We all are the sum total of our life experiences, good and bad. There are tapes that we all play in our own heads. Some of these tapes are things we've discovered or decided on our own, and some of these tapes are things that we've been told or taught by others. Our job is to choose the ones we listen to. Our subconscious minds don't know the difference between fantasy and reality—that's why brainwashing works (and that's not necessarily a good thing!). But here is the beauty about that: we have the power to re-program ourselves. We can control our thoughts. Let's say we wake up groggy and starting the day is a challenge. We can say, "Oh my God. I can't believe I have to go to work." Or we can say, "Hello, world! Fortunately I have a job, benefits, a parking pass, and free coffee." We do more damage to ourselves by what we tell ourselves than anyone else could ever do. And that is one of the reasons that my best friend, Jackie, is so important to me: she reminds me to replace all the negativity with good. She reminds me of all that I've done, overcome, and accomplished, and all that I'm capable of doing. My best friend, Jackie, makes what seems daunting fun!

We talk to ourselves all the time. We should whisper sweet nothings into our own ears. My best friend, Jackie, turns off the old, worn-out, out-of-style tapes that play and replaces them with new, fun, and soon-to-be classics! Here are some of the horrible songs that we sing to ourselves every day:

Ladies and gentlemen: The CD of negative songs playing all day and even while we sleep!

Sing along if you want to: one . . . two . . . three!

> *"Baby Got Fat!"*
> *"I'm a Loser, Baby!"*
> *"It Really Sucks in Herrrrrrrrre!"*
> *"Bitch Girl!"*
> *"Geekie in a Bottle"*
> *"You've Got No Friends"*
> *"The Real Not-Slim Shady"*
> *"Saturday Night's Alright for Sleeping"*
> *"You Pull Me Down Where I Belong"*
> *"I Won't Survive"*
> *"Sisters Can't Do It for Themselves"*
> *"We Are Not Champions, My Friend"*
> *"After the Lovin' I'm Not in Love with You"*
> *"Baby We Were Born to Trip"*
> *"I'm Walkin' on Farm Swine"*

But my best friend, Jackie, helps me write my own anthems. Try this! (Sing to the tune of Destiny's Child's "Independent Women")

> *All the women*
> *Over size eleven*
> *Throw yo' hands up at me!*
> *All the hunnies*
> *With chubby tummies*
> *Throw yo' hands up at me!*
> *All the Mommas*
> *Rockin' big buttocks*
> *Throw yo' hands up at me!*

Girl, I didn't know you could get down like that
Chubby
You're an Angel
Be down like that!

Mmmmmmmm-hmmmmm!

My best friend, Jackie, can take compliments.

My best friend, Jackie, reminds me that I may not know everything, but I'm only an e-mail away from someone who does.

My best friend, Jackie, reminds me how nice it is to have a job whenever I complain about long days.

My best friend, Jackie, makes me feel strong and safe even when I'm scared.

My best friend, Jackie, does not allow low-energy people and actions in my life.

My best friend, Jackie, reminds me not to eat lunch with whiners. It's bad for your digestion. Have a papaya instead of a whina'.

Rules are made to be broken.

There are rules that we as a society all agree on and should follow, laws that keep order and keep us safe, and certain social customs that make life more pleasant for everyone (although laws change all the time, but more about that later). But then there are rules that someone somewhere decided should be "rules" based on their personal opinion or taste. I have a big problem with those! Some of my all-time least-favorite rules are:

- Dark on the bottom, light on top.
- No horizontal stripes if you're above a size six. (If I were a horizontal stripe, I'd be really pissed because seven-eighths of the women in the United States are above a size six!)
- Finish your food.
- Don't make waves.
- Don't speak until spoken to.
- Don't dip your pen in the company well.

I don't always follow the rules that were made by others that I had no part in creating (I'm talking "rules," not laws, rules). I did not vote on these rules. No one called me. Did they call you? If you believe that the rule makers are more capable and more important than you, then you have lost. The rule makers and enforcers like to keep the power that they have over you. The rules are designed to keep you scared and feeling like you're not important, you're not good enough, and you should just shut up. Why do we assume someone else always knows better who we are than we do? For example, when was it decided that only skinny people are fabulous? Why is it such an unbelievable battle for worth and respect if you don't look like a human lollipop (big head, stick body)? Who is so important or powerful to decide that only thin people are beautiful? It's just plain ridiculous and arbitrary. If you don't believe me, go to a museum. Look at the classics. The women celebrated in the great works of art are zaftig, big, beautiful, and cherubic! So how did we get so lost? It's because we allowed ourselves to be told what is beautiful and what isn't; what is valuable and what isn't. And for some reason we stopped asking, Why? Says who?

Just because someone has a master's degree or has a title doesn't give them the right to make you feel bad about yourself—unless you let them. My best friend, Jackie, reminds me that nobody can make me feel any way that I don't let them. Titles don't ensure that someone is smarter than you. They just mean that perhaps someone has some technical ability or authority. Everyone deserves respect, but never more than you give yourself. Nobody in a position of power is a better person than you are by virtue of the position they hold. They may seem to have an advantage over you, or perhaps they may have some authority over you, but that doesn't make them better.

Your value as a person is only diminished if you let your self-image be shaped by someone else's perception of you based on one interaction or a limited relationship. Each one of us falls into this bad habit regardless of where we are in life or how good we feel about ourselves. We have all been conditioned to think that everyone else knows more than we do. Sure, we can all learn from everyone, but the answers to who we are and how we can be great do not lie with someone else. Listen to your own voice. Some call it instinct. Either way, that is where true wisdom lives.

That is, if you are clear about the person you are. You need to get really honest with yourself and really know what you want, who you are, where you're going. And check in with yourself the way you do with your friends and loved ones. Make sure the path you're on still makes sense, make sure the goals you have are still what you want, make sure the shoes you're wearing still fit. Remember, change is good. You can always change your mind about anything. You are constantly learning and changing and adapting, and your perception of yourself and how you treat yourself must reflect that.

Recently my friend Lash and I went window-shopping together. We walked by Betsey Johnson's boutique. I loooooooove Betsey! For years I've dreamed of being able to wear her fabulous clothes, but they don't fit me. For years I've fluctuated between a size twenty-two (on a good day) and a size twenty-six/twenty-eight. But I adore her clothes. Lash and I went into the store to look. I figured I'd check out her accessories—you don't have to be skinny to carry her adorable bags! Well, I saw the cutest, flirty skirt made out of the most delicious soft velvet fabric, and said, "I would love to be able to wear this skirt!"

The saleswoman (tall, thin, gorgeous, stunningly beautiful despite having her arm in a cast) said, "That skirt is so cute on. You should try it."

"Oh no," I sputtered, "I'm too fat to wear her clothes."

As soon as the words came out of my mouth, the poor saleswoman looked as though I'd punched her in the face. "You should really try it on," she insisted.

I was so irritated because I just knew that this wafer-thin girl had no idea what it is like to not be able to squeeze my fat ass into anything in the store. So just to shut her up, I grabbed the damned skirt out of her hand and stomped into the dressing room to prove to her that it didn't fit! I huffed and puffed and pulled my pants down and put the skirt on and . . . zipped it right up! The size-ten Betsey Johnson A-line skirt with the flirty hem fit me! I practically did a cartwheel right there in the dressing room!

I ran out of the dressing room and into Lash's arms! "Can you believe it? Can you believe it fits me?!"

I'm sure the entire mall heard me! I twirled around the store like Cinderella at the ball for a few minutes. Then I changed back into my clothes and proudly marched up to the register to pay for my beautiful new skirt! I felt like I'd just won a medal at the Olympics! I don't think I've been a size ten since sixth grade. I'd worked very hard for this moment! As I handed the saleswoman my credit card, she said, "You know, I probably shouldn't say anything, but I used to weigh two hundred thirty pounds. I know what it's like not to be able to wear anything in this store, and I have to tell you, it's a little offensive to hear someone who can obviously fit into whatever you want say that you can't. You have no idea what it's really like not to be able to wear anything in a store." Lash and I were absolutely speechless! This was my first wake-up call that I needed to check in with myself about how I perceived my physical self.

"Actually," I explained, "I weighed two hundred ninety-one pounds last year and still can't get my head around the fact that things might fit. And it's so ironic that you were offended by my comments, because the *only* reason I tried the skirt on in the first place was because your insistence that the damned skirt would fit was so offensive to me!" We both laughed. I learned a *big* lesson that day: Gotta check in to make sure the place I'm headed still makes sense for the person I am today!

OUR CORE MUST BE STRONG

Opinions and plans change, but your core must be strong. My emotions sometimes get the better of me. I am working on calming myself down. I am working on acknowledging when I am nervous and dealing with it. I am trying to motivate my team and myself every day. Sometimes I have to admit that I don't understand something. I am working on working hard but not forgetting to celebrate. I am working on staying focused and training my rebellious mind to concentrate on the immediate task, but not lose sight of the big picture. My best friend, Jackie, reminds me of my progress.

My best friend, Jackie, knows I am improving all the time. While sometimes I wake up in fear, I try to figure out a way to help myself and have fun. Then the fun will be infectious, and maybe someone else will pick up the fun ball and we can have a good day. So much of my day is about making small decisions. Should I throw the mail on my kitchen table? Maybe I'll sort it and throw most of it away immediately. Should I talk to someone for an hour even though I am swamped with responsibilities? Should I argue or avoid?

There is a part of me that just wants pleasure. I have to adjust my definition of pleasure. For example, I am trying to enjoy writing more. I am trying to enjoy working out. I have yet to get that runner's high, let alone runner's thighs! I have a lot of pain, and very little instant gratification. But I understand the potential long-term gain. I am trying to enjoy eating less at night.

My best friend, Jackie, reminds me that just because I have done something one way for a while doesn't mean I have to do it that way for the rest of my life. Once again, the beauty of life. Every moment holds the promise to do better, be better, try something new, adjust your attitude, meet someone, change a habit, start a new one; it's all good!

My best friend, Jackie, doesn't let me get stuck in a rut. My best friend, Jackie, reminds me that I am always able to work on the "new Jackie." This is a simple way to give myself room to be the person I want to be, and not, out of habit, revert to the person I've been.

The "new Jackie" doesn't panic when she gets bad news.

The "new Jackie" gets to sleep early and monitors her caffeine intake.

The "new Jackie" gives herself a break.

The "new Jackie" is into quality, not quantity.

The "new Jackie" thinks globally but acts locally.

The "new Jackie" wears skinny, stiletto heels.

The "new Jackie" may or may not wear makeup to leave the house—her choice!

The "new Jackie" does not read gossip magazines.

The "new Jackie" doesn't socialize with people who make her feel bad.

The "new Jackie" doesn't waste time.

The "new Jackie" knows when and where to pick her battles.

The "new Jackie" won't brood if someone criticizes the "new Jackie."

LIVING NEXT DOOR AND IN A WORLD
UNDER CONSTRUCTION

I live with the smell of stucco and the roar of the cement mixer. I have to tell you, being under construction can be a dirty business. Huge trucks have invaded my formerly quiet, tree-lined street. I had a view of blue skies. Now I have a view of construction guys. The noise and the banging commence at seven a.m. sharp every darn day, six days a week. The workers are nice enough. They work really hard. They have amazing amounts of energy. They can work and sing and talk all day. The workers also leave garbage every day. Fast-food cups float in front of my home. And when I have to drive out of my garage, I can't see oncoming traffic because of their massive trucks that block everything. A friend told me, "Honey, you have been visited by the ghetto." My best friend, Jackie, reminds me that growth and expansion and change is all around, and that includes me too—and sometimes the loss of sunlight and a view.

The "new Jackie" just turns on a lamp, puts her music on loud, and keeps on keepin' on! In life, you roll with the punches. That's part of being under construction.

INSPIRATION

To be my best friend, Jackie, I have to motivate myself and inspire myself. One of the keys to inspiring yourself is knowing what you like. When I find something I like I say it out loud. This way I reinforce it to the universe and to myself. You have to be healthy of body, mind, and spirit. Music may inspire you. Nature is very inspirational. You have to know when you are trying to inspire your partner or teammate that inspiration is hard to capture, but once you do it will be a tool that can take you all the way. While I was writing this book it inspired me to believe that I could connect with many people. I could possibly help many people. It inspires me to be able to express my feelings and see if others share those feelings. It inspires me to complete a task (writing a book) that is very challenging. It inspires me to watch what I eat and how I expend my energy. It inspires me to know that I can push myself to do what I set out to do. It inspires me to know that I can write another book. I visualize a future where I see people who are moved and who can inspire me and teach me. I am inspired because my mind, body, spirit, and heart are activated and working as one.

This past Christmas I was really sad and missing my mom. I remember those days when the "old Jackie" would escape to the mall—and inevitably the food court. I would lose my mind at the food court. Everything was tasty but deadly. Next to the food court there was a Take Vitamins to Lose Water Weight kiosk. I'd buy some of those. Then I'd buy books or magazines that dealt with topics like "Begin a twelve-month plan to bring order to your life," "Solving your emotional energy crisis," "How to maximize your vagina!" and of course, "My stomach makes me look like Buddha."

Then I would sit down and vibe to the live music of the mall piano player. Here's a guy who performs in front of the Walking Store and the million kinds of fragrance store. I'm surprised someone hasn't been found hunched over from a Chanel overdose or an overPoloexposure. I would hear snippets of other people's conversations. "Sure I lost thirty-three pounds. But what I really value is the lightness of my spirit and heart." "What goes with festive dressing?" "Of course he's an ass. He's a Gemini." Ah, the good old days!

But back to this past Christmas.

Bill and I haven't put a tree up and there are no decorations in our home. There are piles of presents to be organized, wrapped, and mailed. These are the only signs of the holidays. When my mother was alive, she took great pride and joy in decorating, baking, making, wrapping, and writing during the holiday season. I'm afraid this year I am a huge disappointment to her in the glee department. I have eighty-three people on my list this year to buy presents for. I'm overwhelmed. I'm writing a book, starting two businesses, working out, and so desperately sad. I miss my mom! My dad is full of Christmas cheer, but he's in Mexico with his new wife, Judith, and her family. I wish he were here or I was there with all of them. It's raining and I am very busy. I probably won't have a tree this year.

My best friend, Jackie, reminds me that tree or no tree, my mom would be proud of me.

My best friend, Jackie, reminds me that there is always next year. And a chance to do better. Happy Holidays!

CHAPTER SEVEN

Trust Your Self!

*"You don't become what you want.
You become what you believe."*
—OPRAH WINFREY

I THINK IT'S SAD THAT WE LIVE IN A TIME WHEN many people think it's cool not to trust their leaders, their politicians, their police, their industry, their bosses, and maybe even those close to them. Some people say you can't trust anybody. Some people say you can only trust your family or your friends. But first you might try this: *trust your self!*

When you trust your *self*, you get really clear about others too. You will not know who around you to trust until you trust your self. When there is deserved trust, people win. When people trust each other, they defeat groups that don't. When you trust your instincts and intuition, others will trust them. When you believe in trust, there will be trust all around you and people will surprise you with unexpected gifts. Then the fun will begin.

The first casualty of the failure of self is your willingness to trust your self! I believe that fear stops us from being able to trust ourselves enough to try, to take the chance, to gamble. It's always a gamble. Don't let the inability to trust your self stop you. You can change and be the person you know you are because *baby, you're a star!*

You know you best. Do not let people steer you away from your beliefs or what your gut tells you is right for you. It is your own instinct and intuition where your unique wisdom and genius lives. Take the time to listen to yourself. You have the answers. You are the judge, jury, and lawyers in the case of *You vs. Misery*. You must trust that every day is a chance to win your case in the pursuit of justice and truth. Everything you've done up until now in your life makes you most qualified to make decisions about you. You must move obstacles, move forward, drip determination, and trust your best friend, *you!*

Trusting ourselves is hard. It's probably one of the most difficult things to do. It's a full-time job, and at the beginning you don't get paid. As I write this, I'm thinking, "Am I being clear, could I say more, am I forgetting something, does anyone really care what I have to say?" In the end I trust that things will be fine. All I have to do is be myself.

Being yourself means you have to be really connected to who you are, you have to know your self well enough to be honest and aware of who and what you love, what you want to do, what you value, and what you like. This seems like an easy thing to do. So why is it so damned hard? I think it's because to be yourself is to be original, and when you're the only you it may sometimes feel a little lonely. To be myself is to do what seems right to me and not to force my personality, my body, or my soul into a box created by someone else. Unfortunately, often we're afraid that others would like us better if we were like someone else.

For example, it's hard to trust yourself and declare your needs, because you might be called selfish or a nag, or, my least favorite, bitchy. When you tell people that you don't agree with them or they've hurt you, you're often met with a condescending response, like "You're too sensitive." It often seems that the easier path is to just shut up and keep your opinions to yourself. It may seem easier, but I promise, eventually you will pay a terribly high price for not being able to trust yourself! You have to trust yourself enough to trust your original thoughts and your original genius.

Be an original? How do you do that? Emphasize your qualities you most want the world to know about. Do you like to sing? Sing. Are you interested in people? Listen to them. Do you like to draw? Hang your art on your walls. Are you jolly? Be the life of the party. Are you funny? Perform. Have a sense of humor about yourself. See the reactions and enjoy your self!

Without originality, progress is difficult. Martin Luther King Jr. was a leader, a visionary, and a true original. Dr. King trusted that his dreams were worthy of incredible sacrifice. His "I Have a Dream" speech is profound and has forever altered race relations in the world.

It would not be so famous if he did not believe in himself or trust. It would not be so famous if he made the speech "Keep Things the Way They Are" or "I Don't Want No Trouble" or "I Just Want to Blend In."

My character has chosen to be in show business, which is, shall we say, different! It's about as financially and emotionally stable as the guy who searches for gold on the beach with a sand drain or a metal detector. And the health benefits are similar. I could certainly make the case that my choices have been a little crazy. Among some in my family, words like "reckless," "immature," "insane," and "scary" get thrown around about my life and my choices all the time. If I were living my life for them, I would have to say that I'm a complete and total disappointment and failure. It's difficult to constantly fight the fight to "be myself!"

I look around, and many of my friends are married (some are already divorced, and a couple of them have already married a few times!), have kids and retirement plans, own homes, and take regular vacations. Today, I am not married, I don't have children, I don't own a home, I have no gallbladder, I don't have a retirement plan or a 401(k), and I have gone on one vacation (to visit my dad in Mexico) in eight years. But I have a dream, a blueprint for my own success, and I'm building. My character has made some tough choices in order to live the life I've scripted. I find strength in my passions and work hard every day to continue to have the strength and the faith and the belief to keep on moving forward! Believe me, there are days when I think about going and getting my real estate license and calling it a day. But that would be the biggest sacrifice of all—to be anyone other than who I am. I have things to do and I have a plan, so I've got goals! I have made a massive gamble with my *life*. I believe, however, that the most dangerous gamble is to *not* bet on yourself. The safe and secure route is not always so safe. So I trust myself and continue to be "one of a kind." Remember, only in Vegas does anything beat one of a kind! I live in Los Angeles. We'll see if I walk out with any chips, or if the house wins. A tip? Bet on me—you'll live to thank me!

I work to trust myself. I try to use my instincts. And of course, *when people show you who they are, believe them!* All of us have that strong voice within that yells out when something doesn't seem quite right. Some of us have trained ourselves to listen to it, and some of us need to tear down the old walls that muffle it. You know how they say, "Don't go to the grocery store when you're hungry"? Well, I say, *Don't go friend shopping when you're "emotionally hungry!"* How many times have you stepped out of your role as a star or forgotten your best friend or didn't trust your self enough to pay attention to the part of you that was screaming, "Do not trust this person" or "This is not a good situation" or, worst of all, "This offends your soul"? I know that if I'm honest about the times in my life when I've been hurt, set back, had my heart broken, or been blindsided by something, it's usually because I didn't trust myself enough to believe that what I knew to be true was, in fact, true! *Always* a mistake. (If I took my cues from the world around me and didn't trust myself, I'd never leave my house!) Believe what you *know* not what you're *told*.

Trust is better than doubt. That's why our money says "In God We Trust." It doesn't say "In God We Doubt." This would lead to serious inflation.

When you doubt yourself you find yourself doing, saying, and being something you're not. There is an old adage: "If you don't stand for something, you'll fall for anything." There is a lot to fall for. The whole world is about marketing. It's hard to avoid all the puerile, promotional pap. Even people in solitary confinement get junk mail. Tibetan monks get spam! Basically they are saying, "Buy my product and you won't be scared." "Buy my product and you will be pretty, bubbly, and have tighter abs." "Buy my product and your loneliness will disappear." "Buy my product and a powerful man will wrap his powerful arms around you and his pits won't smell because he uses Irish Spring after he does the Riverdance." We have to be mindful and fight it every day because we know that confidence and self-worth aren't things that we can buy; they're earned by knowing, loving, trusting, celebrating who you are, and working every day to learn more in order to be the people that we are capable of being.

We live in a world full of options. We have to trust our brains and our hearts. We are inundated with information and rules and marketing and images that we are told we have to live up to. Says who? Were you ever invited to vote on whether you should want to look like one standard of beauty, love one type of person, drive a certain car, go to a certain school, speak a certain way, dress a certain way? I wasn't, and I've never met anyone who was. I think what's more important than trying to imitate what you see on television, in movies, and in magazines—which is fantasy—is to trust that your life, your dreams, and your goals are important. Enjoy the fantasy if it gives you something. Use the fantasy for inspiration, but always stay focused on what is right for you. You are completely unique. There is nobody else like you. Even identical twins are unique.

Personally, I like people who have a sense of humor coupled with a dash of rebelliousness. What gives each of us our own unique style is courage and independence. So, in a world of facsimiles, clones, sequels, Kinko's, remakes, reruns, retreads, refried, retro, formula, cookie cutter, by the number, play it safe, middle of the road, and knockoff, let's take a moment for some originality. How about in this world of extreme sports, extreme dating, and extreme makeovers we campaign for some extreme independence? Would anyone care for some extreme thinking? Trust that being different is great. Trust that by being different you just might make a difference. Live your life and find pure joy.

I once had a friend who was pure joy. But somewhere along the line she became so busy being everyone else's friend that she forgot to be her own. Today she spends so much of her time worrying about what other people are doing, saying, thinking, and feeling that she has completely forgotten who she is and what she likes. She doesn't listen to herself and she doesn't know who she is anymore.

Recently, I was at a wedding with her and a group of her friends, and I noticed that she was extremely quiet and self-conscious. The laugh that I remembered and loved was gone. The joy and the energy she once had felt like something I'd imagined. I had an opportunity to sneak away with her for a little while, and I asked her why she seemed so restrained and quiet. She told me that one of the "friends" she was with is very critical and gets upset when others get attention. So she pulls back in order not to upset her friend. I was shocked. Could this be the same chica who was always the life of the party and a complete badass? Did I imagine all those sleepovers, concerts, trips to the beach, ball games, and shopping trips that she'd organized when we were teenagers?

As I looked at her I felt so sad, because she seemed so small and weak. And that is *not* the girl I knew! I was reminded of something my mother had said to me right before she passed away: "Jacksie, you have a sparkle that comes from within and that light shines onto everyone around you. There will be people who can't stand to be in your light, but don't ever lose it. Don't ever think that you're doing someone a favor by turning your light off. No one around you will shine brighter by dimming your own light. Let the people around you bask in your light and you in theirs."

My friend had turned off her own light. I felt sad for her, because she thought that by making herself less interesting it made her friend more interesting. I also felt sad for me, because I missed my fun friend. Here's the point: She trusted her friends more than she did herself, and in the process she lost her *self*. Her friends also lost out on the best person that she could be. Everyone loses in that equation.

I battle daily to not be a watered-down, overcompromised shell of myself. I have to combat the easy accommodations because it's convenient. We all have the potential to be the old-fashioned version of a First Lady or an ever-grinning, ever-agreeing Stepford Wife. You clam up because you want to be the perfect partner, friend, trophy, sidekick, support team, number two, bodyguard, confidant, consultant, assistant, or whatever. We all do it because we don't want to lose what we have. The reality is we could lose a lot. We could lose the game before we have even had a chance to play. My goal is to trust myself enough to get in the game and trust myself to make the right plays.

Each of us is occasionally guilty of creating negative history—check in with your best friend about this. Our negative history scorecard chips away at our trust, which weakens our faith, hope, confidence, self-assurance, self-reliance, poise, cool, determination, willpower, strength of mind, resolve, purpose, fortitude, stamina, endurance, staying power, commitment, obligation, dedication, loyalty, devotion, reliability, and dependability.

The way we view our past affects our ability to construct our future. It could be that we are haunted by the loss of others or the mistakes we have made. Then we create our own personal résumé of defeats. Our history of bad decisions or relationships can weaken us. It can chip away at our belief in ourselves. It can stop us from trying new things.

We all have a few times when we felt unprotected, not taken care of, or not told the right thing. One time I was taken to the hospital thinking we were going to visit a sick friend, and then I found out that *I* was the one who was going to get operated on. My grandmother took me to the hospital and left me there to have my sinus cavity cleared out. Not exactly major surgery, but I was only nine years old and I was terrified. She was terrified too. She was afraid to tell me the truth. There was a lack of faith and trust. As I sat in a dark hospital room watching fuzzy television, I felt betrayed and abandoned. I guess that's part of the trust thing. As kids get lied to or feel unprotected, there is a loss of trust. Loss after loss is recorded in our failure résumé, but we don't balance it with our many wins. Balance it and it is easier to trust.

We need to constantly update our positive history scorecard, to remind ourselves of our victories and not highlight the defeats. My best friend, Jackie, doesn't let me stay at the negative party too long. My best friend, Jackie, reminds me that I am a star. I am a star no matter where I am or with whom. My best friend, Jackie, reminds me that I have won more than I have lost. My best friend, Jackie, reminds me that when it rains, it's okay to take the day off occasionally. Eventually the rain will stop and we can get back to our construction. I totally trust my best friend, Jackie!

You are brand-new. You are a new brand. You are a new brand of unique beauty on the shelf of life. Leap off that shelf. Brand yourself a winner. Don't brand yourself as someone lacking in the essentials. Regardless of how bad things seem, you must be confident that confusion will turn to clarity. Once you reconnect to your dreams and your instinct, the choices you need to make will become very clear. We all have a job to do, and we have to have the strength of mind to persevere. I always try to trust that there are many more good people than bad. Sometimes I see bad people get away with things, or I see bad behavior seemingly get rewarded (have I mentioned I'm in show business?), but it's during those times that I remind myself that everything in life is energy. Every thought, every decision, and every action we take holds energy, and life has a funny way of showing us what type of energy we are putting out. I believe that good deeds and goodness and karma provide a nice balance and keep us all in check. It may not happen exactly when or exactly the way I want to see it happen, but it will happen. Therefore I choose to trust in good.

It could be that the less you trust, the less people will trust you. So why not trust and trust often? Don't be afraid. Control what you can and be open to possibilities. I guess it really comes down to whether you believe that people are basically good or basically bad.

Do you believe that given the choice, most people will do the right thing? I believe 100 percent that everyone is good and capable and trustworthy . . . until they give me a reason not to believe that anymore. *Trusting your self* includes trusting your instincts about the people in your life. Remember, when people show you who they are, believe them! Listen to that voice inside of you trying to guide you. Trust your self that what you perceive is, in fact, the truth.

When you label yourself as someone who lacks confidence, you will not inspire those around you. You won't get the trust that could help you win the everyday battle of life. When you label yourself as someone who lacks determination, then those you love and need on your team will be less inclined to rally around you. This can be avoided if you trust in your capabilities and your goodness. You have to believe in your unique talent. You have to have faith and trust your self.

Every day I wake up and say, "Merry Christmas," to Bill. This is because we try to remember that because of the love we share and the bond we've created, every day together is as joyous as Christmas. Every day can be a great day. Yes, sometimes I have momentary doubts, but then I remember it's still Christmas, dammit!

When I trust my self, I trust others. I have sometimes been accused of being a control freak. I am working on this. Many of us are too controlling. It might come from a lack of trust. It could be that if we don't trust ourselves, it might lead us to not trust others, fear others, and try to control others, and then we end up micromanaging and annoying the crap out of everyone around us.

I used to work with a woman who is incredibly bright and very generous. Unfortunately, she was so absolutely incapable of trusting her self that she drove everyone around her crazy, and her talent often went unnoticed. She didn't realize that she was enough. Every time someone would introduce a topic of conversation, she had to say something. Every time someone would suggest a way of doing business, she had to have an opposing position—even when she agreed with the plan, she had to say something. Every time someone commented on how busy he was, she was busier! Every time a new project or task was identified, she had to be the one to do it; even when there was no place for her on the project, she'd insert herself into the process and create unnecessary work and tension. Her inability to trust her self kept her and everyone around her in a whirlwind of resentment, eye rolling, and noise. Eventually people stopped talking to her, they stopped inviting her to join meetings, and she retreated into a nasty, resentful place and became very destructive to the project. She couldn't function if she wasn't allowed to micromanage. Don't be that woman.

Leaders must trust people enough to allow them to perform and excel. That does not mean a "hands-off" approach. One must check in regularly. But the check-in should include praise and inspiration.

Many of my friends are very capable and successful people. They have created beautiful families, successful businesses, and thriving careers. I'm proud of them. One thing I've learned from watching the ones who really seem to manage it all is that they don't try to control others. Rather, they trust themselves when a decision needs to be made. They make a decision and they live with the consequences of that decision. In order to do that, you need to fully and completely trust your self. When you are busy micromanaging and volunteering to do everything, you master nothing. This leads to exhaustion and frustration. If we don't think the people in our lives are capable, then why are they in our lives? As a friend of mine recently said, "Do what *only* you can do." Brilliant! Otherwise your good deed will be punished and people will lash out at you. This will cause you to retreat and lead to emotional separation. Then communication breaks down. Then we have distance, tension, and fear. Then we don't know what the other is thinking, and they surprise you and possibly hurt you with their new actions or path.

As I've said, I want to improve my game. I want to work with the best. I want to position myself so that my ambition and my skills are obvious and I can effect change. I know things will not be handed to me. I put my "game face" on daily. This requires sacrifice and prioritizing. I decided I want to get a house big enough for my family and me. That's my focus. That's why I read up on how to get the house of my dreams. I spend hours with people who have done it. This may mean less time watching a favorite show, *Law & Order: SVU*. Now while I miss the beauty of brooding Christopher Meloni, I know that someday I will have a nice house where I will sit and watch him in style. I visualize success and focus on what I am moving toward, not what I am missing. I trust that

Christopher Meloni and the *SVU* crew will be there when I have the time to visit!

I enjoy working and playing with people who are passionate. I find they make me compete at a higher, more concentrated, intense level. Whether they know it or not, they reveal their secrets to success. Just watch, listen, and ask questions! Listen carefully to what people reveal.

Deep down, people want to reveal. All of us need to express ourselves. This is one way to truly grow and learn to trust yourself. We need to tell our story. We need to hear other people's stories. That's why we hear people say, "Tell me something I don't know." People always leave clues. Just like on *Law & Order*. Criminals always leave clues because they want to be caught.

Well, we all want to be caught. We want to be captured being who we are. Remember in elementary school when a teacher would give you positive reinforcement by giving you a happy-face sticker or gold star? "Caught you being good!" We want our true selves apprehended. We want our innermost part of us to be captured, interrogated, brought to trial, and exonerated in the court of public opinion. Deep inside we want to stand before our peers and be understood and have our say. We want our day. But we protect ourselves with the familiar and predictable; sometimes we confuse familiar and predictable for safe and secure. We wear emotional armor so that we can't be hurt. Sometimes we fear new adventures. We are too tired to think or learn or grow. We fight surprises.

But what we really want *is* surprise. What's better than a surprise gift? Children are interesting in part because there is always something new going on with them. Great actors are great in part because they are unpredictable. Marlon Brando is a legend because you never knew what he might do. His behavior was organic. He was like a cat. Animals have the same unpredictable appeal. Sports do too. We crave newness, but we are terrified. Have you ever heard the expression "Let's change—you first"? When we strip away the terror of what appears to be foreign, the delightful surprises will occur. Surprises happen when we are available to receive them. We must strive to be open and grow. When you're in an unfamiliar situation, trust your self that everything you have done has prepared you for this moment. Trust that you have what you need, and then you can take the experience onto the next phase of your life. Trust your self!

Trust in the long term and don't go for the quick fix.

Do not be a sucker for the latest trends, the newest fad diets, or the current get-rich-quick scheme. Trust that when something seems too good to be true, it always is. You know that; trust your self! You have to be a seeker. Shop around, investigate, and ask questions. The path to happiness and success isn't an exclusive club for those who *know*; it's a very large and always expanding club for those who *seek* and for those who *ask*.

Don't be afraid to take chances. If the very thought of that terrifies you, start small. Try different color combinations with your clothes. Try parting your hair a different way. For one day, go on a negative thought diet—no negative thoughts about yourself or anyone else. Take a walk and look around your neighborhood as if you're an exotic foreigner who is seeing your familiar surroundings for the first time. Turn on some music, shut the door, and shake it like a Polaroid picture! Thank everyone you speak to in a day for the value they bring to your life.

Live a life as unique as you are, and sprinkle your personal flavor into everything you do, and the quality of your life and of your relationships will improve. I have always taken chances with fashion, which means I've also made my fair share of mistakes with fashion. I have an absolute passion for fashion and I have studied the rules, but my character frequently chooses to wear really tight clothes, which my dad is quick to point out sometimes makes me look like a walking *chorizo* (Mexican sausage)—thanks, Dad! I have exposed my butt to criticism, and it has taught me who is open and who is rigid. It's always fun to see how people respond to a haircut. You learn who is in a good mood, who is very wild or conservative. If everyone does the same thing you learn little. Kids know this. Even if they wear uniforms to school, they always add their own flavor (like drawing on their own faces) to make a statement. They are always developing their script. The kids who are different are the ones you remember. They have something wonderful to offer and have not yet been burdened with being self-critical and overly self-conscious. We should all be as free and open and adventurous as children. They trust themselves and you must trust your self!

If you trust yourself you can ride out the daily storms of your job, or your relationships. You can then be available when the breaks start going your way. People frequently complain that they never get a break. They complain that they are not lucky. But if you consider yourself lucky you will get more luck. People like to help lucky people. The more you work, the luckier you'll be. As they say, luck is when preparation meets opportunity. Think, dream, create, and believe, and you will find yourself saying, "I'm lucky." That small adjustment of calling yourself lucky can pay big dividends. It's affordable and can help you cross the finish line. Sometimes it is the little things that can make you a winner.

Life is a game of inches. If you try a little harder, you win a lot more. Trust that you can work a little harder. The difference between winners and losers is frequently 10 to 15 percent more work and dedication. You have abundance. You don't sweat.

Trust in those you trust. They might give you a free tip to improve a small part of your game. Trust that you can accept criticism. This way you can learn and change and build a better life.

I'm always looking to make one small change. Golfers tinker with their swing. Academy Award–winning actors continue to take acting classes. "Small" actions are important. The smallest change can alter human history. If you set sail from the United States for Europe and you are off by one degree, you will end up in Africa. With a change of one degree Columbus would have "discovered" nothing. Baby steps. I say I need thirty hours in a day to get my work done, yet I use up valuable time on long phone conversations in which I listen to my friends and counsel them. I've been cutting down. Now I have time for a walk. I know it's hard to believe, but a twenty-minute walk to my favorite neighborhood coffee place can build health and eradicate a bad mood. Sometimes buying a book will inspire me. Reintroducing myself to my heroes Bill Clinton and Leonardo da Vinci can reignite my passion and push me to work that extra hour or take the stairs instead of the elevator. I have to work on reintroducing myself to my hopes, dreams, and inspiration. I trust that the path I'm on is where I want to be and where I'm headed is where I want to go. Life is cumulative; every little bit of effort counts! Trust that your goals, actions, and choices have a cumulative greatness that will result in victory.

CLOSING OUT THE FOURTH QUARTER

Athletes say closing out games is the key to victory. Many coaches also say closing out quarters in basketball games is the key to victory; players have a tendency to lose focus at the end of a quarter. Some of it may be due to fatigue. But that's when you can lose a game.

In life it is the same. Every four hours you should make sure you are taking care of what you need. You may need a small nutritious snack. You may need to close your eyes for two minutes. You may need to breathe deeply. You may need to stretch. You may need to call a friend. Take care of yourself and trust that others will benefit. Nighttime is a time to be a little careful. When you drive home late at night you have to be diligent. When you eat late at night you have to be diligent. When you drink and lie down with an attractive suitor you must be *really* diligent. This is where you can lose the whole game. It's when you are tired that you ease up and have one too many cocktails and one too many wieners. Acknowledging the exhaustion and taking a moment to understand that you need to get rid of the dirt and oil on your face will go a long way in developing your complexion and your character. Do not become complacent. You can't afford to not get out and do something. Be great, take a chance, and get rid of the dirt and oil in your life!

Trust yourself when you smell the stench of negativity. When some-

I have a passion for fashion.

thing stinks, it stinks. Say you walk into a room and smell something foul. You might say, "Do you smell something?" But someone gives you a bewildered stare and comes back with, "I don't smell anything." Now you are feeling a little foolish. But you persist because you notice there are a lot of dead flowers in the room. You ask others, "Do you smell something?" But nobody smells anything as the paint drips off the walls. You now feel a little hangdog, sheepish, and foolish. "Maybe I was imagining a foul aroma. Maybe it doesn't smell." So you stay in this foul dump. And the longer you stay in this putrid, rancid sewer of negativity, the less you believe that it stinks. After a while you don't even notice the stench. But then one day, someone else arrives with a fresh perspective, and you remember that you knew long before they arrived what they now know—you just forgot to *trust your self!* This stranger opens a window and suddenly everyone is revitalized. Everyone charges toward the window and sucks in the fresh air of life. Everyone except the person who has smelled funk for so long they can't live without it. That funky person immediately drives to the nearest truck stop latrine for a hit of stench. But the others know the truth. Fresh air is better than foul air. The moral of this foul tale is that *you* should be the breath of fresh air. Trust yourself and be fresh and minty. Don't listen to those whose noses may be stuffed or who are too weak to disagree. Be the positive stream in the polluted sea of negativity.

Whenever I am lost or facing a challenge, one of the little tricks I use is to approach my life as if it were a talk show. As the host, I am responsible for asking the questions to get the answers I'm looking for. My audience depends on me to ask the things that they want to know. I try to get as much information as I can, and then immediately incorporate it into my own life so that I can make sure I've understood what I've been told and that I can relate to it. Like the flow of a talk show, always end each segment on a high note.

"Today on *The Jackie Guerra Show* we've been talking to women who have trusted their instincts, connected to their passions, and in the process found and learned to trust their self. My guest is a young woman who learned to walk into a room like Elvis and trust her instincts; when she smelled a smell that smelled, she didn't deny it; she opened up a window and became the breath of fresh air that the room needed. I have to say, you're truly an inspiration to all of us because you've learned to really trust your *self*. We've all been there, where we know something is true but for whatever reason we let the people around us convince us otherwise. And I love what you say when you ask, Why do we give other people more credit than ourselves? It's so true. From now on, when it smells, it smells. Either open a window or get out." (To camera) "When we come back, we're going to learn how we can find love not by searching for Mr. Right but by *becoming* Mrs. Right. Don't go away!" (Applause.)

Some people find solace in saying that their job sucks. This is, of course, another way of saying that they suck. But saying that you suck and your life has been a minefield of catastrophes and you don't like your self or your husband or kids is too horrific to bear. It's easier to say that your boss is an idiot. Negativity is like a cut-rate fake diamond: it gets attention but ultimately has little value. Negativity actually makes your sucky job suckier.

A lot of people are not sure if the job sucks. They only know that they are exhausted. These exhausted folks put on their shoes and comb their hair and pluck areas they won't admit to and shave their legs and put on their "game face." They are heroic and courageous. You are too. *Trust your self!* And dump that sucky job! Life is too short to spend your time building a house you don't want to live in.

Believe in goodness and hope, and trust that hard work pays off. I know this for sure: hard work may not always ensure success, but hardly working will, most definitely, ensure failure.

About one-fourth of all people get very *negative*. They use sarcasm and grumble that the roof is always caving in. Instead of trust, they contaminate the tired people. The vulnerable people. They mingle with the exhausted people, who become confused, and that best face they came in with gets a zit and a stress wrinkle. Then their back hurts, and now three-fourths of the workers are depressed and there is true misery. Misery loves company and can destroy any company. Then you become a last-place, losing team, afraid to make a mistake, dreading every minute, waking up in fear, dragging your tired behind out of bed, and you are waiting out the clock, counting the minutes for the end of the day. When you focus on the things that "suck," then that's the life you lead. This is what happens when you lose hope and trust. It doesn't have to be that way. You deserve better and you can have better. Your best friend knows you're worth more than self-destructive negative thinking, and never forget, *baby, you're a star!* So trust yourself and remember that it only takes one person with one thought, which becomes an idea, which then becomes an action, to change the world for the better. If workers unite and work as a team, they can make a workplace tolerable and even . . . dare I say it? . . . fun! This is a tried-and-true model for success. What do countries do when they are fighting evil? They form coalitions. What do big companies do when they are trying to achieve power? They merge! Merge with people and ideas that amplify the best part of you, the part that you trust is valuable and beautiful.

As we know, there are many people who actually like their jobs. Everyone has a chance to be one of those people. Don't be the person whose job is so horrible that it poisons everyone around her. Make your job interesting or make other arrangements. Also don't be the person who escapes into work to avoid the rest of life. That only works for seventeen years, then you wake up alone, confused, and hungry. You are either happy or miserable. What's it going to be?

Here is a trust story from the wonderful world of show business.

One of the times I had to trust my self was while I was working on a sitcom. The person in charge was someone who, let's just say, did not suffer from low self-esteem. He suffered from high self-esteem. What do I mean by that? Let me explain. . . . He referred to himself as "the boss" (I'm sure Bruce Springsteen appreciates that). He is the type of person who *demands* respect. The concept of *earning* respect is completely lost on him. Although I'd heard he had been fired from many shows, somehow in a way that only Hollywood and corporate America know how to do, he kept getting "fired up." Remember when I mentioned how annoying it is to see bad behavior get rewarded? He is the poster child for it. Every week the writing staff would write the episodes and then send me the script. I'd make notes and then read the script with the other actors while the writers and producers took notes. That's called a table read. After the table read, one of my responsibilities was to sit with the writers and talk to them about my notes. Every week the routine was the same. So after the table read I walked over to give my notes, and he said, "I don't have time to listen to you. Why don't you draft a memo with your notes and send it to my office?" It was a slap in the face, and although I was pretty humiliated, I didn't say anything at the moment, because anything I would have said would not have been particularly productive, and I didn't want to have an argument with him in front of the entire cast and crew. He knew I had to go to rehearsal and did not have time to "draft a memo." This was his not-so-clever way of telling me he wasn't interested in my opinions or suggestions or anything I had to say.

I spent my lunch break drafting the memo. I went through the entire script and listed twenty-two comments and suggestions. I was well aware of his bad mood that day, so I took extra precautions to word everything carefully and respectfully. As God is my witness they were not demands. They were well-thought-out queries. I gave the notes to a production assistant, who took them to him.

A half hour later, during rehearsal, I got a call demanding that I meet him in my trailer—alone! I walked outside and saw that he was already there waiting for me. As I got closer I realized he was bright red, almost purple, boiling with anger. He looked as if every capillary in his head was about to burst. I saw he had my memo in his hand. He didn't say a word; he just opened the door to my trailer and motioned for me to go in first. Then he stepped inside the trailer, slammed the door shut, and blocked the door. There is not much space in a trailer, and I felt very uncomfortable. He then threw my memo at me and yelled, "Here are your f——ing notes!" I felt a little out of body. Is this grown man really having a tantrum? I bent over to pick up the paper. At this point I was so nervous I began to tremble a little. I was thinking, "Be careful; this is the kind of rage that might produce a punch." I stared at the same sentence for much too long, unable to focus because of fear. I read and reread the first line on the page ten or twelve times before I realized he had handwritten the same response to each of my questions: *Go f—— yourself!* This Emmy Award–winning "genius," who was old enough to be my father, had actually taken time out of his life to write *"Go f—— yourself!"* twenty-two times. Now, I'm not easily rattled, but to me it's shocking when you hear those words spoken. It's even more shocking to see them in print.

He was sweating, huffing and puffing, staring at me like he wanted to knock my head right off my shoulders, and he was blocking the door. I had no way out. My purse was on the stage, so I didn't have my cell phone. I tried to lighten the mood. "Well, at least you're consistent!" I said, indicating his comments.

"Who the f—— do you think you are? You don't f——ing know what it takes to run a f——ing TV show! You don't f——ing tell *me* how to f——ing write! You do what *I* f——ing tell you to do. You show up when I f——ing tell you to f——ing show up and you f——ing read the lines that I f——ing write and you shut the f—— up!"

There I was living the big, fancy life of the lead in a sitcom, and at that moment I felt like a hostage. I glanced out the small window of my trailer and saw Diane Wilke and Frank Lombardi, two writers I knew, walking along with Fran Drescher (of *The Nanny*). I watched them walking and said a silent prayer, *"Please, Diosito, if there is any chance for me to send a telepathic message to them for help, now would be a great time."* As if on cue, they saw me in the window and smiled and waved at me and kept on walking. So much for my psychic powers!

A moment passed and I decided, enough is enough.

"I want to leave."

"I'm not done."

"If you don't let me leave, that's called 'being held against my will.' "

He exploded again. "*I'll* f——ing tell you when to leave!"

He opened the door and stormed out. The door bounced off the side of the trailer and swung back and forth. I stood frozen for a moment, still holding the paper, which by now was crumpled and sweaty from my nervous palms. When I was sure that he was really gone, I stepped out of my trailer.

I walked slowly back to the soundstage to rejoin the rest of the cast and crew for rehearsal. I knew that the second I walked in everyone was going to ask me what happened. And I also knew that the way I appeared when I walked back into that room would determine how this situation was going to be resolved. I needed to determine if this house was going to be fixed up or knocked down. I decided to act like everything was fine until I could make my decision. I knew that his behavior was unacceptable, but I also knew that if I got emotional and engaged him in any kind of power tug-of-war, I risked the network shutting down production on our show while they figured out what to do, and every single member of our crew would be out of work in the middle of a television production season, when there are no job openings for them. I couldn't let that happen. I also knew that if I didn't do anything, I would be teaching him that treating me that way was okay, and it most definitely was not. I had to really home in on what my instincts told me to do and trust my self.

I walked onto that soundstage like I was Elvis!

After rehearsal, I called my agent. She was very supportive, and her first instinct was for me to walk off the show because I didn't deserve to be treated that way. I asked her to wait to call anyone until I spoke with the president of the WB Network to try to work out a solution to this disgusting problem. She reluctantly agreed.

I made the call but was unable to reach the president of the network. So I asked to speak to the second in command, and then the third, and finally was connected to the fourth person in charge. Number four said condescendingly, "Now, Jackie, calm down. Remember, you're a first-time sitcom gal." And then she advised me to "go home, take a nice hot bath, and learn your lines." (She no longer works at the WB, by the way.)

This was not exactly helping. My instincts told me to keep calling the president until I finally reached him. He listened without interruption, and then said, "I support you one hundred percent, Jackie. Let me deal with this." I hung up and knew that one way or another he would.

The next day I went back to work, and kept working the rest of the week. After our taping on Tuesday night, the announcement was made that "Mr. Fired-Up" was being replaced. And as they say, *the show went on!*

I trusted my self by trusting my own instincts and my own belief that in the end goodness prevails.

Trust that everything you've done and the foundation you've laid will support your dream house as your "construction" continues. And just know that sure, some days will suck! Once in a while you may need to use manufactured wood instead of Douglas fir, but when that happens, just pull out your plans and keep on goin'! Begin today to trust your instincts, your beliefs, and your feelings. Value yourself and your decisions and be committed not to let the blah days stop you. And above all, trust your *self*! Your destiny is yours. Make it fantastic. I trust that you will.

CHAPTER EIGHT

Never Say Die-t!

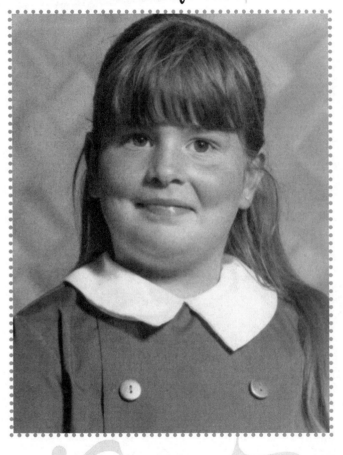

> *"Though no one can go back and make a brand-new start, anyone can start from now and make a brand-new ending."*
> —CARL BARD

WHEN I SAY *NEVER SAY DIE-T*, I MEAN NEVER GIVE UP (never say die), but consider that you might need to rethink how you're going to reach your goal. Be open to a new solution or a new idea. Having an open mind just might bring the gift of an unexpected solution. After a lifelong struggle with weight, I received a well-earned gift during the summer of 2004.

All of my life I've been overweight.

All of her life my mother drowned the memories of her childhood with alcohol.

Despite the fact that I've strived to be happy and live my best life, the one thing I've never been able to do is put behind me my identity as a fat girl. My weight was always a battle between my mother and me; she was thin, and it drove her crazy that I wasn't. Her drinking was always a big battle between us; I don't drink and she was a functional alcoholic. I felt judged by her and she by me. Both my weight and her drinking were the things that at times divided us and at other times united us.

My mother had a mortal fear of being fat. She spent her entire life on a diet and put me on my first diet when I was eight years old. One night after dinner, my dad and my brother went bike riding and my mom and I went elsewhere: Before I knew it I was at my first Weight Watchers meeting.

I took center stage on a scale in front of a roomful of strangers. It was exciting. I had an audience and all eyes were on me. As she shouted out my weight, followed by "Welcome," the meeting leader handed me my Weight Watchers tote bag, complete with passport, stickers, menus, tips, recipes, miniature scale, and, most important to an eight-year-old, more stickers. I was happy to be part of this group that seemed excited by my presence. These strangers actually gave me presents. And lots of stickers! When I skipped back to my plastic chair next to my skinny mom, however, I saw a hauntingly familiar look on her face. It was the same look of shame and disappointment that I saw the day I had eaten the Girl Scout cookies. That look was so painful. I had no idea what I had done this time to make my mom so sad. Now I realize she was sad because her daughter was fat.

My story is not unlike many others. I have led a lifetime of diets. I've lost and gained the same seventy-five to one hundred pounds four times in the last ten years. My entire life I've carried the additional weight of being overweight.

THE MANY STAGES OF CHUBBYHOOD

Until I was eleven, I never thought of myself as anything other than cute and round and strong.

Age Eleven

Then my chubbiness was spotted and I was outed. My obnoxious ballet teacher with a booming, thick, recent-Soviet-defector accent announced to my entire ballet company that I had "thunder thighs!" I beamed with pride and responded, "I know!" I assumed she was complimenting me because I was so strong that even my thighs had the power of thunder. But I was confused by the tone in which my ballet teacher said it and the giggles from my fellow ballet students. My friend was quick to enlighten me. She told me, "Umm, 'thunder thighs' is not a compliment. She means 'thunder thighs' like, you know, like 'jelly-belly,' 'lardo.' She means *you're fat*. You have *fat* thighs." I would never look at my thighs the same way. What a few minutes earlier had been these tanned, muscular legs that allowed me to dance, run, swim, and strut were suddenly something that I apparently should be ashamed of. I was so confused and humiliated.

*Me, my leg warmers, and my powerful "thunder thighs"
during dance class . . . what a feeling!*

Age Thirteen

My friends and I were innocent and goofy. We had not done very much, a-hem, social dancing. Mostly we did a lot of giggling. The eighth-grade dance was a really big deal. We talked and dreamed and giggled about boys for weeks before the dance! This was a *big* step toward womanhood and the achievement of my fashion-magazine girlhood fantasies.

My mom and dad did their usual. They overcompensated by bringing the whole extended family to the house to prep me for the gig and to scare me to death. No pressure!

My friends and I got all dressed up and felt adult. Some of my friends stuffed their bras. I wore some of my mom's Chanel No. 5 and felt very glam. The boys had on way too much cologne and hair gel, but hey, they were my friends and I loved them. There was a sense of anticipation in the carpool. We got to the dance. The excitement was palpable. I figured, we came as a group, we would dance as a group. My heart was full. I felt great and thought I looked good. This was my big night! I love to dance and have always been a good dancer—the night was mine! I felt the music sweep over me and couldn't wait to hit the dance floor.

I did not dance much that night. In fact, I was ignored. None of the boys asked me to dance. The brutal reality of adolescence came crashing down on me as I watched all of my guy friends ask girls who weren't part of our group to dance, and my girl friends systematically get asked to dance by all sorts of guys. I realized at that moment that there are two kinds of girls in junior high: the kind the guys dance with and the kind they are friends with. I was their friend.

When my parents came to pick me up I told them that nobody asked me to dance. My father said, "What are you waiting for someone to ask you for? If you want to dance, dance!" My mom chimed in, "Don't worry, Jacksie. We'll start a diet tomorrow." I know they were trying their best to be supportive and encouraging, but I got the message from my mother loud and clear: "If you were skinny, they'd ask you to dance." She advised me the best she could based on her own life experience. She was a sexy woman and knew that doors had opened for her because she was hot, and I'm sure it terrified her to have a daughter who didn't fit into that category of womanhood. I'm sure she feared that my weight would make my life more difficult than it needed to be. She probably didn't mean to imply anything negative, but it hadn't even occurred to me that the reason I had been rejected and felt miserable was because I was chubby! It didn't make sense, but somehow I knew she was probably right.

And Dad? Dad said, "Let's go get a *sopresita*." "Sopresita" means surprise in Spanish, but to Dad and me, it's our code for a snack. I put on my sweats and we went with my uncles to Jack in the Box.

Age Fourteen

I love fashion magazines. In ninth grade, magazines were kind of like the cool aunt who tells you the stuff you need to survive, like how to get rid of a zit, the latest "do," perfect eyebrows, how to pose for the perfect picture, and so forth. One day I opened a magazine and turned to an article about the dangers of being a chubby chick. I looked at one of those weight-height charts that lets you know if you're normal. My height and weight equated me with an ape. I felt as if I'd been smacked in the gut with a two-by-four. I mean, according to the chart, I was, well, off the chart. I instantly felt like a *total freak!*

I turned the page quickly, as if to make the image disappear, and stumbled onto a story about a glamorous supermodel who maintained her fantastic body by doing something the magazine referred to as "purging." She looked beautiful. She seemed to be successful and have it all. I was sure *her* mother wasn't calling her friends' parents during a sleepover to tell them not to allow her to eat anything after six o'clock at night. I bet she got asked to dance all the time. And that is how I got the not-so-brilliant idea that I could eat whatever I wanted and then throw it up.

At fourteen I had already enjoyed a six-year career as a professional dieter. Purging was the best idea I'd ever heard about how I could lose weight. Forget about being singled out during lunch at school as I hovered over some dumb excuse for a snack or lunch that my mom had sent for me. Gone would be the days of "Mom, I'm hungry," "Have a glass of water, Jackie." I'd be skinny and my mom would be so happy, and maybe, just maybe, she'd stop drinking. Oh yeah. It was a new day.

Unfortunately, the magazine article failed to mention that bulimia is a disease that takes over your life. I didn't read anything that said I'd start to lose my hair, that I'd feel tired all the time, that I'd get leg cramps in the middle of the night due to a lack of potassium, that my teeth would become brittle and start to break or that I'd disrupt my menstrual cycle. The article didn't mention that the more you throw up, the more you have to throw up. I didn't read anywhere that I'd spend the next twelve years of my life burdened with a horrible secret and have to lie to everyone I knew about why I went to the bathroom so much. I never saw one word about the isolation I felt when I'd decline invitations for dinners, parties, or trips because I didn't know if the proper facilities would be available to throw up in. Not a mention that eventually I'd start driving and spend a small fortune on Tupperware for when a bathroom wasn't available, on breath mints and car freshener. There was nothing said about the eventual need to take diuretics and laxatives to make sure that whatever I ate came out both ends. I didn't read about that, but I sure lived it.

The hell of being a practicing bulimic is beyond horrible. It is a very sick and nasty disease that lulls you into a feeling of superiority. I remember thinking for many years that I was so smart because I'd figured out a way to eat, drink, be merry, and never gain weight. But guess what? My metabolism eventually adjusted to existing on very few calories and I gained weight. Eventually the throwing up became less about losing weight and more about the way I lived. I had to do it. I could not physically handle the feeling of being full. I'd feel panicky and anxious, because even though I watched my weight steadily increase, I convinced myself that it would be worse if I didn't throw up. I was very, very wrong.

Eventually I heard all of the warnings about how purging wreaks havoc on your metabolism, destroys your teeth, and affects your heart. But I never believed that that would happen to me. One of my closest friends in high school died in her sleep four months before graduation. Cause of death: Cardiac arrest as the result of complications due to bulimia and anorexia. Even that didn't stop me. I was sad, but it didn't scare me, because when you're sixteen, you can't imagine ever being thirty. When you're sixteen you can't imagine that the day may come when you fall in love with someone and want to have a baby, so the warnings about not being able to conceive never concerned me. When you're sixteen and your teeth are white and shiny and straight after wearing braces for two years, you can't imagine that those same teeth might dry up and become brittle and start breaking in your head.

The horror of bingeing and purging, diet pills, laxatives, diuretics, and waking up in the middle of the night sobbing was my nightmare. I felt like I had been given a life sentence in "fat prison." I just knew there was an active, joyous, inspired woman inside who desperately wanted to live life to the fullest but was confined to a body that didn't make sense.

I finally broke the cycle of bingeing and purging and using laxatives, diet pills, and diuretics when I attended an Overeaters Anonymous meeting with a friend. I was twenty-six years old, sitting in a damp, freezing-cold meeting room at a church in Santa Monica, California, with men and women, young and old, all different races, ethnicities and body sizes there to confront the cycle of self-abuse. I went to support my friend, who felt she could no longer control her binge eating. I sat and listened to each person speak and tell their tale of struggle and pain and remorse. As I listened I focused on one woman in particular, who looked like she was probably around forty-five or fifty and weighed about ninety pounds on her most bloated PMS day. She stood up and talked about her nine-year battle with anorexia, which came to a head the month before when she had a heart attack. She was only twenty-nine years old! I looked at her for so long I realized I was staring. I couldn't stop. She seemed so sad and so scared I felt I could almost hear her shattered soul rattling around inside of her. I knew her story was not that different from mine, and I sure didn't want to be standing where she was in three years, telling a story about something horrible that knocked me into action. I heard it. I felt it. I was ready to stop. She didn't say anything I hadn't heard before, but on that day I was ready to *hear* it for the first time. Sometimes you don't need revelation, just validation. That moment I began my journey to save myself. I didn't stop spinning the dieter's roulette, but I did stop purging.

I never went back to another OA meeting, but I never forgot what I heard and what I saw.

Adulthood

Somewhere early on in my childhood I figured out that by being kind and funny and helpful, people seemed to look past my weight. I developed an instinct for people and situations that could hurt me and I avoided them. I developed an armor of happiness and comfort to protect me from a world that told me every single day that I was less than perfect. I chose to focus on what I could do and shut out the noise of the things I couldn't. The painful sound of doors that were closed in my face because of my weight was my own "secret." I have never apologized for who I am or for what I look like. Despite my battle with weight, I have always strived to live my best life.

My fiancé, Bill, is, because of his connection to me, known throughout the land as a chubby chaser. I guess *Chubby Girl* magazine lists men who date chubbies, and Bill is on the Most Wanted list. His picture must be posted at all the plus-size stores. Whenever we're out together, chubby women flirt with him as if he understands their secrets. When he's alone, the chubby women get very close! The truth is Bill has had a long and distinguished career with all kinds of women, skinny, chubby, cute, and plain old fuggugly.

Bill says that thin women get a disproportionate amount of attention. They are pursued and they think they are better than they are. This makes them *seem* like they have more value. It's the law of supply and demand. Or maybe it's Murphy's Law. You should not have more value or be given a higher rating simply because you have won the genetic lottery or refuse to eat Ho Hos. Even if you win a Nobel Prize or become secretary of defense, if you are not attractive, that's what many people will remember. People will always focus on the looks. People always discuss Senator Hillary Clinton's clothes and hair. They don't really do that for Senator Orrin Hatch. Many people criticized Theresa Heinz Kerry because she's opinionated and forceful. They prefer their women to be nice and proper. Translation: thin and quiet. Excuse my French, but that is a bunch of hooey! Agree with her or not, you have to applaud the fact that women like Theresa are living the script they've written for themselves and not apologizing for it—we could all learn something from that.

Bill says you need a woman who is funny and tough, because after you have sex a couple of hundred times and it's not as exciting, you need a partner who can do a tight twenty (stand-up speak for twenty minutes of killer material), a few impressions, and kick some ass. You need a partner who roots for you! You need a partner who wants to know your friends. You need a partner who protects you. You need a partner who can enjoy a walk around the block with you. You need a partner who will give you the surprise gift at the surprise time. You need a partner who can read your soul. You need a partner who is with you through *thick and thin.* I love him! Of course Bill forgets to trim his eyebrows and take smaller bites. And sometimes he's "Moody Guy." And sometimes he's "Spell Out the Worst-Case Scenario in Graphic Detail Guy." And sometimes he's "Make Up His Own Medical Solution Based on Whimsy Guy." And sharing a bathroom with him in hotels is always interesting. But that's okay. Some of my best friends are moody. Some of my best friends have been superthin—I live in Los Angeles, so really, what choice do I have? Many of my friends, who claim to love me, are people who would rather cut off their own arms than be fat. Am I their token fattie? Hmmmm. Interesting observation or my issue? But they love me. If I had a dollar for every time someone has said, "I never think of you as fat," I'd be a very wealthy woman. I don't even know what that means. I only know that every time I hear it I think of that great scene in the movie *Do the Right Thing,* where one of the Italian characters who has an obvious disdain for the surrounding African-American community talks about his love of Prince. When Spike Lee's character reminds him that Prince is black, he says, "I don't think of him as black—he's Prince." I know that somehow people think that's a compliment, but it hurts. I do wonder, what are they thinking? Many of my male friends have said to my face that they would never be involved with a plus-size girl. They won't even date a "slightly" chubby girl. That attitude hurts.

A friend of mine told me one day that she was surprised that I didn't smell, considering what a "big girl" I was! Although we laughed about how absurd the statement was, it hurt.

When an aerobics instructor very condescendingly asked the class to give me a round of applause for finishing her class (need I mention that I was the fattest person in the class?), I told her that I'd recently lost one hundred pounds. A woman next to me said, "Oh my God. You must have been so fat!" She's stupid, but it hurt.

As I stood in line to pay for groceries one day, a stranger said, "It's a sin that God gave you that beautiful face and you are so overweight. My daughter lost twenty-five pounds by eating cabbage soup for a month." I know somewhere buried in her horrid delivery was a compliment, but it hurt.

Many times I've been offered roles in television shows or in movies that were the "fat girl" roles. By that I mean roles where a character only exists so that other characters can make fat jokes or talk about their own weight. I've turned them down along with the fat paychecks that go with the roles, but kept my dignity. Remember the old commercial where an actor said, "I'm not a doctor but I play one on TV"? Well, I *am* a fat girl but I *don't* play one on TV!

The "fat girl" is a role that I've lived my entire life. I have struggled with my weight my entire life. I have been on every diet and exercise program imaginable. They've all worked, but they haven't lasted. I lose weight, but I've always gained the weight back and more. I have been on a diet, thinking about a diet, talking about a diet, or "blowing" a diet since I was eight years old. Losing and gaining weight is a very public battle but a very private war. You either win or lose at the dieting game, there is no third way, and everyone knows. You either lose weight, or you're a loser. It's a horrible and vicious cycle that has chipped away at my soul. No matter what I've done or where I've gone, the beast to conquer is always there.

Now don't get me wrong—as I've said before, I have never *weighted* to live. I never let my "thunder thighs" stop me from taking and loving ballet. But now it takes effort to shut out the negative path I've been on.

In truth, I had to finally admit to myself that I was tired. I was tired of

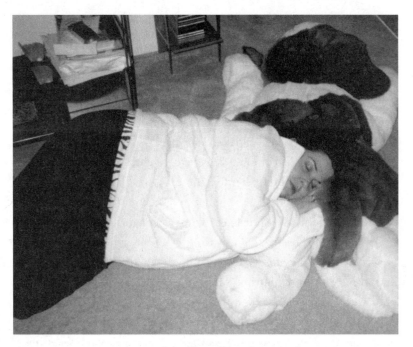

. . . and the "beast" is exhausting!

the constant challenges and obstacles that all overweight people face. I was tired of feeling that I was always trying to drive from the back of the bus. I was tired of waking up every day and having to gear myself up just to summon the courage to step out my front door and into a world that defines me by the way I look. I was tired of not looking like I feel. I was tired of pretending that the constant assault on fat people doesn't affect me. I was tired of being judged and listening to the "helpful" comments and diet suggestions from friends, family, and total strangers. I was tired of getting depressed every time I had to go to an event or a photo shoot or to a wardrobe fitting or to see old friends. I was tired of being so limited in what I could wear. I was tired of being uncomfortable. I was tired of being the fattest person I know. I have a big, loving, and generous heart to share with the world, but I was tired of pretending that I wasn't making my heart work overtime to pump blood through the extra weight I'd carried for so long. And I was tired of pretending to be okay. I was tired of being tired. I knew I was not thinking long term. I knew I had to listen to my needs and *trust my self*. If I wanted to be a *star* in my own movie, I had to get serious. I had to admit that being confident and feeling good about myself was not an excuse to not do better, be better, and feel better. I was not interested in *weighting* for a doctor to one day tell me what is inevitable: *Lose weight or die.*

I remember the last attempt I made to help my mother win her battle with alcoholism. I took her to a therapist whom I adore named Susan Schick. Bill and I had gone to her for a year at the beginning of our relationship. Since we came to each other from difficult relationships, we wanted to make sure that this time we did it right. I think Susan is one of the most phenomenal women on this planet. I asked her to see my mother and try to help her. My mother went a few times alone, and I went with her, my brother drove two hundred miles from San Luis Obispo to attend family sessions, but it just wasn't working. One afternoon during a family session, Susan said, "You guys are not listening to her. Your mother is telling you that she does not want to stop drinking. She is not ready to face her feelings and her fears and her life sober." My brother cried and I was frozen. It was the first time in my entire life anyone had said that. I thought my mother wanted to quit drinking but just hadn't found the right doctor or program. I thought that if my mother had a choice, she'd choose sobriety. On that day, I learned that my mother wasn't ready to quit drinking. She died two months later.

On February 19, 2004, I sat on my couch in the home I share with Bill in a beautiful neighborhood and sobbed because I realized that after all the years of working around my weight and working so hard every day to compensate for the brutal way overweight people are treated in our society, I didn't want to do it anymore. For the first time in my life I was ready to have my inside match my outside. I am very deeply in love with my fiancé, and I want to get married and have children, be healthy and live a long, wonderful, and rich life. I want to grow old with Bill. I want to be my best self possible. I want to ensure my quality of life. And for me, there is no future in weighing 291 pounds. My character is ready for the next act. I decided to do the one thing my mother was never able to do to conquer her battle. I decided to get real, long-lasting and permanent help to conquer my battle with weight. I decided to undergo laparoscopic gastric bypass surgery.

After spending thousands and thousands of dollars on weight-loss programs that haven't lasted, and after having visited nutritionists, swallowed supplements, guzzled protein drinks, restricted my diet, employed food delivery services, and maintained a wardrobe that includes clothes that range in size from fourteen to twenty-eight, I decided to end this cycle for good.

My old attitude toward the surgery was an example of ego-driven self-importance. I used to run into Carnie Wilson at the mall all the time. I spent a lot of time there and so did she. I remember the day she told me she was going to have gastric bypass surgery, and I was, let's just say, less than supportive. I didn't congratulate her. I didn't ask questions. I acted like a jilted lover because that's how I felt. I'm embarrassed to say that I thought, "You would rather have your stomach and intestines altered than be like me?" What the hell was that? I know how wrong that thinking is, but at the time all I did was feel offended and judged Carnie when she didn't deserve it. She was brave to have made the commitment to health and life, but I took it personally and did to her the exact thing that people had been doing to me my entire life. I wanted her to look a certain way to make me feel better about me. I was a complete hypocrite and a total asshole. Sorry, Carnie!

I thought the surgery was a freaky thing done by freaky people who were taking the easy way out. I thought they were weak and I could do better. I thought that I was better. Basically it terrified me to admit that perhaps I was out of control. It terrified me that I would have to resort to something so drastic and permanent, and it terrified me that I would have to have my body cut, my intestines altered, and my stomach stapled because I couldn't stop eating. The prospect of not being able to eat whatever I wanted for eternity felt like a loss. It felt like a death.

Ready for my next act! This is me in my see-through ensemble with my dear friend Lash Fary, the gorgeous and supertalented actress Elisabeth Rohm and foxy host of The Abrams Report, *Dan Abrams, at the Costume Designers Guild Awards. My moment of truth.*

My decision to have surgery was a long, difficult, and deeply personal process. I needed to prove to myself that I wasn't looking for a "quick fix." I did a lot of soul searching and research. The most alarming statistic I learned is that if someone loses seventy-five pounds or more, they have a less than 1 percent chance of keeping that weight off for more than a year, let alone a lifetime! So what the hell had I been doing besides making other people rich and wreaking havoc on my body?

I thought about the surgery for over five years, and I can tell you that it is the hardest thing I ever did and *the best* thing I have ever done for me! I truly feel as if a miracle has occurred for me. I don't think it's for everybody, but I do think that everybody who is even considering it should do their due diligence and research, research, research! Two of the Web sites I found most helpful are www.obesityhelp.com and www.transmed.tv.

Please speak with your personal physician and read as much as you can. I also encourage you to speak to as many people as you can who have had the surgery.

Part of my research included going to support group meetings. I went to a bunch of Wednesday evening meetings held at seven o'clock. It was springtime in Los Angeles and the sun was setting and the cool weather was refreshing and glorious. Normally it would be a great time for a large meal with dessert and tons of coffee and Diet Coke. But my life was going to change. I was leaving behind a world where I had freedom in my eating but shackles everywhere else. I had heard the "call to adventure," but I was the reluctant heroine. "The refusal of the call" was what I was overcoming. In order to face my adventure, I had to admit the walls I had built to keep pain and hurt out were the same walls that kept me trapped in a body that didn't make sense to me. I had to fill myself with positive thoughts.

It was easy to see which room in the hospital the meeting was being held in. A parade of large people walked slowly in one direction. But these large people had heads. What do I mean? You know these special news reports about the dangers of obesity. They always show footage of fat people walking and eating . . . but only from the neck down. I call them the "decapitated fatties." And every time I see that footage I cross my fingers and pray that I don't see myself. I do live in Los Angeles, after all.

In the basement meeting room complete with podium and whiteboard were fifty to seventy-five people who shared a lifetime of struggle. Many could barely walk. Some had suffered strokes, heart attacks, and other obesity-related illnesses. Some had tried suicide. Many cried. Some were so brave that I felt like crying. Some had overcome so much. Seeing looks of sadness mixed with hope was overwhelming. In this basement room were people who cumulatively had suffered for thousands of days. Very few of them were lazy slobs. Very few were mean or vindictive or harmful to the human race. But they had been abused. They had been discarded by much of society. I don't like to think of myself or my chubby brothers and sisters as victims. We are responsible for our actions. We know that we were not born the same way. We were not born with the same metabolism. But some of these people never had much of a chance. This meeting room represented a chance. The specter of death loomed large over many in the audience. Some were afraid they would die without the surgery. Statistically it was extremely unlikely that they would die during surgery. But there are risks. Sometimes you have to trust your self and take a chance.

Couples held hands; some had their kids with them, but many of the future or past patients were alone. I was lucky that Bill went to the meetings. He would take notes and ask questions. Some people were not getting support from their loved ones. Some husbands or wives just couldn't deal with the intensity and the commitment of the surgery. Some couples' entire relationship was based on drinking and eating. They were unwilling to give up the food orgies that provided them with one of life's only pleasures. Some people gorged themselves to take the place of drugs they used to use. Some people feel so bad about their lives they refuse to sacrifice any more, their only source of comfort and joy coming from the instant gratification that food provides them. They are not even sure if they want to live a long, healthy life—just like my mother and her drinking. For many, the limitations that being obese imposes are at least predictable, compared to the hell of forging a new identity and becoming the person they are capable of being. Being thin and vulnerable and expected to take center stage is too much to bear for many. Better to stay confined to the self-imposed fat prison. They are not even sure they love their spouses or themselves. Some people feel "life sucks, so let me eat cake, lots and lots of cake." The thought of never drinking again was too much for some. One man who was essentially housebound because of his weight of four hundred pounds asked if he could have a beer. Then he asked if he could have nonalcoholic beer.

The idea of change terrifies many. Some wondered aloud what would happen once they lost two hundred pounds and became "attractive." Some people had never received any attention. They lived isolated lives of television and food. Some patients were afraid of becoming sexy. Some had only dated anonymously. In other words, they'd have unsatisfying sex with someone who would never be seen with them in public, or with insecure guys who were with the "big girl" for a self-esteem injection, or a meal ticket.

I know that some people think gastric bypass surgery is easy, that the weight just melts away the next day. I was one of those people, but I'm here to tell you that is totally untrue. There was nothing easy about this whole deal. Once the weight comes off you still have to deal with the demons that lie underneath. Be careful what you wish for. The thought of dramatic and possibly permanent weight loss was too much for some of the people who were close to the patients. Some people can handle it and some can't. I met a mom and her daughter who'd both had the surgery. They were wonderful. I saw families bond like they never had before. Some of the patients had become exercise junkies. Some had gotten multiple surgeries, shaved their heads, moved far away, and practically adopted new identities. Some of them had lost a hundred pounds but were still wearing their fat clothes: the shrinking-fatso syndrome. Some of the women wanted to tell their stories privately. Some did comedy routines.

At each meeting, we went around the room and told our personal stories. Some were too enthusiastic. There was a sense of newly found freedom and rebirth. Occasionally the meetings took on an almost revivalist tone. Some of the attendees were so pro–gastric bypass that I had a moment when I felt like I was in a cult meeting. Bill wondered if he would have to give up being a Catholic. A tough broad with a wrist full of bracelets and a leather tan stood up. "My name is Jennifer and I had the surgery six months ago and I have lost eighty pounds." I thought she was going to start throwing uppercuts. There was a round of applause. One person had had the surgery just a few days earlier and was back on her feet. She inspired me. I wanted to do that. I asked questions. I felt better. I made new friends. We exchanged numbers. A real estate agent wanted to show me a home. An actress wanted to find a producer. A producer was looking to find an actress. I left the meeting feeling renewed.

The meetings for the surgeon that I ultimately chose were held in the basement at Providence Saint Joseph Hospital. Maybe it's kismet that I found a new life in the same hospital where my mother lost hers.

I remembered the AA meetings I had been to with Mom. She was a seeker. Maybe I would find the mastery of self that she had often talked about. She always said I had my own style—which usually translated as, "Well, I wouldn't wear that, but if you like it . . ." Maybe I would find the courage she had tried to instill in us. It was weird. I felt a connection to a big beautiful universe. I walked down the halls where years earlier I felt the worst pain I had ever felt. I walked down the halls where years earlier my whole life had turned upside down. Where I had my heart ripped out. Where I was numb. Where the world was working and living and laughing even though my mother was dead. Where outsiders said the right things but I could not hear. Where I just wanted my mom. Where my family lost the soul that kept us together. Where my father lost his partner and wife. Where my brother lost his protector. Where my nephew lost his grandma. Where Bill lost a new friend. But now something beautiful was happening. Something strange and magical was happening. A miracle. As I walked into a gorgeous L.A. night I felt I was very lucky. I felt my mom in a new way and I knew she would be proud that I was finally taking care of my weight by taking care of myself. I was proud and I was, for the moment, at peace.

I made the decision to have gastric bypass surgery based on my own weight-loss history, medical statistics, and the desire to be in control of my own body for the first time since the age of eight. The choice to undergo surgery was mine to make and not anybody else's; my body, my life, my choice. For this reason I decided not to tell too many people, because I didn't want to jinx it, and I certainly didn't want to open myself up to the kind of judgment and treatment I had given to Carnie and others during my more ignorant days. I knew it was a controversial decision, but more important, it was deeply personal. I didn't even tell my dad or my brother, because I knew they would worry and most likely tell me, "You're fine the way you are." That is really loving and lovely, but I was way past that and needed to protect my feelings and my decision. Plus my dad is a big, fat crybaby!

I met with seven surgeons, and ultimately I chose Dr. Philippe Quilici, a surgeon in Los Angeles with a zero mortality rate (always a plus) and a wonderful aftercare program. Once I chose my surgeon and program, I submitted the requisite paperwork for insurance approval.

The process was grueling. The hours seemed like days and the days seemed like months while I waited. Bill and my friend Devin were with me every step of the way: at every doctor appointment, test, and psychological evaluation (the surgeon I chose requires it). They helped me gather proof of past weight-loss programs and history, and prepare the many calls and letters and faxes to the insurance company. Being approved for the surgery was almost a full-time job and took over a month.

The day I got the news that I'd been approved for surgery, I was in Mexico City for a three-day photo shoot for *Latina* magazine. The magazine flew my friend and stylist Penny Nicholakos and me to Mexico City for a story about returning to your roots. They arranged for us to shoot around the city and for a lovely reunion with my dad, stepmother, stepsisters, grandmother, aunts, uncles, and cousins. My dad served as our unofficial location scout, and it was really wonderful.

On April 1, 2004, we had sat down to have lunch at a beautiful restaurant in the Polanco section of Mexico City after shooting all morning at the Villa (the cathedral built in honor of the patron saint of Mexico, *La Virgen de Guadalupe*). Just as our food arrived, my cell phone rang, which in and of itself was a miracle, because I had trouble during the entire trip with reception.

"Hello?"

"Hi, Jackie, it's Debbie in Dr. Quilici's office. I just wanted to let you know that we received approval for your surgery from the insurance company this morning, so I'd like to schedule some pre-op appointments for you as well as your surgery date." I literally leaped out of my seat and jumped for joy! Penny, who was the only person at the table who knew I'd been praying and waiting for this call, got up and stood next to me. I covered the phone and whispered in her ear, "I'm approved!" I started crying for joy, and her eyes welled up too.

"Jackie, are you there?" I heard Debbie say.

"Yes. Yes, I'm here. I'm just so happy and . . . overwhelmed. Thank you!"

"I'm happy for you too," she said. "I had the procedure done three years ago, so I know exactly what you've been feeling and how great you're going to feel."

"How soon can I have the surgery?" I asked.

"April sixteenth."

"I'll be there. Thanks, Debbie." I hung up and said a little prayer of thanks, *gracias Diosito!*

Penny and I went back to the table, where everyone looked at me with curiosity and waited to hear what kind of great news I'd received. My dad said, "Good news, Mija?"

"The best news, Chimi. I'm so happy."

"Can you share your good fortune?" he asked.

"Not yet. I can't jinx it." I looked into my dad's eyes, which were full of love and support. He was so proud of me and so happy that I was in Mexico to share my family's roots in *Latina* magazine. All I could think as I looked at his beaming face was that he had no idea what I was about to do. I felt guilty that I didn't tell him, but I just couldn't risk making him upset or leaving him to worry about me. The guilt was really working on me. I felt the way I used to as a teenager when I knew I was about

Mexico City the day I was approved for my surgery.

to do something that my parents didn't know about. The fear of looking into my parents' faces and seeing disappointment is what kept me in line as a kid. But this time I knew I was doing the right thing. I blurted, "I love you, Chimi!"

"I love you too, Mija. I'm proud of you."

For the second time in ten minutes, I began to cry.

I returned home three days later to a frenzy of meetings, auditions, pre-op appointments, and a stack of reading material to help me get ready for the surgery. I called my friend Beth to tell her what I was planning to do. Her first reaction was "Is Bill working that week?"

"Yes," I said.

"Then I'm coming down to be with you and take care of you when you get home." Beth is one of the greats. She lives in Seattle with her husband and their two boys, Julian and Charlie. She made arrangements with Ronnie to stay home with the kids so she could come down and be with me. That's a friend. Thanks, Ronnie! And thanks, Beth!

The last day I could eat before my surgery was Tuesday, April 13. I decided to have a get-together with a handful of people for my own "last supper." Everyone kept asking me what I wanted to eat, and I couldn't think of anything. I finally decided on chips and salsa, taquitos, guacamole, Lash's famous chicken casserole, and chocolate crème pie. Penny brought some spanakopita and Devin ran out for some last-minute French fries. I felt very supported as I looked around the table, but I found I had absolutely no desire to eat anything. I knew for sure that I was doing the right thing, because I was ready to eat to live instead of living to eat. I didn't feel panicked or sad. I felt relieved and free.

I spent the forty-eight hours before surgery doing what is called a bowel cleansing. It's a process to clean out everything in your stomach and intestine. For anyone who has done it, high five! For anyone who hasn't, be thankful. I'll just say that I didn't see too much of the world during those forty-eight hours aside from my bathroom and the couch.

The night before my surgery, I couldn't sleep. When the alarm finally went off I was wide-awake and leaped out of bed. I showered, got dressed in my favorite velour jogging suit (size twenty-six/twenty-eight), and went downstairs. Bill's a teacher and his class had a field trip that day, so he was going to join me at the hospital after work. He carried my bags to the car and kissed me good-bye, and Beth and I made the drive through beautiful Coldwater Canyon, the canyon that connects Studio City to Beverly Hills, to the hospital. We listened to music and sang off-key and laughed as we pulled into the hospital parking lot. It was six fifteen a.m.

I checked into pre-op and was quickly ushered into a freezing-cold room where a very kind nurse took my blood pressure and went over my forms. At six twenty-eight a.m. she asked me to step onto the scale, just like the one in Dr. Sarang's office—only this time I didn't fear the number. I really wanted to know. I weighed 291 pounds. "The next time you step onto a scale, you'll be so happy, huh?" the nurse said.

"I already am," I told her.

She flipped through my paperwork and suddenly announced in her thick Filipino accent, "Uh-oh. You did not do a pregnancy test."

"No. Nobody told me I needed a pregnancy test."

"Oh, you must do the pregnancy test or Dr. Q cannot perform the surgery," she replied.

I explained to her that short of a miracle of biblical proportions I could not be pregnant, because I had not had sex since my last period. "The last day of my period was Tuesday. I began bowel prep on Wednesday, and please believe me when I tell you that I most certainly did not have sex during that fun fest."

She laughed and explained that she would have to talk to Dr. Quilici to see if he would accept that. My heart sank at the thought of having to go home and come back another day.

"Dr. Q is in the surgery right now, so I will page him. If he tells me it's okay, I will continue. For now, why don't you relax."

Beth and I sat in that freezing room staring at the walls and each other. We were silent. The only noise was the sound of the second hand ticking on the wall clock.

Our silence was broken by the sound of my nurse's voice booming over the intercom, "Dr. Quilici. Your next patient did not do the pregnancy test. She say she did not have the sex since her last menstrual cycle. Patient Jackie Guerra did not have any sex. Can you approve?"

Now, honestly, if I were watching a movie and saw a scene where a nurse hits a wrong button on an intercom and announces to the entire floor that a patient did not have sex, I'd sit in the theater, roll my eyes, and think, "That would never happen." Oh, but lucky me, it sure did! I was approved.

Inside the operating room were Dr. Quilici, my anesthesiologist, three nurses, and lots and lots of machines pumping and humming. The operating table had a plank that stuck out. The orderly explained to me that during surgery my arm would be strapped down to keep it still. I won't lie. As I slid onto the table and he began to strap my arm down, I felt a little like Sean Penn at the end of *Dead Man Walking*. Not the best visual right before surgery.

I remembered that I had read that whatever emotion you feel as you go under anesthesia is the one you feel coming out. Just as someone was about to put the mask over my face, I told the room about what I'd read. "So I'm going to need some fun and laughter from everyone in this room. I'd appreciate a little dancing, please!" They all obliged. The last thing I remember is a bunch of people in green pajamas and masks dancing around like little kids and laughing hysterically. I was laughing as I lost consciousness, and I woke up to the sound of my own laughter in the recovery room. It was nine twenty a.m. and I was in recovery feeling groggy, but grateful to be awake and alert and on the other side of surgery.

"Jackie, how do you feel?" the recovery nurse asked me in a soothing voice.

"I feel fine, just sleepy."

"Your friend is outside waiting for you to wake up," she said.

"I'm awake. Bring her in, please!"

Beth came in with the nurse, and they prepared my bed to make the journey to my room. When we got into the elevator, I asked, "That's it? Are you sure that my stomach is smaller and everything went well?"

In the most calming voice, she said, "Yes, dear. Your surgery went perfectly. Now you're going to feel very stiff today and then sore tomorrow, but you need to get up out of bed and walk around your floor at least four times today."

"I don't really feel stiff, but I am thirsty. Can I have some water?"

And then she dropped the bomb. "You can have some moist gauze to dab on your lips and tongue, but you cannot put anything into your stomach for at least twenty-four hours. Once you've had your X-ray, you can drink and have some broth, but that won't be until tomorrow afternoon."

"That's okay," I thought. "I can do this." We got to my room at ten oh five a.m. For a moment I almost whined, "Not even water?" But I could hear my own voice: "My life, my body, my choice." The "new Jackie" is determined to accept the consequences of her choices and decisions. I was really proud of myself.

"Your floor nurse will be in to check on you, and in about an hour she'll come and take you for your first walk." And with that she said good-bye and good luck to me, and then left.

I fell asleep almost immediately, and was awakened by a voice saying, "Jackie, can you wake up for me, sweetie?" I woke up to find Beth and the nurse standing over my bed.

"Okay, Jackie, we're going to help you get out of bed to take a little walk. Can you roll over onto your side for me?"

I made a move to shift my weight to one side and was greeted by the promised stiffness. It was the first time I saw the drain hanging from the left side of my stomach and the three little incisions being held together by staples. With some help, I got up slowly and a little painfully. I was out of my bed but still hooked up to an IV. The nurse swung it onto a stand on wheels and we were off. I was really stiff and the hanging drain was uncomfortable, but I did it! I took my first lap around the nurse's station at twelve forty-five, just four hours after surgery.

I came back to my room and immediately went back to sleep. The next time I woke up was to the sound of Bill's voice. I was so happy to see him. He hugged me long and hard, and I felt his tears on my neck. It's scary to see someone you love in a hospital bed connected to tubes, regardless of circumstances. On the other hand, I've seen pictures of me that first day in the hospital, and it made me cry too. Hospital chic: not my best look!

The next hours were a blur of Beth, Bill, flower arrivals, "dab, don't drink," nurses poking and prodding me, shots in my lower abdomen (ouch!), sleeping, walks, thirsty, more flowers, very thirsty, more nurses, and most notably, no bathroom activity. One of the reasons my surgeon insists his patients get up and walk every hour is to release the anesthesia. Otherwise, it takes too long for your organs to wake up and you don't have normal function (bathroom). At midnight, when I still hadn't gone to the bathroom, I had to have a catheter inserted. Let me tell ya, it's a joy to walk around a public place wearing two gowns, socks, and slippers, with razor stubble on the legs, no bra, no underwear, no makeup, and dry lips while pushing an IV stand with a bag of pee hanging on it. Hot!

I was discharged on Monday morning. Once I got home, I felt good, but I was very tired and weak. Have you ever gone on a drastic diet and dramatically cut your calories and/or carbohydrates? You know how you feel weak and a little bit like you're in a fog? That's how I felt. I think the fact that I really slept a lot the first week really helped me. Our bodies heal when we rest and sleep. I went for walks every day and drank a ton of water. When I wasn't walking or sleeping, I was peeing!

The first few weeks after surgery were identical: sleep, sip, walk, read, sleep, sip, and walk. The diet after surgery for the first four weeks is incredibly strict. Liquids only for the first two weeks, followed by two to three weeks of mushy foods. You eat as if you're a baby in order to give the stomach time to heal. After that, you begin to introduce new foods one at a time—no fried foods for six to nine months, no sugar or alcohol for twelve to eighteen months.

Each day Bill and I would walk slowly around our neighborhood, and each time we'd check out the construction site next door, and I'd think, "Good work, guys. My construction is going well too." Together Bill and I shared a renewed commitment to a healthier lifestyle. We continued to go to the weekly support group meetings. In fact, I got dressed and went to one the Wednesday after my surgery. I felt like an Olympian!

It took me about three weeks to really feel "normal." But I don't want you to think I couldn't function. I actually did a photo shoot at the beach two weeks after surgery. I went for long walks, went to meetings and appointments, and really felt good. Like I said, I was just tired. I probably slept twelve hours a day for the first three weeks.

I think most of my postsurgery success was due to the fact that I really took time to prepare for recovery. Even when I didn't feel like it, I got up and walked. I drank so much water I'm surprised there's any left in southern California. I put myself on an eating and vitamin schedule and I stuck to it. But most of all I rested. I listened to my body, and when it told me I needed to sleep, I slept. Our bodies heal when we sleep, and I wanted to heal.

Here's a journal entry from one month postsurgery:

It's Saturday, May 15, 2004.

Today is five weeks and a day since I had my surgery. I have five bullet-hole scars on my belly. I had to wear tight jeans for a photo shoot the other day, and my bullet holes were barking. My feet hurt from standing. To be honest I don't even know if I have lost any weight. It doesn't feel like it. In ten days I will have an official weigh-in. I'll start worrying in about nine minutes. Should I be a role model for my chubby friends? The responsibility is to myself. In the past, as a big girl, when I saw famous people lose weight, I came face-to-face with the green-eyed monster, but then I realized I was embarrassed that I was not doing what they were able to do. We all want to be healthy. No one says I want rolls of fat hanging over the top of my pants when I put them on. No one says I hope I have to lie down on my bed to put on my pants. On hot days I bleed from the rash created by the friction of my thighs rubbing. I walked the AIDS walkathon, and I had to call in sick to work the following day because my thighs were bleeding like Jesus for the last ten miles. I walked twenty miles because I am so competitive.

June 2004

    What I almost know.

    I have been mad at my body for so many years.

    I used to be pissed because I couldn't wear tank tops and have summer fun with skinny girls eating ice cream.

    When I eat hot food I hiccup. That's annoying.

    My identity is in flux. Who am I? Am I the big, jolly girl? Am I the quiet person, the patient person, the motherless person? Lots of thoughts are floating around. Will I ever be able to have sugar again?

For me I think the hardest part after surgery has been to remember to eat slowly and chew each bite thirty-two times! I practiced for about three weeks before surgery, and I still forget sometimes. The same anxieties or compulsive eating habits sometimes rear their ugly heads. I have to breathe and relax. In the past I used to dive into my meals. I always loved the feeling of a big bite of warm food. Whether you've thought about it or not, I bet you do too. You know, the way it feels to take a big bite out of a cheeseburger or a heaping spoonful of rice and beans. I can't do that anymore, because two or three big bites and I'm done. I have to take small bites and chew, chew, chew! I have to be careful.

The reason that sugar and alcohol are restricted for the first year after gastric bypass surgery is because for most people the part of the intestine that breaks sugar down has been removed, and it takes between twelve months and eighteen months to regenerate. Sugar and certain other foods cause what's called "dumping." Dumping is when you eat something that your intestine can't break down. It's a hideous, scary, disgusting thing when it happens. Luckily it's only happened to me twice, once when I ate macaroni and cheese in a restaurant and another time when I ate melted cheese. Foam came up through my throat, my legs felt like cement pylons, and I couldn't walk. I was dizzy and hot and then cold. It's unlike anything I've ever experienced. Some people throw up. I didn't. I just leaned on Bill, breathed, and tried to relax. It was over in about twenty minutes. It's the kind of thing that, once it happens, you never want it to happen again. So caution is the mantra.

Bill and I go out to restaurants and he orders food that I can eat too. We often share a meal. Bill has lost thirty-two pounds since my surgery. I've also rediscovered foods that I didn't used to eat or like. Remember my mom's "diet dinner" of tomatoes and cottage cheese? For years, I've hated tomatoes—hated them! Now I eat them almost every day.

I feel better, not restricted.

The biggest surprise is how little I eat. Everybody told me I'd fill up fast, but I just thought, "Yeah, right! I can eat a lot more than the average bear!" But it's true. The other thing is that it took me a good month to get used to the schedule (vitamins, supplements, protein drinks, and so on). I found that to be a big challenge, because it isn't something I'd done before.

So the lessons I've learned and like to impart are numerous.

Don't confuse confidence with defiance.

Don't be afraid of change.

Seek help when deciding on something.

Do your homework. I did a lot of research before the surgery.

Don't see obstacles. See challenges that when accomplished will make you proud. Don't be afraid to be proud of yourself. And don't be afraid to sacrifice the short term.

When you take the path less traveled, the benefits can be numerous and surprising.

Believe what you know, not what you're told.

And what is the biggest benefit? OMG! Where do I start? I feel great. I have a lot more energy. I have a lot more free time (it's amazing how much time I spent eating!). I have a better attitude in general. Specifically, I'm not as irritable as I used to be, and I don't think I worry as much as I used to, because I'm not constantly stressed out or defensive about my weight. I never thought I'd say this, but I think I'm actually going to enjoy this new, smaller house I'll be living in. Downsizing is not always a bad thing!

CHAPTER NINE

Put Your Mask on First!

"Self-love, my liege, is not so vile a sin, as self-neglecting."
—WILLIAM SHAKESPEARE

IF YOU'VE EVER BEEN ON A PLANE, YOU KNOW YOU GET peanuts and a warning. "In the event of an emergency . . . *put your oxygen mask on first before coming to the aid of others.*" But why wait for an emergency? You absolutely must put yourself first. Why? For exactly the same reason that the airlines tell you to put your mask on first—because if you don't take care of yourself, you won't be available for anyone else.

My mentor at the union was a verbose, philosophical gentleman. He said, "Take care of number one. Then you can take care of number two. Take care of first things first. First you have to take care of yourself. People will respond better if *you* take care of *you.*" My mentor asked, "What do people like more? When you drag your sick self over to help, or when you dance over to help?"

Now, if you are a horrific dancer, then you must choose another example. But generally, I agree. The more you take care of yourself, the more the universe takes care of you. When you are healthy the world seems healthier. You have the ability to see beyond the horizon. You have the ability to dream. The good overwhelms the bad. The positive defeats the negative. Obstacles are replaced by opportunities. When you are healthy you can make nice, make money, and make love. When you are sick you focus on sickness, and coughs, and count all the sneezes you hear. When you are happy you see the universe as full of possibilities. You can believe that things happen for a reason. Someone once said, "Smile and the world smiles with you." I say, "Frown and you end up the centerfold for *Frownie Frumpy* magazine." And who wants that?

In the past I have been known to not take care of myself. In the past I have been known to not be honest about what I needed. In the past I have been known to not put my mask on first. That is scary to the people who love me and depend on me. The people who love you want you to be healthy and happy. People who love you would rather attend your party than visit you in the hospital. Unless you throw *really* bad parties.

Sometimes you forget how important you are to your own survival. You worry about *everybody else* except yourself. You care about what everyone else needs and thinks. You might value their opinion more than your own. You might even change your well-thought-out course based on someone's snap judgment. If you do this long enough you can lose yourself. If you do this long enough you are putting *their* mask on first. If you do this long enough you will forget how to "put your mask on first," and it will put you on the survival highway instead of the happy highway. The happy highway is where you will thrive, instead of barely survive.

To put my mask on first, I always have to evaluate what I need. What is the priority? Be clear about your needs. What is important? Remember that *baby, you're a star!* Write your script and know what you want. If you don't figure out what you want, the everyday "negative options" will overwhelm you. You will be overwhelmed and numbed by "happy" meals. You will be supersized into a carb coma. You will watch so much "reality" TV you will lose your own reality. Don't make the mistake of waking up one day without a plan and suddenly find yourself being an extra in someone else's movie.

When I worked as an organizer for the Hotel and Restaurant Union, I loved being constantly active and belonging to a group that served people in need. But after eighteen months of nonstop work, I stopped learning, growing, and having fun. I became tired, demanding, and sometimes unreasonable. I realized I needed to leave the group.

Sometimes when you belong to a group you feel powerful because you are not nagged about your own *personal* insecurities. You feel powerful because you always have "backup." You are artificially never alone. Your life is the *group*. You are focused on the *group* goal. You know what the *group* wants. The outside world doesn't exist. It's a good way to focus and it's a good way to escape. Escaping into your career is commonplace. Sometimes when you belong to a group, you don't think for yourself. Sometimes you end up volunteering for everything and being responsible for nothing. Sometimes you are never fully appreciated. Sometimes when you belong to a group, you gain over one hundred pounds. Sometimes when you *don't* belong to a group you can gain over one hundred pounds. In any case, you have to take the time to look inside. You cannot afford to forget to take care of your prime property, *you.*

Many times I have allowed weeds to grow on my prime property while I thought I was helping the universe. Maybe I did a little bit, but ultimately I cheated everyone out of the best me I could be. I know that working hard and throwing myself into my work seemed like the right thing to do, but in the long run doing that helped nobody except the pizza delivery boy, who received my big nightly tips. If you need a time-out, take one.

Every day I talk to women who don't have anyone who truly listens to them. Every day I talk to women who are wiped out. They are drained because they feel responsible for their grandparents, parents, siblings, or thirty-three-year-old musician son who forgets to turn off the air-conditioning in *their* home. I look in their eyes and they are desperate. Meanwhile the sick grandparents, guilt-tossing parents, needy siblings, or thirty-three-year-old musician son with bad credit has no clue how put-upon these women feel. We have to speak our minds. We have to tell people that their bad planning or bad choices are not our emergencies. We have to practice saying potentially harsh things, like "Why would you say that to *me*?" "Now is not a good time for *me*." "I'm saving *my* money for *my* retirement." "I don't want to spend *my* only vacation listening to you complain."

You can only play the role of the martyr for so long before you become the martyr who has been played out. Some people love to play the role of the martyr. That's a tough movie to be in. They say they give everything to their jobs, spouse, kids, or volunteer work, and they don't get equal value in return. We all have a little martyr in us. The idea of sacrificing yourself for something other than you is said to be noble. It can be the highest form of love. But it can also be a trap to let you off the hook. It can be a way to give up your responsibility to yourself. It can be a way to give yourself an excuse for not taking care of yourself and your dreams and desires. Being generous and considerate is important, sacrifice is important, but self-sacrifice is actually quite selfish. When you don't take care of yourself first, you're not around to take care of the people and the things that you claim to love so much. It doesn't do anyone any good when you sacrifice your happiness, because it always catches up to you. The resentment and frustration build and build, and one day when you least expect it, they'll explode. You and everyone in the line of fire at that moment will be covered in the shrapnel from the explosion caused by many years of denying that indeed you needed to *put your mask on first.* If you're sacrificing and complaining, that's not satisfactory sacrifice. That's a sack of crap. If you're giving and not getting equal value, that's not good giving—that's not even good living.

I sacrificed a lot in my union organizing days, searching for something greater than myself. I wanted powerless people to feel powerful. I believed in fighting for equity in the workplace. I made relationships that I would never trade. There were times, however, when I definitely did not take care of myself. I worked and learned, but there was pressure that never stopped. I was threatened and yelled at, and my colleagues and I were spit on. The environment was hostile. We picketed a major hotel for well over a year, and the people there hated us. It was difficult for me because I love people and I love hotels and I *really* love room service. But it was for the greater good. I miss the excitement of working full-time on campaigns. I miss the members, and I miss my friends at the union, but I don't miss the spit.

What about putting on your mask first when you are a parent? Aren't you supposed to sacrifice for your kids? My mom did. But you can't sacrifice to the point where you black out from lack of oxygen. What good would you be to them? When you're so busy teaching, loving, and caring for your kids that you forget to teach, love, and care for yourself, you lose and—believe it or not—your kids lose. Your kids lose because you're inevitably teaching them that you're not as important as they are, and, even worse, you're teaching them to sacrifice their lives for the happiness and well-being of others. This may seem like a nice thing to do, but what happens when you run out of steam? My mom kept going and going and giving and giving. She didn't stop to put her mask on first. My dad, my brother, and I always came first. Our needs, our activities, our crisis of the day were always more important than anything going on in her life. As a kid I may have benefited from that, but it was a terrible trade-off, because as an adult I don't have my mother to share my life with. She'll never know her grandchildren because she didn't put her mask on first. I don't care if you drive a $500 car or you have a brand-new $200,000 Bentley. If you don't put gas in the tank, neither of them is going anywhere. So, moms, please, for the sake of your children, *put your mask on first!*

Many moms say their kids are the most important thing, and meanwhile their spouse becomes number two, three, or four in their lives. Some women rate their hairstylist as more important than their husbands. I want the number of that hairstylist! But I totally understand. A lot of women out there are living in unfulfilled relationships. Sometimes staying in a relationship is putting your mask on first and sometimes it isn't. I had a relationship that was so unfulfilling I took laps around empty malls, during the mornings, by myself, and bought nothing. That's like hanging in Vegas and not gambling. I was trying to figure out what was best for me. I was in a relationship with a guy who screamed and stomped around and broke things and threw things, and I stayed because I thought he needed me and that I was taking care of myself by being in a relationship. That's cra-zay! I finally woke up and realized I didn't need to be in a relationship to be whole. I needed to take care of myself and know myself and love myself. I had to leave the relationship in order to put my mask on and be whole. I wouldn't tolerate that now. Taking care of yourself and being honest with yourself in a relationship are the hardest jobs you can have, because sometimes taking care of yourself in a relationship means you have to end it.

Putting your mask on first means handling obstacles that are not always in your face, otherwise known as dormant bummers. Dormant bummers are not daily problems, but rather ones that we ignore, pretend don't exist, or don't bother us until we least expect them. For example, people you don't see regularly but who are a bummer when you do, like a bully relative.

Putting your mask on first means you don't let anybody trample your feelings, beliefs, or dreams. Don't suffer silently when someone says something cruel.

Remember the class bully in sixth grade? That brat grew up and is now an adult. The kid who used to walk by your desk and kick it just because he could is now an adult. Adult bullies aren't as obvious as the ones in elementary school. They are too slick to kick. Adult bullies kick with words. They say things that are offensive and inappropriate and hide behind claims like "I'm just joking" or "You're so sensitive," or my all-time favorite, "What? I just tell the truth." Well, the truth is that it's not okay for anyone to kick your life. Period!

There is someone in my family who is a bully, and for some reason everyone in my family just puts up with her bad behavior. Whenever anyone in my family tells me a story about something she did or said that hurt them, I always ask the same question: "What did you say to her?" For years I've heard the same excuses: "That's just her personality. She doesn't even know she's a bully. I don't want to make her feel bad." She hurts people and ruins every event with her mouth, and they don't want to hurt *her* feelings? Everyone in my family needs to put their mask on first and realize that *their* feelings are more important than whatever momentary discomfort she may feel when she's told to stop. Agggghh! I decided that this was it. I'm going to put my mask on first, and hopefully others in my family will follow. I've had it!

I was at a family wedding sitting with a group of my older relatives, who were simply enjoying the day, when one of my younger relatives—let's call him Jose—began to tell us a story about how one of our favorite uncles had really helped him out with a problem. Just then my bully relative—let's call her Sneaky—sat down. I was on red alert and knew that if she opened her mouth to say anything inappropriate, I was ready to put my mask on, because no way was I going to let her ruin the wedding and ruin my day. The conversation went like this:

> Jose: *"I was feeling really confused and upset about being fired, but then I spoke to Uncle Rey for about three hours on the phone the other day. He gave me some great advice that definitely helped me out. He is so smart."*
>
> Sneaky: *"Rey spent three hours on the phone with you? That's a shock. He never has time for anybody."*
>
> *I felt the tension and could see my older relatives, who all adore Uncle Rey and spend every family gathering trying to ignore Sneaky's bullying comments, begin to look around and shift uncomfortably in their seats. This was my cue to bust a move.*
>
> Me: *"Excuse me, Sneaky. What do you mean by that?"*
>
> Sneaky: *"What? Hmm? I didn't mean anything. I'm just telling the truth. Rey is always busy and never has time for anybody."*
>
> Me: *"Well, what exactly is your concern?"*
>
> Sneaky: *"I don't have a concern. I'm just saying that the only time I ever see him is when someone dies or gets married."*
>
> Me: *"So then what you're concerned about is that Uncle Rey never spends time with you."*
>
> *Silence. After a few uncomfortable seconds, Sneaky had a comeback.*
>
> Sneaky: *"Yeah. I guess."*
>
> Me: *"Okay. So you're upset because you never see him, but it isn't true that he doesn't have time for anybody. Right?"*
>
> Sneaky: *"I guess so."*

Two simple questions—"What do you mean by that?" and "What is your concern?"—and she was forced to explain herself. My relatives tried to conceal their smiles and looks of relief that Sneaky got shut down. There was no drama, and I'm happy to say that I had a great time, and so did everyone else, because Sneaky was shut up. Normally the day after a family gathering is full of phone calls and e-mails about Sneaky's bad behavior, but not this time. I'm sure I'll have to ask her those two questions many more times, but it doesn't matter. I put my mask on first and put up a "bully roadblock." Sneaky didn't have anyone to pick on, so she found another game to play, just like the sixth-grade bully.

It's simple. A bully is a bully until you put up a bully roadblock. Then they either go away to find some other target or they stop and join the rest of us in the human race. I'm not suggesting that you lower yourself to become like them or go out of your way to create drama, but I do suggest you do something to protect yourself or remove them from your life. Don't let bullies become dormant bummers; put your mask on first.

A dormant bummer can also be that person with whom you have "unfinished business," like the friend you don't speak to anymore, but can't remember why you stopped speaking. You're out with friends, feeling cute and having a good time, when out of nowhere, bam, there she is, right in front of you! She gives you a dirty look and you feel the life has been sucked right out of you; that's a dormant bummer. The to-do list that never gets done is a dormant bummer that makes you feel like you're always a failure. The relative who only calls you when they need something from you—namely, money—is a dormant bummer. That visit to the dentist you've been putting off because you know you will be X-rayed, lectured, strapped down, tilted, sedated, humiliated, yanked, and, worst of all, unable to eat or talk, is a dormant bummer.

My weight has been a dormant bummer and an active bummer. It's dormant when some of my clothes don't fit. It's active when none of my clothes fit. After years of struggle I knew I could not continue gaining and losing weight. My past, present, and future were all becoming filled with dormant bummers. Losing weight, not losing weight, it was something that was always in the back of my mind. And no matter what else was going on in my life, I felt like a loser for not losing (weight).

The "old Jackie" was antisurgery. She wanted to have her big meals with Bill. The old Jackie wanted to have the freedom to eat, drink, and be merry. The old Jackie thought that if she could eat and drink she would be merry. The old Jackie thought that gastric bypass surgery was a desperate choice made by desperate people. The old Jackie felt she had to prove to everyone that she could still lose the weight permanently, even though she had tried and failed many times. The old Jackie was concerned people would think she is a freak who has no discipline. The old Jackie used to be offended if people did not think she could lose the weight. The old Jackie wasn't honest about needing to put her mask on first.

The new Jackie decided to summon the courage to have the surgery. It is almost a year later, and though I can't use aspirins or cold medications (some have sugar), I haven't needed them. Emotionally and spiritually I feel strong because I have passed a big test. The new Jackie is very grateful every day for the medical technology that has made it possible for her to have a new, smaller stomach and a new life. The new Jackie knows that regardless of what people may think, life is much better for her since she *put her mask on first*.

Putting your mask on first requires prioritizing. Here's an illustration. Bill teaches in an elementary school. Every morning we wake up at six fifteen. Call me old-fashioned, but I make his breakfast and lunch. I do it because I want to spend time with him before work. It's not about "serving Bill." It's not about giving Bill what he expects. It's that my life with Bill is very important. My time with him is something I value. Loving Bill is effortless. So waking up early to make his breakfast and send him to work with a yummy lunch isn't sleep deprivation. It's fueling *me* with love for the day. It's PYMOF.

Sometimes my priorities change. Occasionally I sleep in. The other night I was at an event until one in the morning. I did not wake up at six fifteen. Bill understood totally. He loves to see me in the morning and get served his meal like a king, but he also loves it when I am well rested. He derives pleasure from a relaxed Jackie. So he is also putting his mask on first by letting me stay in bed while he makes his Lean Pockets and packs his own turkey and Swiss sandwich. He wants me happy. He loves to see a smile on my face. Each of us is putting our mask on first; this is a winning situation. He wants my mask on first. I will have energy to love him more. I won't be grumpy and tell him to take smaller bites and use his fork properly. He is therefore protecting himself and us.

Now, what could happen if I didn't put my mask on first? If I always sleep in and don't see him, then I feel disconnected from Bill. I don't get to enjoy the extra-strong coffee with him. I don't get the morning kiss as he leaves. I don't get to remind him to carry his cell phone. I don't see him for long stretches of time. Then we may grow a few inches apart. Inches become feet, and before you know it Bill is living in a basement apartment across the street from school with a wet-haired teacher's assistant, and I am luxuriating in Beverly Hills with a plastic surgeon. Nobody wants that. Now, let's be clear, my friends. I am not saying that if I don't make him a Lean Pocket we're going to break up. I'm not saying I wake up to save our relationship. I'm saying that priorities may change from day to day. Sometimes the priority is an early wake-up, and sometimes it's rest.

I am putting my mask on first by putting my relationship and me first. Sometimes it's the nice little things that keep a relationship in balance. PYMOF requires honesty about priorities. That is why I share this scintillating slice-of-life story of Jackie in the kitchen. Questions? Send your thoughts to Lean Pockets dot com.

In a relationship there is mutual dependence that requires mutual well-being and discipline when it comes to health. Other people depend a lot on us. If you aren't in good physical and emotional health, that other person also may suffer. So, if you've taken on the role of a friend, lover, confidante, mistress, or bootie call, you've also accepted a responsibility to put your mask on first. That means taking care of yourself physically, emotionally, mentally, spiritually, and financially.

TAKE CARE OF THE ONE YOU LOVE—YOU!

As far as your health is concerned, prevention is paramount. Your own physical illnesses should be treated fast. Regular checkups are especially important. Aches and pains and more serious stuff can be active or dormant bummers. Be honest with yourself. Don't fool yourself. And do not say that you don't have time to get regular checkups. You don't have time not to.

I ignored inner pains until I needed emergency gallbladder surgery. I could have prevented a prolonged hospital stay. I didn't have to miss out on plans made and tasks left undone if I'd put my mask on first and paid attention when my body started telling me to sit down. Sometimes you have to put yourself on the bench, and only you can decide when to come back into the game. Sometimes a few days on the bench can give you a chance to see the game differently. Perhaps you will return with a greater appreciation for the game of life or even a new play. Love yourself completely, and use the time while your body is asking for rest to check in with yourself. How's your script going? Don't rush back before you are ready to play like you mean it. You have to be physically and emotionally ready to be effective in the game of life.

I know it's not easy, but maintaining emotional and mental health is key to putting your mask on first. Emotional health is the shy sister to other forms of health, but its importance is often overlooked.

Emotions are often conflicting and confusing. You may feel rage, guilt, impatience, hopelessness, love, and dislike all at the same time. You may tell yourself that some of these are "positive" feelings and others "negative." Don't judge your feelings. When you are emotional you are not in a good position to judge anyway. Don't despair because of feelings. Just live them and give yourself a break. Don't beat yourself up because you lost your composure. We all screw up. Hey, it's a fine line between expressing your feelings and "losing it."

I have a friend who is always proclaiming that she's "freaking out." The first ten or twenty times it was interesting. Now I find myself avoiding her. But holding in your feelings is not always the answer. I have held in my feelings to the point where I became goo. Then I would just be stepped on, and people would be upset because they had goo on their shoes and then threw the gooey shoes out. Don't end up the goo on the bottom of someone's shoes.

I guess it's about balance. What I try not to do is to judge and condemn my feelings. That's the goal. Have the thought. Don't judge it. Move on. Most feelings are normal. Accept your feelings. Don't waste energy trying to talk yourself out of having a certain feeling. Frequently I have gone from feeling bad to feeling guilty to depression to melancholy, and then anger, and then deep, unresolved hunger. These feelings hang out at your pity parties, but they are not your friends. Be nice to them and then escort them to the door.

Remember, if you are sad about something, you can bet a neighbor or a friend is experiencing something similar. We are not alone. Your situation may be unique, but you don't have to live it by yourself. Many other people have these same feelings about their situations. It may help to have a close friend, or group, or confidant whom you can call every day. There is no shame in asking for help. When you need it, get it. Friends have helped me many times when I've felt sad or confused, and I love them for it. So speak up!

Have a plan for those times when you get blindsided by the blahs. I remember when I broke up with my first boyfriend. I didn't want to go anywhere that he might be. It was summertime, I was sixteen, and my mom was determined to get me to move on. She told me, "You better have a plan to cope. You're going to run into him, so you might as well be ready." I've always thought that that was great advice for life in general. Life is going to surprise you. There will be many times when you'll need a plan to cope. It may be the fear of running into someone you don't want to see. It may be a situation where you forget to be your own best friend. Whatever it is, be ready and have a plan to cope.

A coping technique can be anything from rubbing lotion on your feet or listening to music to dancing alone, cleaning a closet, or taking a brisk walk. If you have a technique, you are ahead of the game. Sometimes redirected sad feelings can lead to something worthwhile. Miracles do occur. Be open and objective. Find a hobby and make it your routine for dealing with feeling frustrated or down. That's partly why I started to make jewelry. I found that it focused me on something other than the pain I was going through at the time. Later on it became a business venture. It became an opportunity to meet some great people. If you don't have a hobby, try it. You'll like it!

Take a breath, take a walk, call a friend, find a distraction, and try to

My hobby, my passion . . . my jewelry!

be open to new experiences. Reading and listening to music often help me. Sometimes I'll contact people who can advise me and help me think about things clearly. Sometimes I talk to my dad. Sometimes I have to talk to people about my dad. People's roles can sometimes change.

Who has time for all this? It's a reasonable question. There are ways to combine your efforts to achieve balanced health. For instance, a daily walk with friends or a weekend excursion with a hiking club provide exercise, social interaction, and perhaps even emotional support. A reading group might offer food for thought, emotional support, spiritual uplift, and personal affection. Hobby groups may also discuss current events. It may be difficult to change your lifestyle immediately to achieve real putting-your-mask-on-first success. You have to be patient. You have to count the little victories. You have to believe. You have to believe in the comeback and fresh starts. So get started; select at least one or two areas to work on right away. Make that overdue doctor's appointment, or accept your neighbor's offer to help you have a yard sale. Get rid of the old to make room for the new. Get going on some activity for yourself.

In other words, set a realistic goal for yourself to improve the quality of your life, and regularly check your progress toward that goal. Make sure your priorities make sense given whatever project you're working on. The more you focus on your big project, the less time you have for things like chub gen. Remember chub gen? The "always number two" syndrome? Always a bridesmaid but never the bride? Be the bride. In fact, be the bride-to-be. Ever watched a bride-to-be? Nothing gets in their way on the way to the altar. Nothing. Nothing deters the laserlike focus of a bride-to-be—nothing. Every single project in your life deserves that kind of commitment. And so I now pronounce you . . . ready to tackle your goals and priorities!

As I began to write this book, I had to set a goal to write every day. In order to make room for writing, I had to put my mask on first and make a shift in my priorities to give myself the time to think about my life and organize my thoughts and just sit with the experiences and lessons in order to make sense of them. I value my friends and family, but I had to sacrifice some of the social time I normally spend with them in order to complete my goal. It's a question of balancing two right answers: stay home and work on my book or spend time with my friends and family. Like a bride-to-be, I needed laser focus and could not be distracted. Most everyone in my life has been wildly supportive and understanding. A couple of them have been surprisingly uninterested and frankly mad that I've been, as they say, "underground." But it's taught me which people love and support me and want me to succeed, and which are constantly humming the old Janet Jackson song "What Have You Done for Me Lately?" It's been difficult and sometimes a struggle to stay focused, and not run around trying to make the ones who say they feel abandoned feel better. If they're truly my friends and our friendship is strong, it will remain so until I finish my book, and I made the right choice. If not, then I obviously made the right choice too.

Interestingly enough, there is one person who has complained more than all the others combined. "I know you're working on your book, but I feel abandoned." Our friendship has been incredibly one-sided for a long time. After we speak I'm often left with a bad taste in my mouth, like spoiled milk. Our conversations are always me listening to her complain about her job. "I'm not being used to my potential. I have a much stronger work ethic than everyone else." She is frustrated because she craves a relationship but hasn't been able to meet anyone. "All the men in L.A. are superficial. I'm just too real for them." Her other friends and her family irritate her too. "Everyone is so needy. I'm so tired of having to feed everyone else. Nobody feeds me." The problem is that she has relied on me to feed her for some time. She doesn't know how to feed herself. When I suddenly wasn't available for her regular feedings, she got hungry, grumpy, and then she was mad. She can't understand why she always feels empty and disappointed. Yet she doesn't consider that the common denominator to everything in her life that leaves her feeling empty and unsatisfied is her.

In all fairness, our friendship began when I was emotionally hungry.

We met during a period of my life when I acted like an extra instead of the star of my own movie, so the bulk of our scenes together were all about her. While I was a card-carrying member of chub gen, I was willing to put up and shut up. I was her go-to gal. That is the person she enjoys being friends with. But that is not the person I enjoy being. I have known for some time that speaking to her has felt more like a chore than joy. A good friendship is nourishing. A good friendship helps build a strong you, like a nutritious and refreshing protein drink. It doesn't always taste delicious, but that's okay, because in the end it's good for you. You shouldn't burp up bad feelings for hours or days after spending time with someone. I kept fooling myself into thinking that my upset stomach was the result of something I ate and not what was eating me. I convinced myself I was being impatient because I was busy and felt pressure to meet my deadline—I doubted what was loud and clear, my own instinct. She told me who she is many times—but I didn't listen.

She didn't change; I did.

I kept sipping from this relationship long past its expiration date, even though it tasted like spoiled milk.

This particular friendship isn't nutritious any longer. In fact, like all things that have spoiled, it began to poison everything else in my fridge. I put my mask on first and allowed myself permission to reprioritize and check in to make sure that my priorities still made sense. It's not easy, but when a relationship is past its expiration date, you have to let it go. Otherwise you are lugging around spoiled milk, and that stinks!

Put your mask on first and you gain a sense of control over your time and your life. It's when you feel disgusted, unloved, misunderstood, and not listened to that you are most likely to wear down or waste away. These are the times when you move less and eat more. Of course there will be times when you and I will be sad or lonely. That's when you need to announce to your inner circle that you are going for a drive down Lonely Street, and if you don't come back in an hour, you need to be "picked up." The people who pick you up are the nourishing friends you want in your life. These are the ones who can keep you on the right track. Then the next time you go for a drive, it will be down a beautiful sun-drenched highway to happiness. And *then* you can help someone else because you *put your mask on first.*

CHAPTER TEN

Think Globally, Act Locally!

"Great minds discuss ideas; average minds discuss events; small minds discuss people."

—ELEANOR ROOSEVELT

G E T   O U T   A N D   D O   S O M E T H I N G ! ! ! In a world that seems so huge, where we can feel so powerless and insignificant, those words are transformative and full of the promise of accomplishment. Those five little words are proactive and empowering. Life is what you make happen and not what happens to you. I wonder if my mom and dad fully understood how valuable the lesson was.

For as long as I can remember I've wanted to make a difference in the world. I think we all do. Nobody wants to be insignificant. There's a whole big world out there *under construction* that needs us to do some work in it. But to get out and do something and make a difference in the world can seem overwhelming. That's why we have to "think globally, act locally." It's simple, it's exciting, and it works!

Each one of us affects more people than we can ever really realize. Now that you are ready and you've got your mask on, use everything we've learned to make your body, your mind, your heart, your home, your family, your community, your town, your state, our country, and the world a better place. *Think globally, act locally* starts by taking care of yourself, living the life that you've *scripted*, being your own *best friend*, not *weighting to live*, and *putting your mask on first!* Once you've done those things you're ready to get out and do something for the world!

When you take care of yourself and respect yourself, you will undoubtedly care for and respect others in a much more deliberate and valuable way. When you value your own needs, dreams, and desires and act like the person you're capable of being, you treat others as the people they're capable of being. And when that happens, the world is a better place—one person at a time. Just like Cesar Chavez said, "You change the world the same way you eat tortillas, one bite at a time or one person at a time."

If you've ever doubted the impact that one person can have on the entire world, let me drop a few names on you: Eve, Jesus, Mohammed, Susan B. Anthony, Rosa Parks, Billie Jean King, Nelson Mandela, Cesar Chavez, Albert Einstein, Harriet Tubman, Gloria Steinem, Oprah . . . the list goes on and on.

So how do we make a difference? *Think globally, act locally!* Think about the ways you can envision a better world. What are the things that matter to you? What do you want to change? What do you want to improve about the world? Once you've decided, start at home and, as Gandhi said, "Be the change you want to see in the world."

When I was a baby organizer working for the Center for Participation in Democracy, my duties included voter registration and education. I spent a lot of time on the streets talking to people about the importance of registering to vote and, of course, voting! I was always amazed at the gap most people felt between their needs for quality of life and the voting process. Unfortunately, politicians, candidates, and elected officials don't always do the best they can to bring their messages or services "to the street." So often the rhetoric during an election cycle seems so far removed from our everyday lives! When most of us are worried about a paycheck, health care, our kids, feeling safe in our homes, and being able to plan for the future, the politicians are talking about trial lawyers or swift boats or who smoked pot when and inhaled, and who didn't. It's ridiculous! At the same time, we as voters have to take some responsibility too. If we see ourselves as consumers and the politicians as salespeople, consider your vote to be your money. You aren't going to spend your hard-earned money on something you don't want or need, right? But if you don't make your needs and wants known, how can someone offer you a product that will be useful to you? So be heard!

About ten years ago, I heard about an amazing group of young guys who really epitomize thinking globally and acting locally. They're called the Surfriders. Twenty years ago these friends, who regularly surfed on the Santa Monica shore, became increasingly frustrated that beaches were being closed due to contamination. They got organized and started asking questions. Who was interfering with their ability to surf? What businesses were polluting the beach? Why was that okay? They turned their questions into action and took their concerns "to the street." They started circulating petitions throughout their community, and eventually made it all the way to the state capitol. Today, the Surfriders are one of the most powerful and influential lobbying organizations on behalf of environmental issues, with chapters throughout the world. They cleaned up the beach so that they could surf, and in the process helped clean the water for everyone. They have made a difference. Check them out at www.surfrider.org. Aside from the fact that they've been able to influence legislation and get the beach cleaned up so they could surf safely, they've inspired surfers and beach lovers all over the world to get out and do something!!! And they inspired me to *think globally, act locally.*

And that's how it starts. A very wise person once said that the greatest change happens for selfish reasons; the Surfriders wanted to surf! They were a bunch of guys who followed their own script, trusted themselves, and, as a result, made the world a better place for all of us. I think it's worth repeating that when we get really connected to who we are and what we want and do, to the things we know are good for us, the positive effect on those around us extends far beyond our own immediate world. And how about the people in your immediate world who through their actions have made your world a better place—your parents, friends, teachers, neighbors, clergy? We are each able to make the world a more loving and safe place for so many. The world's smaller, we're all connected, and our actions have repercussions. "Local" actions have global implications. "Grassroots" actions create change. And it all begins with one person asking why something is the way it is and having the courage to take the first step to make a change.

Have you ever heard the story about the boy collecting starfish on the beach? The boy was walking along the beach surrounded by stranded starfish. He worked feverishly to pick them all up and put them back into the water to save their lives. As he'd put them into the water, another wave would wash in a bunch more. A man walked up to the boy and said, "What are you doing? You're wasting your time. Every time you put one back another washes up. You can't save them all. You can spend your whole day putting them back into the water and you won't make a difference." The boy picked up one more starfish and put it back into the water. He looked at the man and said, "I just did."

I recently read an article in *The Week* magazine about the positive effects of voting. "Voting is good for your mental health, researchers say—even if your candidate loses. That's because voting makes you feel that you have more control over your life, and that feeling reduces stress. The poor, in particular, benefit from the feeling of involvement that voting provides, since the poor are most likely to feel powerless." "Of course it's better if you win," said political scientist Lynn Sanders. "But there is still a positive effect from voting."

I have been involved in campaigns and I love how it energizes people to get out and do something. Hollywood says that politics is showbiz for ugly people. Political folk say that showbiz is politics for dumb people. But it's always fun whenever the nation's ugliest and dumbest get together on a campaign. People come together to think, debate, and put their beliefs on the line. Politics is a form of expression that frees the spirit and makes us feel connected to something larger than ourselves. It can bring out the passion that makes you think and communicate better.

Sometimes you have to allow your indignation to take over. It is a powerful tool if handled properly. Indignation can increase your circulation to produce an aerobic effect, which can put you over the top and get you where you eventually want to go. Sometimes when you are angry you can put your argument together more effectively than if you are passive and analytical. Use your heat. Be aware of your anger. Now, don't go crazy. Be smart with your anger. Be smart with your art. Great art comes from rage. Great art emanates from "rage against the machine." Find the emotional appeal of your beliefs. People need to feel the emotion. Don't always try to control your emotions or the emotions of others. That is exhausting. If you can sell your point of view with passion and intelligence, you can win the election of life.

Though I've always believed strongly that it is not just my right to vote but, as a citizen, my responsibility, I too get frustrated sometimes during the election cycle. I especially resent it when candidates give lip service to the truth that teachers are one of our nation's greatest resources. I completely agree, but I rarely see anything beyond campaign rhetoric to demonstrate that they are a priority. Bill is a fifth-grade teacher at a public elementary school in North Hollywood, California. Don't let the name "North Hollywood" fool you; his school is in a very humble neighborhood and his students are the daughters and sons of the working poor in Los Angeles. I know firsthand how hard the teachers at his school work, and I also know they don't do it for the money; they do it because they too want to make a difference in the world by teaching kids just like they eat tortillas: one at a time.

Bill is by far one of the greatest people ever to walk the face of the earth. He is honest and caring and smart and kind and funny and hot! But that's not the point. The point is this: the school and the surrounding area are under construction. The school is filled with kids who have recently arrived in the United States from Mexico, El Salvador, Honduras, and Guatemala. The kids are full of hope and fifth-grade angst. They are changing from little kids to little people at the dawn of their teenage years. They are much more worldly and streetwise than I ever was at their age. Every day Bill and the other wonderful teachers at his school battle language barriers and help the kids prepare to make the transition from safe elementary school to (what seems to them to be) scary middle school. Every day they work in a school that is constantly *under construction*, where the teachers are bombarded on an almost daily basis with new tests from the federal government, new tests from the state government, new forms that must be filled out; sick kids, crying kids, kids who have had their hearts broken for the first time, happy kids, neglected kids; no physical education program, no music program, no art program—but no child left behind! Every day these people we call teachers get up and go to work, and in Bill's case are responsible for thirty-two young lives for eight hours a day in a small, dusty classroom with no computers and not enough books across the street from a crack house. There is no parking lot, so the brave women and men who teach at Bill's school drive to work, lock their cars, and cross their fingers that their cars will be there in one piece at the end of the day. They gather their bags, coats, corrected homework, lesson plans, books, and supplies and then dodge traffic, crime, and desperation to make the walk from wherever they've found a parking spot in the surrounding area to go teach the future. The budget was cut so dramatically at Bill's school that the teachers are now responsible for buying their own supplies for their classrooms. Despite these circumstances, these teachers take their job very seriously. Their job is to help other people's children become the best people they can be. And the teachers do it under extremely sparse and stressful circumstances. These are people who worked hard to put themselves through college and believe strongly in the value of education and the value of good teaching.

Bill and his fellow teachers are, in my opinion, the real unsung heroes of our country. Elected officials and political candidates know this too. They know that our public school teachers are overworked and underpaid, and they know full well that it is nothing short of reprehensible. And that's why every election cycle there is always a ton of rhetoric flying around about how we need to "protect one of our nation's greatest resources: teachers." And every morning after the election the rhetoric stops, the conditions stay the same, the teachers don't get raises, and, as far as I've seen, their situation worsens. And our governor and our president are surprised that fewer and fewer college graduates are choosing to pursue careers in education. Hmmm, I can't imagine why.

It really breaks my heart to watch this happen over and over and over again. It is so upsetting. And then I get indignant. And then I get angry, and I realize that I have got to do something! How can I *think globally, act locally* on this one? And so I got to thinking, "What can I do?" I can't give each teacher a raise. I can't bring music, art, and physical education back to Bill's school. I can't move money around in the budget to buy computers for the school or enough books for every student. So how can I do something to make the experience easier for the teachers and therefore better for the students? I started thinking about some of the incredible teachers I had in elementary school and how much they shaped my life. I began to think about how much it affected me when my teachers were happy, and more important, how scary it was when they weren't.

That night I asked Bill, "What is the one thing you wish you had at work that would make your life a little easier—besides fewer students in a classroom, music, art, and physical education programs, enough textbooks and school supplies, computers, a place to park, and a raise?" Without hesitating, he answered, "A nice bathroom."

The next day I stopped by Bill's school to visit the kids in his classroom and to do a little investigative work! After talking with the kids for a few minutes about my fabulous career and answering all of their questions about whether or not I "loooooove Mr. Torres" (they're a little obsessed about the fact that Mr. Torres "looooves me" and I "loooooove him!"), I went in search of the faculty bathrooms. There are two. One is inside the coordinator's office, which itself is about the size of a bathroom, so the coordinator knows exactly for how long and how frequently each teacher uses that bathroom. The other is on the opposite end of the school, inside the faculty lounge.

As I stood inside that tiny beige bathroom with the square wax paper toilet tissue and brown paper towels, I was immediately thrust back into elementary school and fully expected the hall monitor to burst in and give me a detention slip for being out of class without a note, again. I really wanted the teachers at Bill's school to know they are appreciated, that I think they're special people who deserve to be treated like they are wonderful. Bathrooms are a workplace issue for everyone. People can't be denied their right to take care of their "business." I heard the call to action and was encouraged to act locally. *Bathroom duty!* I decided to personally beautify the faculty bathrooms at the school by stocking them with all the amenities you might see in a hotel. It's not a raise, it's not more staff, it's not computers, textbooks, a security system, or a gym, but it's something the teachers need and use every day. And maybe, just maybe, if they have a few nice moments a day in a bathroom that looks nice, smells good, and makes them feel special, it'll put a smile on their faces and their students will get a little extra out of their already hardworking teachers! It was certainly worth a try!

I knew my plan to give the kids happier teachers by giving the teachers a nice bathroom was going to work when, on my way home, I stopped by a local coffee shop to get my daily latte, and a total stranger walked up to me and said, "You look so pretty." It put a smile on my face, I felt momentarily elated, and found myself tipping a little extra when I ordered my coffee. And that's how this works . . . someone does something kind for you, you feel good, and you do something nice. And so I figured, if I do something nice for the teachers, they'll feel good and they'll be happier in their classrooms and will teach the kids even better!

I went home and flew through my cupboards, drawers, and closets. I gathered all of the travel-sized soaps, lotions, gels, toothbrushes, toothpaste, and mouthwash I'd collected from hotels all around the world. All my life my friends and family have made fun of me for collecting these. I've taken their ridicule because I knew that someday I'd need them for something. That day was today! I grabbed a bowl, a bag of potpourri, some room spray, two-ply fluffy toilet paper, my favorite Kleenex Viva paper towels, some mints, some vitamin C, some hand sanitizer, and some scrap fabric (which I also save because, of course, I'm going to make something with it someday). And then I had another idea: I grabbed an empty frame and handwrote a note that read, "I hope this bathroom puts a smile on your face and brightens your day. Please enjoy the amenities and feel free to take whatever you like as a thank-you for all of the work you do for so many to make all of our futures brighter. Love, Someone who is very grateful for all of you!" I put the note into the frame, packed everything up, and headed back to school.

It took me about fifteen minutes to clean and decorate the bathroom and place everything nicely for the teachers. And then, outside the bathroom, I waited. . . .

Teachers would literally come out of the bathroom beaming! Some of these teachers almost never smile—they're too tired! Some of them are the teachers who have scared generations of students. Heck, some of them have scared generations of teachers! But for a moment they were transformed. For a moment they probably forgot about being overworked and underpaid. And for a moment, they probably were a little nicer to their students. And who knows? On any given day a little extra kindness, one additional word of encouragement, a beat of extra patience could be the thing that influences a kid for a lifetime. This could lead to generations of more productive people! Pampered, moisturized teachers who feel acknowledged and appreciated could affect hundreds and hundreds of students. Then the kids have a better day; they're more productive. If they're more productive, they feel a sense of accomplishment. If they accomplish more, they're validated. If they're validated, they're more confident. If they're more confident, they're better behaved. And if they're better behaved, the parents win too! All of this goodness is just because of a nice bathroom in the middle of kids and a school that are under construction.

The teachers at Bill's school were so happy and grateful for their new bathroom that they themselves enacted a program to "Beautify the Bathroom." They each took responsibility for the bathrooms for a week and stocked them with nice things and good toilet paper. Eventually books and inspirational quotes were added, and the "potpourri of the month" was added to the bathroom adventure. Community and bathroom activism all rolled up into one. It was different, fun, and very inspiring, and it was most definitely an example of *think globally, act*

locally. I felt as if I had done something to address a very big (global) issue on an individual (local) level. It felt good to do and to give. And,
dare I say, it was a welcome relief at the school!

I get so frustrated sometimes when I read a newspaper or watch the
news. Take the congressional hearings on steroid abuse in Major
League Baseball. I know there are young boys who have been affected by
this and that families have suffered untold tragedy because their sons
wanted to be like their favorite baseball players and thought that ste-
roids were the shortcut. At the same time, I was so mad that while we're
at war, when teachers are scarce, Social Security is in danger, we're still
dependent on foreign oil that is more expensive than ever, and the environment is being severely neglected, our elected officials were holding these hearings. I wonder why steroid abuse by professional athletes
got this kind of attention. Was this really the best use of their time and
our money? When was the last time Congress held hearings on the horrible images that young women are bombarded with and the resulting
eating disorders? Bulimia, anorexia, abuse of diet pills, diuretics,
colonics, laxatives, chronic dieting—how many young women have to
die before our elected officials pay this kind of attention to them? How
many American children need to be diagnosed as morbidly obese before our elected officials look at the way junk food is marketed to kids
and in schools? I am so mad about all of this. When will Congress hold
hearings on self-image abuse? When will Congress hold hearings on
legal speed that is marketed to young women and men for them to lose
weight? When is that going to happen? It'll happen when enough people who employ the elected officials (voters) tell them that it is their
job. Those hearings are a priority because our president is a former
Major League Baseball owner. This is an agenda-driven hearing.

Okay, I have an agenda too. I know exactly what it is to live the hell of
an eating disorder. I know exactly what it is like to turn on the television and be told in words and images that because of your body type you
are ugly and worthless. I know exactly the pain that shoots through your
heart when you go to a comedy club with a group of friends and the

punch line for every lazy comic is "fat, fatty, fat bitch, fat ass." I know exactly what it feels like to be invisible. I know exactly what it means to get up every single day and work to lose weight: prepare meals ahead of time, measure everything, weigh the food, go to a restaurant and order everything plain, steamed, broiled, and a side of plain lettuce. I know what it's like to work and work and work to try desperately to fit into a world that is constantly telling you that you are gross and disgusting. I know exactly the heartache of being judged not for the person you are or the joy you bring to the people you love but for the size of your ass or the amount of cellulite on the back of your legs. I know exactly how much time and life is wasted worrying about what you look like, whether people are laughing at you, whether someone will make fun of you. I know exactly what it's like to have a disagreement with a grown man and have him end an adult conversation by calling you a "fat f#@*ing c*@#." I know exactly what it's like to be ignored and dismissed because you're not a skeleton with boobs. I know exactly the toll that being the butt of jokes takes on your soul. I know exactly how brutal it is when we allow there to be one standard of beauty. I know exactly how terrifying it is to allow the world to define your value by your physical appearance. I can't control Congress. I'm not the president. But I

Your vote is your voice!

am a taxpaying, voting citizen of the United States, and I am writing this book to say to young women and men that *you* decide who you are. *You* decide your value. *You* decide to live a fantastic life. *You* decide how your government spends *your* time and *your* money. *You* decide who is allowed to govern. *Your* vote is *your* voice!

Thinking globally, acting locally is a way to look at something that seems way too big or too complicated for one person to have an impact on and see that is never true. Any kind of change begins with one person, and there is *always* someone or something that needs us. The world is under construction, and how great it is depends on each of us and what we're willing to contribute. Our quality of life is cumulative. Every little bit counts, so *get out and do something!*

CHAPTER ELEVEN

Live Like You Mean It!

"Yesterday I dared to struggle. Today I dare to win."

—BERNADETTE DEVLIN

WHEN I STARTED WRITING THIS BOOK A YEAR AGO, I weighed 291 pounds, and outside my window was a gigantic mess of a construction site. One year later, the construction is nearly finished, this book too is coming to its conclusion, and today I weigh 143 pounds. For the first time in my life I got rid of my "fat clothes." I now realize that each time I went on a diet and lost weight in the past, I set myself up for failure by holding on to every piece of clothing that I accumulated on the way down and then back up again. I was never able to keep the weight off, so I held on to my "fat clothes" and the beliefs that kept me fat as well. Each time I opened my closet, those size-fourteen overalls reminded me of the five minutes in 1993 when they fit—*big dormant bummer*. They competed for space in my cramped closet with the size twenty-sixes and twenty-eights from my all-time high (ironic that it was an all-time high when in fact I was at an all-time low) in 2003 and everything in between. I got rid of all of them. *¡Adios, mis amigos!* I finally found the strength and courage to give them away because I don't need them anymore. I am never going back. *I can see clearly now, the weight is gone!* Surprise!

I've cleared up the clutter in my life in order to create space for new things. *Hola, new amigos!*

I continue to adjust to life after gastric bypass surgery. It was the most difficult decision I ever made, but I truly feel reborn. My stomach only holds six ounces of food at a time now, so those six ounces have to count nutritionally. Due to my public speaking schedule, I travel a lot. It was my choice to have gastric bypass surgery to create a permanent barrier between dangerous foods and me. But boy oh boy, airports sure make it difficult *and* expensive! I can't imagine how a family traveling with kids and luggage and a budget manage to balance time, money, and nutrition.

I read in *USA Today* that in 1976, 4 percent of the children in the United States were obese—I *was* one of them. Today that figure is a staggering 17 percent. It is obvious to me as I make my way through the nation's airports why this is the case. The airports have an abundance of food: fast food, fried food, fat-filled food, and all of it smells delicious. I have spent so much time at airports, everything I own smells like a Cinnabon.

Being at the airport is like being Charlie at the cheese-oil-fructose factory.

I pass the fried cheese sticks, the funnel cakes, the unbelievably seductive smell of fresh-baked cinnamon rolls smothered in butter and icing, the pretty bins of candy and sugar- and oil-drenched nuts, pizza, fried burgers, French fries. Ahh, French fries, my old friend. In one terminal I saw regular fries, fries with cheese, chili-cheese fries, and fries smothered in gravy.

One of the last times I ate at an airport, I took a shot at a fast-food "Mexican" restaurant (although I don't know how "Mexican" anything that suggests you "run for the border" really is . . . but I thought it would be worth a try).

"Hi. Are your beans fried in lard?" I asked.

"Yep," the caustic teenager with his polyester cap cocked to the side to give his work uniform some hip-hop flavor said as he chewed on a piece of skin hanging from his cuticle. He's telling me who he is and I believe him. Beyond gross with the cuticle, but kudos on the personal style!

"Can I get a bowl with some lettuce, green sauce, and a scoop of the ground beef you put in your tacos?" I asked.

Hip-Hop stared at me with wide eyes for a beat and informed me that he'd have to ask his manager if he could do that. I didn't realize that I'd asked for something that requires special permission.

"Okay, but I have to charge you for three tacos," he informed me upon his return.

"So let me get this straight. If I want the inside of one taco minus the cheese, I have to pay for three tacos? Why don't you give me one taco with no cheese and some green salsa on the side? How much will that cost?"

"Let me ask my manager." At this point my frustration gave way to sympathy. I actually felt sorry for the cuticle snacker.

"Let's make life easy," I suggested. "I'll take one taco, no cheese, and a medium unsweetened iced tea."

"The iced tea is already sweetened."

"Okay, how about a bottle of water?"

"I can put some water in a cup for you, but I have to charge the same price as soda."

"I'll just take the taco. Thanks."

Given this, I'm shocked that 83 percent of our kids aren't obese. It's all how you look at it. And it's about what you do after you've looked around.

We are more powerful as people than we sometimes realize. As consumers we have some rarely used muscles to flex too. This is a real TGAL (*think globally, act locally*) opportunity to improve the quality of our own lives and make a difference for others too. It's encouraging to know what can get done if you just ask.

I had a TGAL experience at a restaurant that my friends refer to as my home office away from home, the Daily Grill. After surgery I'd order an entrée at full price, but could only eat about one-fourth of the food. I asked to order from the kid's menu, but the choices were too fried and cheesy. I spoke with the manager and explained that I was wasting food and money, and asked him if they would prepare smaller portions for me at a reduced price. He agreed and they did. Now I can still order from the "big kids' menu." I get half the food for half the price. I pay for what I eat, and I don't waste money or food.

Others are doing it too.

Twice I've overheard customers explaining to their server that they require smaller portions. Both times, I heard the server respond, "Oh, yeah, we offer smaller portions for gastric bypass patients." I watched as a woman went from a self-conscious whisper to exclaiming, "How wonderful. Thank you!" *"You're welcome,"* I thought as I smiled proudly at the TGAL progress. There is no need for any of us to keep our needs quiet and suffer silently. *Put your mask on first* and speak up. You just might help someone else in the process; TGAL, baby! Your mouth is not just for chewin'; it's for speakin' too. Ask for and get what you want! You know what's good for you; *trust your self.*

I continue to build my positive history scorecard, complete with unanticipated surprises.

Today when I look in the mirror, I see the same body I saw before. I know it's smaller, but I still have to work every day to see myself as I am and not as I was. My doctor suggested that I go into stores I avoided in the past to try clothes on so that I would have hard-core evidence of my progress. Wait, did my doctor just prescribe shopping? Yee-ha! I better put my mask on first! I told you life is good these days!

I can now walk into any store and find clothes that fit—even on the sale rack! It's thrilling to put on Bill's jeans, which are now *baggy*, when since the beginning of our relationship I've never even been able to fit into his T-shirts. *Never say die-t!* You just may double your wardrobe by wearing your partner's clothes. Sure, he might cry a little at first, but he'll get over it. Surprise!

I sprinted from one end of the airport in Atlanta, Georgia, to the other to make my connecting flight. I wasn't winded, I didn't have to stop to rest, I wasn't drenched in sweat, and I made my connection. Surprise!

In the past, if I couldn't fly first class, I wouldn't fly. Not because I'm a diva and must travel *first class or not at all, darling!* That's not why. Simply said, it was because my ass didn't fit into the seats in coach, *punto y final* (period)! And on those occasions when I'd have to fly coach and squeeze myself into the seat, I'd always have to ask the flight attendant to get a seat belt extension strap for me. Let me tell you, it's a joy and not at all humiliating to ask for one of those. Ha! Nobody stares or looks at you in disgust or anything. I'd spend the entire flight pinched tightly into the seat, stressed out and embarrassed because I knew I was making the person next to me uncomfortable. Not to mention, I couldn't put my tray down to eat, because it wouldn't lay flat over my stomach and thighs. I didn't dare eat on the flight. I'd suffer silently and wait to land, and then I'd gorge and soothe myself with food. The short-term relief I got from the food did nothing to relieve the pain and bruises I'd have on my hips for at least a week to remind me that I was *too fat to fly*—literally. I recently found myself stuck in the middle seat in coach during a cross-country flight. I sat down, buckled the seat belt, and even pulled the strap to tighten it with so much room to spare. What, no pinching, no extender, no drama? *Who am I?* And by the way, I had extra room in my seat, and even crossed my legs while my tray was down. Glory! It is a pleasure to fly now, and a lot less expensive too. Surprise!

My entire life I've been "two-bag-minimum Jackie." When I traveled, even if it was just for a weekend, I packed a minimum of two suitcases. Now I'm half my size and my clothes take up half the space, and so I am officially "one-bag Jackie." Surprise!

I love to dance. But in the past after an evening of bustin' a move, I'd wake up the next day with sore hips, knees, ankles, and the balls of my feet would be bruised and swollen. Apparently my feet and joints were really pissed about having to "get jiggy" with an extra one hundred fifty pounds of Mexican. Now I dance all night pain-free. The next day the only evidence of the night before is my memory of a good time. Big surprise!

I didn't weight to start my jewelry business, and recently when I was having a rough week or three I received another surprise. Anyone who has ever started any kind of business knows it's a challenge. Some days my hands look like they were stuck in a paper shredder and my back is sore from making jewelry. I worry about the fact that I've invested all of Bill's and my savings into this business and turned our home into a warehouse and sweatshop. Those are the days when I really count on my best friend, Jackie, to remind me to *trust myself* and keep on keepin' on! Working hard may not always ensure success, but not working will most certainly ensure failure.

I know that jewelry can't change the world, but the girls and women who wear it most definitely can. TGAL is making the world a better place, one piece of jewelry at a time.

I sent Carrie Underwood some of my jewelry, hoping that she might wear it during the competition for *American Idol*. I love the show because it's nothing short of people with dreams and the drive to work for those dreams, living them. I knew that she was inundated with diamonds and jewelry from top designers from all over the world, but I took a chance.

On the last night of the competition, Bill and I watched along with fifty million other people as Carrie walked onto the stage to become the American Idol wearing *my jewelry.* Surprise!

She doesn't know me. She chose a necklace and a pair of earrings I had made because she liked them. In fact, the jewelry she chose is from my "Joyce" collection, named after and inspired by my mother. My mom was always my biggest cheerleader. I like to think she brought some good luck to Carrie on her big night too. Carrie became the American Idol and Bill and I felt like we won too. Victories are everywhere—just look.

Bill and I were on a cattle-call flight from Los Angeles to Little Rock, Arkansas, via Las Vegas to the LULAC (League of United Latin American Citizens) conference, where I was scheduled to be the keynote speaker at their annual Youth Awards Banquet. On the connection from Vegas to Little Rock, it seemed everyone was drunk, just married, just divorced, or had just lost their life savings. What happens in Vegas does not *always* stay in Vegas. Sometimes it ends up drunk and throwing up next to you on the plane. I sat by the window while Bill sat on the aisle, in the desperate hope that nobody would want to sit in the middle seat and we'd have the row to ourselves. Nice fantasy, but the reality was that the flight was full. At the very last minute, a Vietnamese man who spoke no English sat his four-year-old-son next to us and then disappeared to the nearest empty seat about ten rows away. Apparently I was in the middle of an in-flight babysitting service. Victories are everywhere?

"Hello, my name is Minh Lee," he announced, and then, just in case we might be unclear, he proudly spelled it out for us, "M-I-N-H!" "I can count to one hundred. One . . . two . . . three . . ." He counted from one to one hundred, three times in a row. "I can spell too many words." Minh proceeded to spell "too many words," and then challenged us to give him words to spell. We obliged our charming traveling companion with every single-syllable word we could think of. He was absolutely right; he could spell too many words.

When Minh finished with his in-flight spelling bee, he told us about his friends "Jimmy, Tommy, Phong, and Jenny." He told us all about his older brother and sister in Vietnam. From the second he sat down he focused only on what he *can* do. He acted as if Bill and I were so lucky that he sat next to us. He was Elvis. Forty minutes later he asked, "Do you have any questions for me?" "Where were you born?" I asked him. "United States of America," he said, and placed his right hand over his heart, as if he were about to break out into the Pledge of Allegiance. "I'm an American!" He said it with such sincere pride both Bill and I were moved by this tiny little dynamo. "You sure are. You're an Ameri*can*, not an Ameri*can't*. Always remember that," I told him. He let out a big, loud four-year-old belly laugh. Apparently he thought that was the most hilarious thing he'd ever heard. I felt glad that we met pre-kindergarten Minh. Sometimes victory is spelled M-I-N-H. Minh, *baby, you're a star!*

At baggage claim I glanced over to a mother and her two young boys under the age of four waiting to get their luggage. She wore a beautiful white peasant skirt, while her boys spilled their juice boxes and stepped all over her. Could there be a victory here?

"You're brave to wear white while traveling with two little boys and two juice boxes," I said to her.

She smiled. "Hey, it can always be bleached."

She reminded me that it's better to take a chance and have to do a little cleanup than to wake up one day with the regret that you never wore that beautiful skirt. *Don't weight to live!*

My cell phone rang. It was my friendly cable service provider calling to ask me why I hadn't paid my bill. Can a cable bill be bleached? My cable service provider was not amused.

Bill and I arrived at the Peabody Hotel in Little Rock, Arkansas, where the LULAC conference was being held. The first thing we saw in the enormous lobby as we entered was a gigantic poster welcoming everyone to the conference with huge pictures of the conference speakers. At the top was former president Bill Clinton—and who was right next to him? Me! Gulp . . . no pressure!

LULAC is an organization that is dear to my heart, and I wanted to do well for them. There would be many people I hadn't seen in a long time at the conference. Although I've been onstage thousands of times and have given many speeches to groups all over the country, this time was different. In many ways this was the debut of the "new Jackie."

I was scheduled to speak after the Reverend Jesse Jackson and before former president Bill Clinton, two of the greatest public speakers in the world. How did I get sandwiched in between them? Bill Clinton clearly had home-court advantage, and Jesse Jackson may well be the motivational speaker heavyweight champ. But then again, *I'm Elvis!*

My stomach began to grumble. *Feed me!* I realized I hadn't eaten a meal since the night before. I gulped an entire bottle of water, mmmmm, delicious and refreshing. Isn't it the worst when you're hungry and someone suggests a "refreshing glass of water"? Ugggggghh!

When I walked into the large banquet room, there were about two thousand people from all over the country excited to be together meeting, networking, exchanging ideas, being inspired. There were some familiar faces and a lot of new ones. The chatter was all about what a great speech Jesse Jackson gave. No pressure!

Bill and I were seated at the president's table with LULAC president

Hector Flores and his lovely wife, Tula. They have dedicated their lives to the civil rights movement while raising a beautiful family and building the great organization LULAC. I was honored and terrified, because if I laid an egg onstage, I'd have to return to their table and sit next to them while I pretended that it didn't stink. No pressure!

The stage was gigantic. There were fifty-foot video screens on each side of the stage to ensure that everyone in the room could see every tick, every trickle of sweat, and every sebum-filled pore on my face. I was so nervous, and I couldn't stop drinking water. Great, now I had to pee! A woman from the production crew came to my table to put my microphone on and touch me a lot. My speech was being recorded. Another reminder of how important this speech was. No pressure!

No pressure!

I stood up while "Ms. Microphone" fumbled to place the microphone pack onto the back of my pants. Without warning, Ms. Microphone lifted up the back of my shirt so that everyone could see that although the "new Jackie" wears low-rise pants, the "old Jackie" hasn't yet abandoned her favorite granny panties. As I struggled to cover the fact that my underwear rose higher than my pants in a real-life "Bridget Jones" moment, a group of students gathered to take a picture with my grannies and me! For purposes of my own dignity, I *choose* to believe that nobody saw anything . . . *please, God!* As I tried to make a break for the bathroom, a group of ten vibrating, enthusiastic, college-aged Texans stopped me. The "Texas Ten" hit me with some headline news regarding the slashing of funds for college-bound kids in their state, and the unspeakable violence against women in their state's border towns, which the national media ignores. My head was spinning, but the Texas Ten and I had a real *get out and do something* moment as we exchanged ideas for what could be done. We all agreed that it's not just our right to enjoy all that life has to offer; it's our responsibility to build our own best lives and aid in the construction of those who need it most. We're Ameri*can*s, not Ameri*can'ts!*

I tried again to drag my grannies and me toward the restroom, and at that moment I suddenly heard Hector say, "Please welcome our keynote speaker, actress, author, activist and *la mera-mera*, Jackie Guerra!" I went up onstage and he gave me a big hug. "Shake 'em up, Jackie," he whispered into my ear. No pressure!

The lights were blinding, but I could see cameras recording me for the tape that was going to my *brand-new* agents. Hector's words were ringing in my ears. I was jet-lagged, hungry, and sporting a frizzy pompom on the top of my head that I tried to pass off as a ponytail. I was acutely aware of every clinking dinner plate, the murmur of conversation in the room, and even some babies crying. The weight of expectations knocked me off my feet, and I stumbled. My rhythm and game were off. I was too concerned with the outcome. I needed to remember that I was there for one purpose: to be of service.

As I looked past the nervous and fidgeting Bill I could see the Texas

Me and two of the "Texas Ten." Ladies . . . another reason to
think globally, act locally!

Ten. I was thrust back to that night twelve years earlier at Rage with a
group of workers from Local 11. Just like on the night of my very first
time onstage, when I glanced at the workers watching me with looks of
hope, I saw the Texas Ten looking at me so hopefully. I remembered
how powerful that first night onstage was when I found my passion for
performing and was able to inspire folks who had stopped in for a drink
to *get out and do something.* That night was a good night for chubby
Mexicans—maybe tonight would be too! And in that second I didn't care
about the cameras, I didn't care about the noise of dinner being served,
I didn't care about my granny panties, I didn't care about the potential
corporate partners, I wasn't hungry, I didn't care about the frizz ball on
top of my head that I call hair. I didn't have to compete with Jesse Jackson

or Bill Clinton any more than they had to compete with me; we're each unique. Instead of being distracted by trying to please thousands of people and my agents, I focused on the Texas Ten. I got really clear about my intention; TGAL, baby! Give them a reason to be inspired to *get out and do something.*

The "new Jackie" set aside the old script and wrote a new one right there in the moment and from the heart. You know, we never see things as they are. We see things as *we* are. And I'm different. As we grow and learn and change, we have to rewrite our scripts. We can't always rely on what's worked before, because who we are today may not be the same as who we were yesterday. I am different. Old scripts, old tapes, and old habits may no longer apply. I had to change the script to reflect who I am today and what I want to say. In my movie, my character is here to make a difference. I wanted my performance to reflect what I've learned and the progress I've made this year.

I found my rhythm and got into my groove and was aware that the chatter and noise stopped. I delivered my speech to three standing ovations. Just like that first night, I was seduced all over again. My forty-five minutes on that stage were pure food for my soul. I wasn't hungry anymore. When I finished, LULAC presented me with their Service Award for 2005. I felt great—not because I was given standing ovations and an award, but because I did what I was there to do. I didn't allow the circumstances to dictate the quality of my experience. Proof that I'm on the right path. Follow that, Mr. Clinton!

And follow he did.

For the purpose of clarity, I will now refer to my fiancé, Bill, as Bill T., because we are going to meet Mr. Bill Clinton. I don't want to confuse the two Bills.

Bill T. and I were escorted to a checkpoint that would lead to another checkpoint that would lead to a room where we would meet former president Bill Clinton. Everything happened really fast and really seriously. Just like the signs at the airports that read "no jokes, please," there is not a big call for levity and comedy when dealing with the Secret Service.

Before we knew it, Bill T. and I found ourselves being ushered into a private area by Secret Service agents to meet the former president.

Bill T. and I were as giddy and wide-eyed as kids waiting in line to see Santa as we floated into the hallway, where we were briefed on what not to do by "Mr. Huge Serious Secret Service Guy," including the fact that I'd have to check my purse, camera, cell phone . . . and on cue, my cell phone rang.

"Hello?"

"Hello, Miss Guerra. This is a courtesy call from Cingular Wireless. Your account is past due. Are you able to make a payment by phone right now?" my friendly cellular carrier asked as I prepared to meet one of the most revered figures in the world.

"Not right at this moment," I whispered.

"Miss, you'll have to leave your phone at the door," Mr. Huge Serious Secret Service Guy repeated impatiently.

"Gladly!" I smiled as I clicked my phone off. "It's all yours!" I said as I handed him my cell phone with its unpaid bill.

Note to self: Don't weight to live and don't weight to pay bills. Got it!

We were taken into a classroom-sized room. Mr. Clinton was front and center, like a teacher about to address his waiting students. When I caught my first glimpse of him, I was impressed by his elegance. He stood tall and looked healthy and happy, eyes sparkling as he met each person. He appeared to be deeply interested in everyone who made their way through the line to meet him. There we were, Bill T. and me, along with decorated military heroes, community leaders, politicians, CEOs, and the twice-elected, forty-second President of the United States, Bill Clinton. I felt very proud.

We stood in line. I watched two people at a time walk up to the president, stand on either side of him, say a few words, shake his hand, glance at the official photographer, smile, click, big flash, and leave. My heart was pumping. My mind was racing. President Clinton was ten feet away, and then eight feet away, and then Bill T. and I were next. We were next. It was our turn.

Hector Flores introduced us to Mr. Clinton. "Mr. President, this is Jackie Guerra and Bill Torres, two of our best and brightest. Jackie tore it up at the Youth Awards Banquet. She is a very talented actress, a dynamic speaker, and a true activist for our community."

He shook my hand and then put his other hand onto Bill T.'s shoulder. I cleverly opened with, "It's an honor, Mr. Clinton. I worked for you in 1992."

He smiled and said, "Well, thank you for your hard work."

And then I heard myself say quite loudly, "You look fantastic!" Umm . . . did I just tell the former leader of the free world that he looks *fantastic*? While I gathered my own thoughts, I heard, "We're from L.A., and we love you, man!" Umm . . . did my fiancé just call the former commander in chief *"man"*?

"Thanks, man." Umm . . . did a president of the United States just say, "Thanks, *man*"? Is it 1981?

Bill T. was on a roll. . . . "I love your book. I listen to it on CD while I work out." Umm . . . did my fiancé just tell a Rhodes scholar that he listens to his autobiography while he sweats?

Mr. Clinton laughed and said, "You do? That's great!"

The Secret Service agents were starting to talk into their sleeves. I felt I had to end our "briefing" and I wanted to make it count. Somehow my mouth took off before my brain was finished carefully deliberating the possibilities, and I blurted, "Can I hug you?" The man from Hope smiled at me, stretched out his arms and said, "Come on now."

I went in for the presidential hug and life was good. Bill T. and I posed with Arkansas's favorite son for the official photographer. Smile. Click. Big flash. Bye-bye! We thanked President Clinton for the tenth time and floated out of the room. We didn't stop smiling for an hour. It was a perfect moment.

When President Clinton addressed the conference attendees, I was especially impressed by the way he spoke about his new friendship with former president George Bush. In spite of their intense competition for the presidency in 1992, today they are friends who respect each

Bill T. from the Bronx, Bill C. from Arkansas and one happy Mexican-American Valley Girl!

other. I thought this was especially important to hear, because it's proof that while it's important for us to understand our differences, it's much more valuable to build upon what we have in common. It's what we have in common that connects us, so that our differences can be shared and settled. President George Herbert Walker Bush and President William Jefferson Clinton are living proof that what we have in common is so much more powerful than what separates us. That's a choice. It's true we don't live in red states and blue states. We live in the United States. That's my choice.

Take criticism *seriously* but don't take it *personally* was a big theme throughout President Clinton's speech. I couldn't help but think about the fact that we all have the *choice* to see criticism as a learning tool. He is the perfect example of choosing and scripting his own life, even through adversity. "It can always be bleached." While *all* of us have made mistakes and done things in private that we'd be mortified if anyone knew about, here is a man whose most private moments and personal mistakes were international news and part of history. And yet, he got up every day and *chose* to do his best. And when he left office, he *chose* to travel the world and make public appearances. Why? To be of service. His choice.

My dad once told me that life is about what you do when you have a choice. My point is you *always* have a choice. You may think you have to do this or that. But you choose the way you feel, think, plan, and eventually what you do. We have a choice. We can choose to believe in possibilities or not. You can choose to hate or congratulate.

My friend Lash has a magnet in his office that reads GAY BY BIRTH, *FABULOUS BY CHOICE!* I love it because it makes clear that we *choose* the quality of our lives. The quality of our lives is not determined by our circumstances or the situations we find ourselves in, but rather how we *choose* to see our own value and define our successes. Clearly there are accepted definitions of what success looks like: fat bank account, skinny body, and *mucho* bling. That's *a* choice, but it most definitely is not the *only* choice. When you see your life as an adventure, you know that being under construction means that your life is a work in progress. Every step of the way it's your choice to determine who you are. You decide what your intention is, and that, my friends, determines the quality of your life. Bank, body, and bling? *That's it?* That's insane. Does it make sense that that's the only way to define success? Absolutely not! By that narrow and absurd definition we should all just give up and go live in a cave. My waterwings and I will join you there. Oh yeah, you didn't think I could lose nearly one hundred fifty pounds and escape the hanging skin syndrome, did you? I call the skin on my arms my "waterwings." See, I *choose* to be amused: my life, my script, and my choice.

At size twenty-six or twenty-eight I often joked that I had the opposite of anorexia, because when I looked in the mirror I didn't think, "Gross." I didn't see a body that I was ashamed of. I saw sexy! I didn't feel self-conscious about my body. I felt then and I still feel that wherever you are in your construction, you have to rock it, and I chose to rock it. But being strong and feeling sexy is not an excuse not to improve the quality of your life. Confidence and pride should be the tools you use to build your life, not attitudes that shield you from your own potential. *Love where you live but always be open to a little home improvement!*

As a society we judge fat people meanly and harshly. And we need to stop it. If you're fat, stop criticizing yourself and find the right cure for you. If you're not fat, think about how being critical of fat people is making your life better, because I am sure it's *not.* We all deserve to be happy and healthy, and it begins with stopping all of the criticism—*now!* Be kind and generous with yourself, *be your own best friend,* and you'll be amazed at how easy it becomes to be generous to others. Remember, we tell people who we are and how to treat us by the way we treat ourselves, and they believe us.

Obesity is a disease from which I suffered for most of my life. I chose surgery as the cure for me. Low self-esteem and feelings of low self-worth are a cultural ill for which we can each be a part of the cure. One person at a time who *puts their mask on first* is a big step. I hope this book can be a part of curing the cultural ill of people suffering from low self-esteem and struggling with issues of self-worth. You don't have time to be self-critical and filled with doubt—*you're Elvis!* Each of us is unique and filled with divine potential. *Live like you mean it!*

Many people have inspired me to work to become the person I'm capable of being. By sharing my stories I hope to repay the many people who have taught me so much and have been so generous. I hope I have been able to help or maybe even to inspire you. Reading books has kept me entertained when I have needed it the most. They have provided intimacy and comfort and fun and have enlightened me when I was in the dark. The fact that I have an opportunity to *get out and do something* in the form of a book is an unexpected gift for which I am forever grateful.

I didn't write this book because I have all of the answers. I wrote it because I want to work on some of the questions. Only by asking the right questions will we ever get the right answer. In the end, I wrote the book that I needed, to remind me that through it all I am *under construction.*

I called my friend Beth this morning to tell her about my week.

"Wow, you finished your book and met Bill Clinton in the same week? You're kind of done," she said.

"Nope," I said. "I'm just getting started!"

Acknowledgments

WOW! HOW CAN I BEGIN TO THANK ALL OF THE INCREDIBLE PEOPLE in my life who have inspired me, laughed with me, and motivated me? I should play it safe and just give a big ol' *muchas gracias* to everyone but there are some to whom I owe such a debt of gratitude that I can't let this go without mentioning them by name. Here I go . . .

Thank you to Angela Lee for your brains, your heart, your faith, and your *never say die-t* spirit. *Go get some sleep!* Kyle Crowner, thank you for your calm during my many storms. *Now stop yelling at me!* Lee Kernis, for being my manager and my friend. *I'm back, you love me!* Krista Parkinson, you taught me more than you can know. *It's big, really really big!* Jeff Glieberman and Penny Salomon, my 8-1-8 "mezpuchah," I'm honored to call you my amigos. *Mazel tov!* Tracy Bernstein, my brilliant editor, your wisdom and extreme patience have carried me through this process. I could not have completed this phase of my construction without you. *Gracias!* Sonia Jeantet, you're right, *maximize passion and minimize resistance.* It works—*Adelante!* Beth/Loula and Ronnie, you've been with me through thick and thin. I love you both. Hey, Ronnie, *remember when you had it going on?!?* Panagiota Demetrius Nicholakos, *mi amiga Griega! Don't clay for me Argentina!* Pam and Felix, your honesty and generosity have touched me in a way that I didn't know was possible in a friendship. *¡Gracias por vida!* Aryton, I love every freckle on your face, *Smelyton! The sun is out. It's a new day. Time to go out and play!* Jessenya, *baby, you're a star!* I love you. *How about the girls?!* Jasmine, welcome to the world! John, you are without a doubt a hero and I love you. Leticia, thank you for loving John and for bringing more Grrrrls to our *familia!* Aunt Judie, Uncle Taylor and Jodi, how do I thank you for teaching me to live like I mean it? I love you very much. *Mmmmm, bye-bye, we out!* A gigantic Distinctive Assets celebrity gift basket of thanks to my bon vivant *petit fleur*, fabu-Lash Fary. You've sprinkled your

"Fary dust" in my life with laughter, brutal honesty, and a latte when I needed it most. I love you. *I am not a crybaby!* My father, Ramon, who has always made me feel safe, loved, and as if I can do anything. You're the toughest, smartest, wildest, most sensitive, wise, and affectionate dad a girl could ever have. I love you Chimi, *give it hell!* My mother, Joyce, who taught me to give everything I have to everything I do and still guides me from heaven. Guess what I'm going to do today, Mom? I'm gonna *get out and do something!* Grump-grump stinky feet and Annie live on. I love you!

And finally, Bill. You are the most wise, funny, kind, honest, tender, courageous, and earnest person I've ever known. Pleek, pleek! Truth be told, your name should be on the cover of this book because your faith and commitment and belief and discipline are what got us here. *Tu eres todo para mi.* You are my rock, my partner, my soul, my heart; your love is why I believe in abundance. *I love you not only for what you are but for what I am when I am with you.* Even while under construction, I love where we live because it's where you are. *Hi, Pumpee. It's me, Peli. Good morning! I love you! Gracias, Diosito, for my healthy Pumpkin, who I love so much. Merry Christmas Perfect!* Do you want to play?

Muchisimas gracias to the posse of people who have inspired, supported and taught me. Uncle Pepe and Uncle GoGo and the entire *familia* Guerra, Judith Palacios *por su apoyo y amistad—quieres botaniar?* Sugar, Aida, Bob, Jim, Rich, and the entire Torres *familia;* thank you for being my family too, Peter Soby Jr.; thanks for the songs in June! My Polish *hermana* Maya: that is so last Tuesday! LMRP, CD, Uncle Jerry, Bruce Toms, Pete Astudillo, Paula and Annie Fary, the mighty Devin Gonzalez, Jennifer and Barry Gribbon, John Redmann, Maria Elena Durazo, Karine Mansoorian, the members and staff of Local 11, Victor Griego, Sue and Jim "Parky" Parkinson, Dyana Ortelli, Ricki Lake, Gina Lombardi-Donald, Ed Cancel, Becca Kovacik, Odilia Gonzales, Rob Strauss, the Quintanilla family, Suzy-Q & A, Cristina Saralegui, JL Pomeroy, Leeza Gibbons, Daniele Baker, Jennifer Roe-Reyes, John Edward, Mel Berger, Brad Bessey, Gail Steinberg, Muriyetta, Tom Fineman, Gregory Nava, Barbara Martinez-Jitner, Nancy de los Santos, Dan Guerrero, UFW; *¡Sí, se puede!*, LULAC; *¡Sí, se pudo!* NCLR, the Girls Scouts of America—*courage, character and confidence!*

If I didn't mention you by name, I thank you just the same. Remember, I'm not perfect; I'm *Under Construction!*

Keep on Keepin' on!

¡Adelante Comandante!